THE POLITICS OF PRAISE

While the revelation of God's name is a central theological topic, its ethical and political significance are often overlooked. In a world filled with violence committed 'in the name of God', how might invoking God's name enable peace, community, and hope?

The Politics of Praise argues that the redemptive potential of naming God lies in how this event transforms friendship. It breaks new ground by tracing the connections between naming God and friendship in the work of Thomas Aquinas and Jacques Derrida. Advancing an innovative reading of Aquinas on the divine names, the book explores how Dionysius' mysticism shapes Aquinas' appropriation of Aristotle's ethics, then retraces how Derrida's reading of religion renders possible an alternative conception of friendship. These explorations lead to a surprising convergence between Aquinas and Derrida on the conditions of friendship.

ASHGATE NEW CRITICAL THINKING IN RELIGION, THEOLOGY AND BIBLICAL STUDIES

The *Ashgate New Critical Thinking in Religion, Theology and Biblical Studies* series brings high quality research monograph publishing back into focus for authors, international libraries, and student, academic and research readers. Headed by an international editorial advisory board of acclaimed scholars spanning the breadth of religious studies, theology and biblical studies, this open-ended monograph series presents cutting-edge research from both established and new authors in the field. With specialist focus yet clear contextual presentation of contemporary research, books in the series take research into important new directions and open the field to new critical debate within the discipline, in areas of related study, and in key areas for contemporary society.

Series Editorial Board:

Jeff Astley, North of England Institute for Christian Education, Durham, UK
David Jasper, University of Glasgow, UK
James Beckford, University of Warwick, UK
Raymond Williams, Wabash College, Crawfordsville, USA
Geoffrey Samuel, University of Newcastle, Australia
Richard Hutch, University of Queensland, Australia
Paul Fiddes, Regent's Park College, University of Oxford, UK
Anthony Thiselton, University of Nottingham, UK
Tim Gorringe, University of Exeter, UK
Adrian Thatcher, College of St Mark and St John, UK
Alan Torrance, University of St Andrews, UK
Judith Lieu, Kings College London, UK
Terrance Tilley, University of Dayton, USA
Miroslav Volf, Yale Divinity School, USA
Stanley Grenz, Baylor University and Truett Seminary, USA
Vincent Brummer, University of Utrecht, The Netherlands
Gerhard Sauter, University of Bonn, Germany

Other Titles in the Series:

Nietzsche and Theology
Nietzschean Thought in Christological Anthropology
David Deane

Law, Liberty and Church
Authority and Justice in the Major Churches in England
Gordon Arthur

The Politics of Praise

Naming God and Friendship in Aquinas and Derrida

WILLIAM W. YOUNG III
Endicott College, USA

LONDON AND NEW YORK

First published 2007 by Ashgate Publishing

2 Park Square, Milton Park, Abingdon, Oxfordshire OX14 4RN
711 Third Avenue, New York, NY 10017

Routledge is an imprint of the Taylor & Francis Group, an informa business

First issued in paperback 2018

Copyright © William W. Young III 2007

All rights reserved. No part of this book may be reprinted or reproduced or utilised in any form or by any electronic, mechanical, or other means, now known or hereafter invented, including photocopying and recording, or in any information storage or retrieval system, without permission in writing from the publishers.

Notice:
Product or corporate names may be trademarks or registered trademarks, and are used only for identification and explanation without intent to infringe.

William W. Young III has asserted his moral right under the Copyright, Designs and Patents Act, 1988, to be identified as the author of this work.

British Library Cataloguing in Publication Data
Young, William W., 1972–
    The politics of praise : naming God and friendship in Aquinas and Derrida
    1. Thomas, Aquinas, Saint, 1225?–1274 2. Derrida, Jacques 3. God – Name 4. God – Knowableness 5. Friendship – Religious aspects – Christianity
    I. Title
    231'.042

Library of Congress Cataloging-in-Publication Data
Young, William W., 1972–
    The politics of praise : naming God and friendship in Aquinas and Derrida / William W. Young.
        p. cm.—(Ashgate new critical thinking in religion, theology, and biblical studies)
    Includes bibliographical references and index.
    ISBN-13: 978-0-7546-5646-3 (hbk)
  1. God—Name—History of doctrines. 2. Thomas, Aquinas, Saint, 1225?–1274. 3. Derrida, Jacques. I. Title. II. Series.

  BT180.N2Y68 2006
  231—dc22
                                                                                      2005037732

ISBN 978-0-7546-5646-3 (hbk)
ISBN 978-1-138-37601-4 (pbk)

For Melissa, and friends everywhere

Contents

Acknowledgements		ix
1	Introduction: Naming God and Friendship	1
2	Proper Names and the Logic of Friendship	21
3	Names and Proofs: Modes of Signification in Aquinas' *Summa Theologiae*	55
4	Charity, Friendship and Justice in the *Summa Theologiae*	99
5	Naming the Impossibility of Friendship: On Jacques Derrida	139
6	Conclusion: In the Name of Friendship	179
Bibliography		207
Index		217

Acknowledgements

All scholarship is collaborative on some level; a work on friendship is perhaps more self-consciously so. This work, in many ways, is the result of conversations and friendships with diverse colleagues holding very different religious views, and with disparate philosophical commitments. The engagement between Derrida and Aquinas is an outgrowth of these conflicting yet overlapping friendships.

As this work has grown out of my doctoral dissertation at the University of Virginia, I would first like to acknowledge Gene Rogers, for his tireless support of the project and his careful, constructively critical readings of numerous drafts, especially in the early stages. From Gene, I learned the importance of situating one's reflection within a theological tradition, while being conversant with those outside it, but even more importantly, a way to read Thomas that loosened his apparent ontological rigidity. What follows in this work is, I hope, a confirmation and furthering of this approach. Without Gene's trust, work, and encouragement, I could not have undertaken this project as it stands, and for that I am deeply grateful.

In addition, my committee members have been highly supportive, both of this work and more broadly. Peter Ochs has pushed me to keep this project going, often reminding me of its potential significance during difficult stretches of the work. Jamie Ferreira and Walter Jost provided numerous helpful comments and suggestions, and encouraged me to further pursue this in the subsequent revisions that have been made.

There are also many friends whose collegiality has contributed in many ways, both material and spiritual, to this project. Gitte Butin has pushed me to read Derrida more deeply and critically than I would have otherwise; Terry Baker and Mark Ryan have both provided encouragement and an ear at appropriate moments, and John Bugbee and Jon Malesic, along with Beth McManus, were very helpful as readers in early stages.

Less directly, my colleagues over the last few years have been enormously helpful. Colleagues at both Loyola College of Maryland, and King's College of Pennsylvania, helped me to see the value of a technical work on friendship, and encouraged my pursuit of this project to its publication. In particular, Fr. Tom Looney, CSC, provided tremendous encouragement and support, Joel Shuman helped me to think through Thomas in some important ways, and Phil Muntzel gave me important insights on the affective quality of Thomas' ethics. In the Society for Scriptural Reasoning, several colleagues have been quite influential for the shape this has taken: Bill Elkins, my co-editor, Basit Koshul, Martin Kavka and Randi Rashkover, Rachel Muers and Chad Pecknold have all encouraged this on various levels, even when I have perhaps wondered aloud over its feasibility. Janet Martin Soskice has been a valuable conversation partner. I am also grateful to Bob Gibbs for his reading of an early draft of a chapter, and what I have learned from his work more generally over the years.

Above and beyond the specific scholarly dimensions of support mentioned above, I am truly grateful for the friendship and time that those mentioned above have given me. I have been incredibly fortunate to have not just wonderful colleagues, but colleagues who are wonderful people; my interest in friendship, as a philosophical and theological issue, is largely because I have received such friendship from them, and I hope to have given to some degree in return.

This work focuses extensively on the issue of friendship with those beyond the limits of a community. Here, again, it is a testament to friendship. My life and thought have developed largely through interaction with those outside my Christian upbringing and community. The tension between this experience, and many religious (or philosophical) formulations of friendship, has been palpable. My work, here, should thus be read as gratitude for these friendships, and as a recognition of the central place of such friendships in our lives. While I cannot name all of these friends here, Noora, Avi, Daniel, Joe, Ethan, Ajit, and Randy are some of those whose friendship has inspired the concerns of this work.

My family has been a constant and steady stream of support. I am grateful to my parents and my sister Joanna for their belief in the project. And, above all, Melissa, my wife, has provided encouragement and her editing skills, along with incredible patience for a project that has taken a substantial portion of both of our lives.

Finally, my thanks to Ashgate for agreeing to publish this work. In particular, my thanks to Sarah Lloyd bringing this through the process, when I may have been somewhat unsure as to how exactly to proceed. Also, thanks to Philip Hillyer for his careful editing and scrutiny regarding final revisions and stylistic consistency.

Portions of chapter 3 draw on material from "From Describing to Naming God: Correlating the Five Ways with Aquinas' Doctrine of the Trinity," *New Blackfriars* 85 (2004): 527-41. I would like to thank *New Blackfriars*, and Fergus Kerr in particular, for their permission to reprint this material.

Chapter 1

Introduction: Naming God and Friendship

I. What's in a Name? Dimensions of Significance

This essay explores the connections in religious thought between the naming of God and friendship. As studied within Jewish, Christian, and Muslim theology, and as invoked in practice and devotion, divine names shape both human relationships to God and relationships within communities. As events of revelation—given by God—names of God signify who God is, how God relates to the world, what we understand of who God is, and how we thereby relate to God. Furthermore, as signs given by people to one another, divine names also shape relations between people, serving as mediums of communication that open new possibilities of community. Like any sign, then, a name of God: 1) relates to other signs; 2) gives knowledge of God—the referent of the name; and 3) establishes relations between the users of the signs, in this case God and a community (or communities). Names of God thus bear several dimensions of significance: syntactics, semantics, and pragmatics.[1]

While, like any other name, names of God relate to other signs, they embody distinctive, unique constellations of semantic and pragmatic significance. I will illustrate these unique constellations through a brief commentary on Exodus 3, one of the seminal texts for reflection on naming God. As the giving of the Name reshapes linguistic practice and calls for political and communal change, the Name which God gives to Moses has both semantic and pragmatic dimensions. On holy ground, in front of the burning bush, Moses receives the Name as part of his commission to go and free the Israelites from bondage in Egypt:

> But Moses said to God, "If I come to the Israelites and say to them, 'The God of your ancestors has sent me to you,' and they ask me, 'What is his name?' what shall I say to them?" [Ex. 3:13]

Here, Moses dwells intimately with God; he has been called to serve God by freeing the Israelite people from bondage and slavery. Moses asks for God's name for several reasons: first, so he can call on God, acquiring some power over God. However, to name God as one names things brings God into the realm of one's subjectivity and agency. Possessing a name of God thus risks idolatry. Second, more positively,

---

1 For further discussion of these dimensions of semiotics, see Robert Gibbs, *Why Ethics? Signs of Responsibilities* (Princeton: Princeton University Press, 2000), pp. 6-10.

having the name signifies Moses' own proximity to God for others, giving them a sign of whom Moses represents, allowing him to testify on God's behalf. Third, he asks so that this intimacy and its promised deliverance can be *shared* with the Israelites, as a sign he can give to them in their suffering. The Name thus serves as a sign of God's intimate presence which Moses can share with others:

> God said to Moses, "I AM WHO I AM." He said further, "Thus you shall say to the Israelites, 'I AM has sent me to you.'" God also said to Moses, "Thus you shall say to the Israelites, 'The LORD, the God of Abraham, the God of Isaac, and the God of Jacob, has sent me to you.'"
> This is my name forever,
> and this my title for all generations. [Ex. 3:14-15]

The semantic dimension of naming God has received the majority of the philosophical and theological attention devoted to this passage from Exodus 3. Semantic readings focus primarily on its cognitive import. Translations of the Name as "I am who I am" often emphasize its signification of God's transcendence and ineffability—the inability of any human name to grasp or conceptualize who God is. On this level, the revelation of God reveals God's utter transcendence of our world. It signifies, and lets us know, that God is "unnameable,"[2] signifying "absolute existence,"[3] "Being," or the infinity of divine freedom. The overemphasis on this semantic dimension is epitomized by Gordon Kaufman who writes that the Tetragrammaton signifies "the ego-agent par excellence."[4] The name of God, interpreted semantically, would be at the heart of a "metaphysics of Exodus," a glimpse of an unfettered otherworldly power that can be neither comprehended nor controlled—a divinity free from all relation to the world. Alternatively, the human cognitive potency embodied in the power of naming encounters its limit in this name that God gives. Such a "recession into infinity of the referent," in Paul Ricoeur's words, subverts Moses' desire to know and appropriate God for himself. As Ricoeur writes, "To the extent that to know a god's name was to have power over that god, the name confided to Moses is certainly that of the being whom humanity cannot really name, that is, hold at the mercy of our language."[5] The Name lets one refer to God as one unknown.

While the semantic dimension emphasizes God's transcendence of the world, a more complex picture emerges when one attends to the pragmatic dimension of the Name, which is more broadly embedded in the narrative progression of the story. For example, Philo interprets the Name as signifying God's uniqueness

---

[2] Pseudo-Dionysius, "The Divine Names," in *The Complete Works*, ed. C. Luibheid (New York: Paulist Press, 1988), pp. 53-5.

[3] Moses ben Maimonides, *The Guide for the Perplexed*, trans. M. Friedlander (New York: Dover, 1956), pp. 89-95.

[4] Gordon Kaufman, *God the Problem*, cited by Janet Martin Soskice, "The Gift of the Name," *Gregorianum* 79 (1998), pp. 231-46.

[5] Paul Ricoeur, "Naming God," in M. Wallace (ed.), *Figuring the Sacred* (Minneapolis: Fortress, 1995), p. 228.

and transcendence, but emphasizes that the name is given by grace, for our sake, so that we may call on God.[6] Likewise, Franz Rosenzweig's and Martin Buber's alternative translation of God's Name— "I will be there with you as I will be there" —suggests this pragmatic dimension, as the Name becomes a *promise*.[7] As Exodus 2 records it, God appears to Moses because God has heard the suffering cries of Israel. God's Name is thus a sign of God's presence with Israel in times of suffering, and the promise of deliverance from suffering.[8] The Name provides a promise that God will be with (*ehyeh imach*) the Israelites, and that God has chosen Israel as his people out of freedom; God's name (*ehyeh-asher-ehyeh*) indicates God's ineffability even while indicating God's free self-determination to be with Israel.[9] Further, the Name is also a sign that Moses can *give* to others. The Name both signifies divine deliverance and enables Moses' activity as an agent of liberation. Historically, the Name's promise of deliverance and liberation has been taken as a sign for others who are suffering; in American history, it functioned most notably as a sign of hope for African-Americans living under slavery. Thus, the Name shapes Moses' own relation to God, Israel's relation to God, and the relations between peoples. In light of the pragmatic dimension of naming, the Name no longer signifies just an otherworldly transcendence of God, but rather God's free self-determination for the freedom of an enslaved people and for relieving their suffering.

In its pragmatic dimension, naming God is political, establishing and reshaping human community. Again, Exodus can be our guide. In Exodus 33, Moses speaks to God in great intimacy once more. Requesting to see God's glory, Moses and God speak "like a man and his friend" [Ex. 33:15].[10] From this friendship proceeds the law, through which God relates to the community as a whole. As Kornelis Miskotte has written:

> As the first tablets contained the "writing of God"... as the two later tablets bore a derivative human script, so the speech which the Lord and Moses engage in here in the mystery of person-to-person, face-to-face encounter is an independent, antecedent secret, *a friendship*, as it were, a relationship that possesses a far higher degree of immediacy than the relationship to the people.[11]

---

6 My thanks to Janet Martin Soskice for conveying this point to me, and in her essay "Philo and Negative Theology," in M. Olivetti (ed.), *Théologie Négative* (Padova: Biblioteca dell'Archivo di Filosofia, 29: CEDAM, 2002).

7 See Franz Rosenzweig, "The Eternal: Mendelssohn and the Name of God," in *Scripture and Translation* (Bloomington: Indiana University Press, 1994), p. 104.

8 See Peter Ochs, "Scriptural Logic," in G. Jones and S. Fowl (eds), *Rethinking Metaphysics* (Oxford: Blackwell, 1995) p. 73, for this interpretation (as put forward in medieval times by Nahmanides).

9 Peter Ochs, "Three Postcritical Encounters with the Burning Bush (in memory of Emmanuel Levinas)", in S. Fowl (ed.), *The Theological Interpretation of Scripture*, (London: Blackwell, 1997); see esp. pp. 132-5.

10 Gregory of Nyssa, *The Life of Moses* (New York: Paulist Press, 1978), pp. 111-20.

11 Kornelis Miskotte, *When the Gods Are Silent*, trans. J. Doberstein (New York: Harper and Row, 1967), p. 392, my emphasis.

In the "face-to-face" encounter of receiving the Name, Moses achieved the height of human intimacy with God; to receive the Name is to move toward a transcendent relation of friendship with God. What Miskotte's text does not capture, however, is that even if they do not establish face-to-face relations, the "derivative" tablets nonetheless draw Israel, as a people, into God's presence: they provide a way for the community to dwell with God. Neither Moses nor the people will see God directly, but through the Name's signification, they are drawn closer. As Emmanuel Levinas writes, "The square letters [of the Name] are a precarious dwelling from which the revealed Name is already withdrawn."[12] The Name's withdrawal leads to individual transcendence, but also serves as a sign *for others*, enabling communal transcendence as well. Through the Name, the Law becomes a mode of sanctification, drawing the community toward God and one another, and opening new forms of friendship and community in ritual practice.[13] As Gregory of Nyssa writes, "If anyone wishes to be a friend of God, let him be a friend of me, the Law (for the friend of the Law is certainly the friend of God)."[14] Naming God intensifies communicative relationships, enabling *epektasis* and the journey toward holiness.

Ultimately, the semantic and pragmatic dimensions (along with the syntactic) of God's names are equally significant. However, in the preceding interpretations, the emphasis on the semantic dimension in the philosophical tradition has often obscured or effaced the pragmatic, relational dimensions of naming God. It therefore becomes necessary to think further about how the pragmatic and semantic dimensions are related. At its height, religious thought brings these two dimensions together, recognizing God's ineffability while affirming God's freely-chosen friendship for humanity, especially in the face of human suffering, and as a deliverance from oppression and death. As Janet Martin Soskice writes, "In the hands of great theologians like Gregory of Nyssa or Dionysius this unknowable God who dwells in 'brilliant darkness' and hidden silence is also and always the God of intimate presence too."[15] Before God's singular name, the rupture of human conceptuality and the healing of community go hand in hand—but how we conceive this connection remains a problem for study.

---

12 Emmanuel Levinas, "The Name of God According to a Few Talmudic Texts," from *Beyond the Verse*, trans. G. Mole (Bloomington: Indiana University Press, 1994), p. 121. For more on this text, see William Young, "Ritual as First Phenomenology: A Response to Robert Gibbs," *Modern Theology* 16 (2000), pp. 335-9.

13 This is the case in the work of Martin Buber; see, for example, Roland Goetschel, "Exode 3,14 dans la Pensée Juive Allemande de la Première Partie du xxème Siècle," in *Celui Qui Est: interpretations juives et chrétiennes d'Exode 3:14* (Paris: Les Editions du Cerf, 1986), pp. 265-76. Here, p. 275 (my emphasis): "Une telle présence de Dieu parmi les hommes signifie l'abolition de principe de tout comportement magique *puisque Dieu se révèle comme un partenaire des hommes*, comme le protecteur d'un peuple dans une histoire dont il est l'unique souverain."

14 Gregory of Nyssa, *The Life of Moses*, p. 108.

15 Soskice, "The Gift of the Name," p. 243.

While Exodus 3 has been central to the interpretation of naming God in both Jewish and Christian thought, Christian theological reflection on divine names often takes its bearing from Christology—as Christ is the "Name" of God. To name God by affirming Christ *as* God, and seeing the life of the Trinity at work in and through Christ, has grounded the central affirmations of Christian faith and guided theological reflection. Much as God names God's self for Israel in Exodus 3, as Christ names God "Father" in the eschatological sense, a renewed intimacy with and a rich understanding of God emerge from this scriptural event. Like in Exodus, the name of Christ has a pragmatic dimension. Both scripturally and in the tradition, the identification of Christ with the Name given in Exodus has been at the heart of Christian belief in God's fulfillment of the covenant, enduring fidelity to Israel, and the mission to the Gentiles in liberation from the slavery of sin.

This pragmatic dimension of naming God is frequently articulated in terms of friendship. As seen in John 15, faith in Christ opens onto a transition from servitude to friendship; the crucifixion and resurrection found (or confirm) a communal politics of self-sacrifice, martyrdom, and mutual generosity. Christ's kenotic devotion is understood to transform human friendship, raising it to a greater participation in the divine life. As Aelred of Rievaulx writes, when friends seek to be joined in the "sweet name" of Christ, then "charm may follow upon charm, sweetness upon sweetness and affection upon affection. And thus, friend cleaving to friend in the spirit of Christ, is made with Christ but one heart and one soul, and so mounting aloft through degrees of friendship with Christ, he is made one spirit with him in one kiss."[16] Semantically, the name of Christ allows for knowledge of God's will for humanity; pragmatically, it shapes relations in the Christian community, serving as the "medicine of life," in Aelred's words, by establishing friendship that relieves the pains of human suffering. It also shapes relations between communities, by enjoining the command to love one's enemies (Mt. 5:44).

In sketching these different dimensions of naming God, differences in interpretation have emerged between these varied theological positions. What is common to them all, however, is that the semantic understanding of the name of God shapes, and to some degree determines, the pragmatic dimension of this event. A focus on God's difference from the world, or immutable and impassive self-sufficiency, will downplay the pragmatic dimension of the giving of the Name, in the context of repair and response to suffering. By contrast, an interpretation that foregrounds the Name's promise, and its proximity to the people, renders one more attentive to relations within community. Thus, how one understands the naming of God, and its cognitive significance, directly affects how one conceives of the pragmatic dimensions as well. How one understands naming God enables, or disables, the imagination of particular constellations of community. The gift of revelation unsettles and reshapes human patterns of exchange and sociality.

---

16 Aelred of Rievaulx, *Spiritual Friendship*, trans. M. Laker, SSND (Kalamazoo: Cistercian Publications, 1977), pp. 74-5.

Assuming this correlation between the semantic and pragmatic relations, the question then becomes where one finds an appropriate mode of expression for the pragmatic correlate of naming God. To be sure, religious language shapes and transforms other relationships within a community besides friendship: erotics, punishment, economics, hospitality, and more. However, as already suggested, several aspects of divine names point to friendship as an appropriate correlate. First, the name of God is a singular term, a unique name for a unique being, as God, in Thomas Aquinas' words, is without genus or species. Likewise, friendship is a singular relation, to another in his or her uniqueness. Second, as a name that exceeds the cognitive, magical, or utilitarian meanings of language, the name of God allows relation to God for God's sake, exceeding or reshaping human intentionality. Friendship, likewise, at its highest level, is a relation to the other for her sake. Like naming, friendship may involve cognitive and utilitarian dimensions, but it must exceed these dimensions as well. Thus, in both interpreting the names of God, and reflecting on the relation of friendship, one conceives of a certain mode of singularity with regard to language and ethics. Naming God and friendship thus embody the place of singularity within the semantic and pragmatic dimensions of religious thought, and it is the correlation between these two topics that this work will explore.

II. Correlations

As we have seen, the interpretation of divine names oscillates between a semantic, cognitive focus and a pragmatic focus that highlights the relational dimensions of naming. As Rosenzweig says, naming makes God "addressable," even if God is only known as one unknowable. Following the work of Rosenzweig, Barth, and Levinas, this essay argues that the relational dimension of naming God should take priority. As address and prayer, naming God is primarily an issue of relation. If God is unnameable and unknowable, the primary significance of naming is to enable relation to God, in ways that also shape relations between people. Knowing God, then, is a function of relation to God; the reference of naming God, it will be argued here, is the enabling of friendship.

Since naming God and friendship illuminate the semantic and pragmatic dimensions of theological inquiry, these issues can also crystallize and highlight important differences between theological perspectives. This essay moves toward a comparison of the work of Thomas Aquinas and Jacques Derrida by exploring the correlations between naming God and friendship in each author's work. Drawing on Dionysius' mystical theology while incorporating Aristotelian grammar and metaphysics, Thomas' work represents the height of medieval reflection on the naming of God. At the same time, Thomas develops and enriches theological ethics through the reworking of Aristotelian virtue and friendship in light of scripture and the patristic tradition. While his ethics and theology are often treated in isolation from one another, Thomas' view of charity as friendship with God—the centerpiece of his theological ethics—embodies the practical outgrowth of his understanding of the naming of God in faith through sacred doctrine. In both language and practice, Thomas seeks to order the particular acts of naming and love toward God's eminent transcendence. Systematically correlating naming God and friendship with God therefore provides insights into the semantic and pragmatic coherence of Thomas' theology.

In deconstructing the philosophical tradition's emphasis on self-presence, identity, and cognition, naming God and friendship have been central topics throughout Derrida's work. On both topics, Derrida sees philosophical reason as effacing singularity, and thereby failing to conceive responsibility, generosity, and love. Philosophy "fails to conceive" in a dual sense: philosophy and theology (in the onto-theological sense) do not think these ideas properly, but thereby they also fail to put them into practice. As set forth in his debates with Emmanuel Levinas, Paul Ricoeur, and Jean-Luc Marion, Derrida emphasizes how naming God *testifies* to God's singularity without rendering it presently graspable. This linguistic deconstruction finds its pragmatic correlate in his conception of friendship as a testimonial, inexhaustible relation to the other that cannot reach stasis or a determined limit. There is a structural openness to both naming God and friendship that destabilizes them in their very occurrence. Through the deconstruction of these concepts, Derrida's work points toward an alternative politics and ethics of singularity.

These correlations between naming God and friendship within each author's work enable a new comparison between Thomas and Derrida's poststructural religious thought. Given the emphasis on pragmatics of this essay, it may seem strange to focus on these two authors. Thomas' focus on beatific knowledge of God, his discussion of analogical language, and Derrida's critique of a metaphysics of presence, seem to indicate a cognitive focus far from the concern of this essay. Yet, for both authors, the politics of the names of God are of central concern, and both constructively and creatively adopt the language of friendship as a way of transforming both divine–human and intrahuman relationships. How one praises God, for both, shapes community and relations between community; there is a political dimension to praise.

Moreover, this comparison is highly pertinent for contemporary theological reflection. While Derrida's work has become prominent in recent philosophical theology, a rigorous comparison of his work to Thomistic theology on these topics has not been undertaken. Reflection on Derrida has more often been undertaken in comparison with Barth and other twentieth-century theologians.[17] However, since Thomas' complex theological reflections on language and signification speak to many of the issues central to Derrida's work in a way that much of contemporary

---

17 See, for example, Walter Lowe, *Theology and Difference: The Wound of Reason* (Bloomington: Indiana University Press, 1993); Graham Ward, *Barth, Derrida, and the Language of Theology* (Cambridge: Cambridge University Press, 1995); Isolde Andrews, *Deconstructing Barth: A Study of the Complementary Methods in Karl Barth and Jacques Derrida* (New York: Peter Lang, 1996).

theology does not, a comparison of their views is quite pertinent.[18] Further, the contemporary movement known as "radical orthodoxy" posits an opposition between postmodernity and medieval and patristic theology, arguing that a theological, analogical ontology provides an alternative to the nominalist, nihilistic thought of modernity and postmodernity, such that the relation between Thomas and Derrida is presumed to be an opposition. While Derrida's and Thomas' conceptions of naming and friendship diverge, a detailed exploration of the pragmatic and semantic correlations between these issues reveals surprising convergences as well. As shall be discussed further, for both authors, in contrast with many voices within Christian theology, the command to love one's enemies carries *political* as well as private significance, testing the boundaries of Christian community. While unsettling the presumed Thomas/Derrida opposition, this political interpretation of friendship carries deep significance for contemporary theological reflection on friendship and community. Thus, while the relation between naming God and friendship is the primary thematic focus of this work, the particular correlations established here complicate and enrich the positioning of Thomas' work with respect to contemporary theological reflection.

Perhaps against expectation, this essay will show that in their linguistic reflections, both Thomas and Derrida provide a way to orient semantic study toward pragmatic reflection. Even in their abstract linguistic work, the politics of praise never fully recede from view. As will be argued below, the emphasis on the relational dimension of naming God gives renewed theological significance to the importance of apophatic and deconstructive approaches to theological language. Apophasis is important for two reasons. First, as would generally be acknowledged, it is a corrective of onto-theological or essentialist understandings of God, bringing humility to the philosophical theologian. As Matthew Levering has recently argued, for Thomas metaphysical reflection is a way of remotion that serves as a critique of idolatry, identifying the unique God of scriptures.[19] Secondly, and more deeply, it instills an awareness of the distance of God, the alterity in and through which God approaches us in friendship, and the otherness and separation in which we may approach one another as well. As such, it both opens the possibility of a greater *intensification* of relationships—denying a self-satisfied stasis—and promotes the *extension* of such relationship, delimiting a community of friends and opening it to outsiders. In short, it enables relations across distance, striving toward the uniqueness of each other, in a self-diffusing, communicative way that reflects and reciprocates the divine gift of friendship toward humanity. For both Aquinas and Derrida, the critical, deconstructive moment of naming God is necessary if such a transformation

---

18 On this point, see Bruce Marshall, who argues that Aquinas' logico-semantic approach to Christology enables a richness of reflection not found in either either Rahner's transcendental reflection or Barth's christological dogmatics. See Bruce Marshall, *Christology in Conflict* (Oxford: Blackwell, 1988).

19 Matthew Levering, *Scripture and Metaphysics: Aquinas and the Renewal of Trinitarian Theology* (Oxford: Blackwell, 2004).

of friendship is to become possible; troubling the boundaries of our language is crucial to maintaining a hospitality toward those beyond a community's borders.

This surprising convergence of Derrida and Aquinas bears great significance for contemporary Christian theology. Reading Aquinas as seeking understanding through reasoning about and from scripture, it challenges the contemporary movement of radical orthodoxy at several crucial points. First, the emphasis on divine distance serves as a corrective to the Platonizing tendencies of radical orthodoxy's penchant for participation-language. On occasion, this emphasis on our participation in the divine life seems to obfuscate the difference between our mode of participation, and the triune life itself.[20] The uniqueness of God—and the uniqueness of our friendship with God—can be obscured as a result. Attending to the distinction between God's simplicity and our mode of knowing and loving God—which is central to Thomas' work—counterbalances this tendency.

Second, one of Milbank's most significant contributions to the contemporary debate is his articulation of a gift as constituted by reciprocal exchange, analogously to the exchange between the persons of the Trinity.[21] As he argues persuasively, a gift is given when it attends to the particular recipient, and enables a response on the part of the other. Milbank's points here are important, and provide an important counter-argument against the unilaterally-conceived gift of Levinas, Marion, and Derrida, as shall be discussed more in the final chapter. However, one might ask if this conception of the gift downplays the superabundant generosity of God's activity, even within the Trinity, as a pattern of relations in which giving is infinite, and thus in some sense without return. In light of this possibility, Derrida's deconstruction of the gift can be (partially) retrieved in the face of Milbank's critique.

Third, building on the emphasis on participation and reciprocity, there is a pronounced emphasis in radical orthodoxy on friendship *within* the Christian community, with little mention of how friendship with those beyond its borders might be of theological significance.[22] For instance, in *Being Reconciled: Ontology*

---

20 For a helpful example of this argument that the difference is lost, see Lawrence Hemming, "*Quod Impossibile Est*! Aquinas and Radical Orthodoxy" in L. Hemming (ed.), *Radical Orthodoxy? A Catholic Enquiry* (Burlington: Ashgate, 2000), pp. 77-82.

21 John Milbank, "Can a Gift Be Given? Prolegomena to a Future Trinitarian Metaphysic," *Modern Theology* (1995), pp. 119-61.

22 In the *Radical Orthodoxy: A New Theology* volume, David Moss presents a view of friendship that, like Milbank's own, strongly prioritizes friendship within the Christian community, as modeled by Anselm and his fellow monks. Such friendship, Moss argues, is a way into the contemplation of God—as he says, somewhat provocatively at the end of the essay, "Would, then, friendship give the site for a most radical recollection today: a remembering of the *analogia entis*?" David Moss, "St. Anselm, Theoria and the Convolution of Sense," in John Milbank, C. Pickstock, and G. Ward (eds), *Radical Orthodoxy: A New Theology* (Oxford: Routledge, 1999) p. 140.

This will be addressed more fully in the conclusion, but it is worth indicating how the interpretation set forth here will differ from radical orthodoxy, though I am essentially in agreement that friendship and contemplation do go hand in hand. For, the contemplation of

and Pardon, Milbank strongly contrasts his own sense of reciprocal friendship, within the realm of the same, with a poststructural emphasis on unilateral relation to others. He does so, in part, by contrasting his reading of John with Derrida's emphasis on Luke's unilateral love of enemies:

> This [Luke 6:32-35] is Derrida's favoured focus for the Christian essence, and yet it is surely to be contrasted with St. John's gospel, where there is no mention of loving enemies, where love seems to ceaselessly circulate amongst friends—I in you, and you in me ...
>
> Now it may very well be argued that Christianity has combined both perspectives on giving, *but if it has done so it is surely more fundamentally under the aegis of reciprocity*, even though the eschatological character of this goal requires "an absolutely unilateral" moment for the gift in our present time ... for the manner in which he dies for his friends is indeed not that they should live their self-possessed lives...but rather in defence of the truth he has secretly proclaimed to them ... a truth only maintained and indeed fully taught in Christ's resurrected return.[23]

Milbank describes his account of gift-giving as "asymmetrical reciprocity,"[24] incorporating a unilateral element within the scope of reciprocity. However, his tendencies to treat unilateral giving as such as sacrifice, and to see reciprocity as directed toward a harmonious union and rest, suggest that unilateral action must ultimately be overcome in his ontology.

While Thomas does emphasize reciprocity in drawing on Aristotelian categories of friendship, I will argue in chapter 4 that this emphasis on reciprocity and friendship within the community is displaced in the order of charity, which impels and propels one toward seeking friendship with enemies and strangers, as a component of emulating divine grace and charity. As shall be shown, where Milbank reads Luke in light of John, Thomas' reading of Luke on love of enemies shapes his reading of John 15, and is logically prior to it in his scriptural interpretation. As will be shown, these questions were clearly important to Thomas, yet they receive less treatment and emphasis within the radically orthodox appropriation of his work than they deserve. Moreover, in Derrida's later work the Levinasian emphasis on the welcome of the other emerges as a trope of friendship that raises questions about the relation of Christian friendship to its surrounding world of others. The possibility of a counter-convergence between Thomas and Derrida thus emerges, in the idea of a "reciprocal unilateralism," in which giving to the other, without reserve, moves one toward greater participation in divine generosity, in part only through the recognition of the finite, deficient ways such participation occurs.

This essay focuses on two conceptual arguments, and the plan of this book reflects these dual goals. The goals are the following; first, the essay establishes a

---

God must come to its fullest realization, in recognition of both participation in God's life *and* our distance therefrom, in friendship both within and beyond the community.

23 John Milbank, *Being Reconciled: Ontology and Pardon* (London: Routledge, 2003), p. 160, my emphasis.

24 Ibid., p. 156.

correlation between the semantics of naming God and the pragmatics of friendship for Thomas and then for Derrida. Through this correlation, it implicitly argues that these issues provide a methodology for articulating the links between the semantic and pragmatic dimensions in others' works as well. Second, in light of these correlations, I re-evaluate their relation to one another and the implications for contemporary theology, as outlined above. To accomplish these goals, it is necessary to provide a philosophical framework and explicate the conceptual terminology for discussing naming and friendship. To this end, chapter 2 develops the Aristotelian conceptions of proper names and friendship. Chapter 3 then develops Thomas' views on theological language and divine names, and chapter 4 explores his views on charity and friendship. These chapters trace how charity and justice serve as the pragmatic dimensions of sacred doctrine's eminent naming of God, while also clarifying how Thomas both adopts and reshapes Aristotelian philosophy on the semantic and pragmatic levels. Chapter 5 then studies Derrida's approach to these issues, establishing a correlation between his understanding of singularity in terms of the impossibility of properly naming God as such and the singular, appresentative relation of friendship. In light of these analyses, chapter 6 develops the comparison between them, and the work concludes by situating each author's work in relation to contemporary theology, especially the work of Milbank and Jean-Luc Marion. The conclusion argues that it is in the dual concern for the particularity of virtue and the supplicating address of testimony that one avoids both an idolatrous materialism and an idealizing analogization. In the tension between Thomas' eminent discourse and deconstruction, one names God in a way that leads to a friendship open to alterity.

III. Returning to the Name: Postcritical Theology

The interpretation of divine names has been a defining issue of twentieth-century religious thought. A brief sketch of this history will situate this study within the trajectory of contemporary theology, and show how the movement toward pragmatic interpretation has been central to postcritical trends in theology. The centrality of naming God in contemporary thought is partly attributable to modern, Enlightenment theology's idealistic tendency to ignore or elide the linguistic particularity of God's names. It is, in short, an outgrowth of the "linguistic turn" in contemporary philosophy. For example, as Thomas Carlson has argued, Hegel's effacement of the naming of God is one of the defining marks of modernism in his theology. On Carlson's view, Hegel's decision to privilege the being of God over the name of God is intimately connected with his effacement of the finitude and temporality of the human subject in the "death of death" he describes in the speculative Good Friday crucifixion.[25] While other thinkers have treated "Being" as a name for God, ultimately for Hegel, "God" is a name for Being; in this move, Hegel subsumes

---

25 Thomas Carlson, *Indiscretions: Finitude and the Naming of God* (Chicago: University of Chicago Press, 1998), chs 2 and 3.

singularity under the conceptuality of the universal.[26] A similar disregard for the concreteness of names is found in the work of Kant, Schleiermacher, and Feuerbach, among others, and one could see Tillich and Bultmann as the descendants of this trajectory. Briefly stated, then, the modern turn to subjectivity has also been a turn away from the verbal, particular practices of naming in religious communities. As modernist and liberal theology have marginalized the importance of naming God, challenges to a modernist approach frequently return to this issue to articulate an alternative rationality that is more attentive to singularity.

Historically, two of the most prominent challenges to this modernist logic are found in the work of Karl Barth and Franz Rosenzweig, both of whom turn to naming God in the context of challenging Hegelianism. Barth's challenge is exemplified in *Anselm: Fides Quaerens Intellectum*, his reading of Anselm's *Proslogion*. On Barth's reading, Anselm's "ontological proof" works because Anselm invokes God in prayer, transforming "that than which nothing greater can be conceived" into God's name: "And *thou* art this being, O Lord our God. Thou so truly art, then, O Lord my God, that thou canst not even be thought of as not existing."[27] As this passage demonstrates, the phrase becomes a name in the address *to* God, breaking with predication while retaining its form. Barth writes, "The lever in both cases, the *argumentum* in his analysis of both parts of the *Proslogion*, is therefore the Name of God that is presupposed."[28] When invoked in prayer as God's name, this formulation becomes the joyful language of praise, a language that seeks to understand what it already believes (*fides quaerens intellectum*).[29] Understanding is thus always already in relation to the other, and divine freedom and agency take priority over human cognition.

For Barth, Anselm's joy over the proof signifies the relationally transformative dimension of the name of God. Through the proof, Anselm discovers that he and the fool (who says in his heart, "There is no God") seek the same thing. The surprising result of the proof, then, is that the theological method makes us *more* human, creating solidarity and relationship among humans in a recognition of our finitude and dependence upon God. The invocation of God transgresses the bounds of our language and knowledge, but not as a simple negation of humanity. Rather, God's name brings about an incarnational transcendence, placing us more immanently within the history, language, and community from which understanding proceeds in light of the event of prayerful address. Anselm's "speculative" proof opens onto

---

26 That is, if religion is a "picture" of that which comes to consciousness in the unfolding of absolute spirit, then "God" names Being, which must then be apprehended in the movement of consciousness.

27 Anselm of Canterbury, *Proslogion*, ch. 3. In E. Fairweather (ed.) *A Scholastic Miscellany: Anselm to Ockham* (Philadelphia: Westminster Press, 1956) p. 74.

28 Karl Barth, *Anselm: Fides Quaerens Intellectum*, trans. J. Robertson (Richmond: John Knox Press, 1960), p. 73.

29 Barth, *Anselm*, pp. 73-5. For a discussion of how Anselm's formulation breaks with ordinary thematic description, see Cora Diamond, "Anselm's Riddle," in *The Realistic Spirit* (Cambridge: MIT Press, 1991), pp. 267-89.

relation to the world. In the relation of Anselm and the fool at the conclusion of the proof, Barth discovers the following: faith seeks understanding as a form of joyful charity toward the neighbor, to glorify God and spread the light of God's love in the world.[30] "That than which nothing greater can be thought," through and beyond its semantics, opens onto an infinite pragmatics, as partially elaborated *in Church Dogmatics*. Even if its status as a "break" from his dialectical thought remains debatable, Barth gave this book and its reflections on naming God and theological method a privileged place in his opus throughout his career.[31]

Much as Barth's work reshaped the field of twentieth-century Christian theology, the New Thinking of Franz Rosenzweig made the naming of God a central locus for twentieth-century Jewish philosophy. As a rejection of idealism, Rosenzweig's work demonstrates the connection between the pragmatic and semantic dimensions of naming God, and it is in terms of these connections that he has influenced both twentieth-century theology and this study in particular.[32] Rosenzweig's work analyzes the independence of humanity, world, and God, the three of whom are distinct entities, yet can only fully be themselves in relation to one another. His most systematic and widely read work, *The Star of Redemption*, begins with these elements in apparent isolation from one another. In this isolation, nihilism and the impossibility of relation mark the limit of human existence.[33] Only in revelation, God's meta-physical revelation into the grammar of speech,[34] is the isolation of the elements revealed to be creation—*already* revelation and the very possibility of redemption itself. As Rosenzweig writes: "The ground of revelation is mid-

---

30 See Barth, *Anselm*, pp. 159-60: "Anselm did not ascribe it to any quality of his own, but to the grace of God, that he himself was not an *insipiens* doing the same thing and that for him the inner impossibility was at the same time an outward one. For that reason the otherwise fearful reproach, 'Thou art a *stultus et insipiens*' is not a direct reproach ... It is with just this reproach on his lips that Anselm takes his place as near as it is possible to be and therefore with as much promise as there could possibly be, alongside this fellow mortal whose action is so unintelligible."

31 Two readings that argue for the decisiveness of the Anselm book are George Hunsinger, *Karl Barth and Radical Politics* (Philadelphia: Westminster Press, 1976), pp. 219-21, and Hans Urs Von Balthasar, *The Theology of Karl Barth*, trans. E. Oakes (San Francisco: Ignatius Press, 1992). For a recent reading that discounts the discontinuity of the Anselm book with Barth's early dialectical theology, see Bruce McCormack, *Karl Barth's Critically Realistic Dialectical Theology: Its Genesis and Development 1910-36* (Oxford: Oxford University Press, 1995).

32 For more on Rosenzweig and his influence on continental thought, see Robert Gibbs, *Correlations in Rosenzweig and Levinas* (Princeton: Princeton University Press, 1992), and *Why Ethics? Signs of Responsibilities* (Princeton: Princeton University Press, 2000). See also Stephane Mosès, *Système et Revélation: La philosophie de Franz Rosenzweig* (Paris: Éditions du Seuil, 1982).

33 Franz Rosenzweig, *The Star of Redemption*, trans. W. Hallo (Notre Dame: University of Notre Dame Press, 1985), part I.

34 As discussed by Rosenzweig in the Grammar of Eros—his phenomenology of the Song of Songs. See ibid., part II, pp. 173-204.

point and beginning in one; it is the revelation of the divine name. The constituted congregation and the composed word live their lives from the revealed name of God up to the present day, up to the present moment, and into the personal experience."[35] In response to God's loving word, Rosenzweig sees humanity as bound together and bound more intimately to the world. The Name opens a future, "into Life" in the famous closing words of the *Star*.[36]

In *Understanding the Sick and the Healthy*, a short book that followed the *Star*, Rosenzweig makes a more pointed contrast between the diseased life of idealistic philosophy, in its concern for unreal essences and abstraction from speech, and a "healthy" form of thought. By contrast with idealist philosophy, the healthy life of the "New Thinking" seeks to live in light of the Name and the concrete, lived relations of language. Rosenzweig diagnoses the philosophical problem as follows:

> Philosophy has always claimed, since time immemorial, that the general concept is given, even if it is not perceptible. The "butter in itself" is the "idea" of butter; it is what the butter is "essentially." Actually, no one has ever seen this "ideal" butter which is always "present." On close inspection, it vanishes. It becomes only a subordinate line, attempting to connect two points: yesterday's butter and today's.[37]

In its concern for the essence, philosophy overlooks the apparent way in which objects maintain their continuity for us: via their names.

> Only the name was yesterday, is today, and will be tomorrow...how can a person, any person, be so faithful to himself as to remain faithful to another? But as soon as the "person" becomes "John"—well-defined by his name—the doubt disappears. The name is not the "essence." Yet, although the name and the essence are not identical, the name is as permanent as the essence is supposed to be. And common sense in action is concerned that the name, not the "essence," remain.[38]

Via the name's persistence in memory and through time, one relates to persons and the world, avoiding the disease of abstraction that seeks out the essential at the price of the actually existent. Yet the name is not the thing: even as it makes real relation possible, the difference between sign and thing also opens a distance between humanity and the world in which the disease of abstraction may fester.

For Rosenzweig, the crucial step in curing this "disease" rests in God's name. The names of things and persons are bound to them, holding them together across time. Names, generally exist for the sake of their bearers. The name of a person, a proper name, is given so that the person may be called and brought into the world. On the other hand:

---

35 Ibid., pp. 187-8.

36 Ibid., p. 424.

37 Franz Rosenzweig, *Understanding the Sick and the Healthy: A View of World, Man, and God*, trans. T. Luckman, ed. N.N. Glatzer (Cambridge, MA: Harvard University Press, 1999), p. 48.

38 Ibid., pp. 48-9.

God does not have a name so that he may be called by it. To him it is irrelevant whether His name is called or not ... *He bears a name for our sake, so that we may call Him.* It is for our sake that He permits Himself to be named and called by that name, since it is only by jointly calling upon Him that we become a "We."[39]

God's name does not serve God, but *us*; it is God's being for us and with us. Through the Name, the language that relates the individual to the world becomes a language *through which persons relate to each other* (a "We"). The Name provides a certainty that not only grounds one's own language, but links it to the language of others as well. It does not give an essential or eternal certitude, nor does it give God endurance; rather it makes our language and world endure by making them the language and world for others as well. Moving through time and language, it unites diverse speakers in the formation of a community. It unites the things named as well, creating the fabric of a world in creating a human community, even as humanity and world remain distinct.[40] Only through this unity of speakers, in speaking the Name (in whatever language this may be), are idealism and nihilism finally cured. For Rosenzweig, as for Barth, God's name opens the possibility of living religiously in the world, in human friendship and community. The work of both authors is highly suggestive as to how the semantics and pragmatics of naming God challenge the subjective emphasis that has predominated in modernist theology.

IV. Postcritical Pragmatics: Ricoeur and Levinas

In the work of Barth and Rosenzweig, the pragmatic and semantic dimensions of naming God interlace with one another. Barth's Anselmian theology and Rosenzweig's New Thinking have both opened paths of reflection that have deeply influenced contemporary and postmodern continental thought. Several thinkers of particular importance, for the issues we are discussing, are Kornelis Miskotte, Paul Ricoeur, and Emmanuel Levinas. While Miskotte precedes both Ricoeur and Levinas, his work is particularly noteworthy because both Barth and Rosenzweig strongly and explicitly shaped his reflection. In *When the Gods Are Silent*, Miskotte gives special emphasis to the Name of God as the potential antidote to the modern threat of nihilism. Miskotte interprets modernity's turn to the subject as collapsing into a nihilistic loss of value, as the projects and projections in which we place value are discovered to be precisely those projects in which we place value with no value in and of themselves. Taking assurance of the value of the world only from within ourselves, the valuation of the world by the ego becomes meaningless. By entering our language from beyond our subjectivity, the Name holds the possibility of a liberation from an ego that sees only itself in the world:

---

39 Ibid., p. 91, my emphasis.
40 Ibid., pp. 91-2.

> Nothing makes the Scriptures and especially the Old Testament so acutely immediate and contemporaneous as the quiet and insistent, loving and mighty NAME; nothing can be such a liberation for the intellectually tormented as the death knell of religion sounded by the theophany of YHWH. When the gods and also the god whom we have constructed for ourselves by our autonomous thought go on exercising their depressive and destructive silence, it must become clear that they have always been silent gods who will always drive us to atheism, total alienation from meaning, the emptying of life, and the eclipse of "God." Nihilism is the necessary consequence of "our Christianity." And from that point of view, the word "our" can be legitimate; indeed, it even forces itself upon us as a confession of solidarity.[41]

For Miskotte, the modern forgetting of the Name in its turn to the bourgeois subject collapses Christianity into the realm of human projection. In the light of the Name, life in the world and in history take on a new value precisely because it is the site for relationship and love. This importance of the Name leads to Miskotte's affirmation that YHWH is the Godhead, and that without the Name humanity would stand in silent isolation separated from both God and one another. In the Name, a "confession of solidarity" becomes possible, both in the recognition of the empty silence of subjectivisim and the possibility of life in the Name.[42]

Likewise, in his reworking of modern hermeneutics, Paul Ricoeur has recognized that the naming of God poses special challenges for biblical exegesis, theological interpretation, and ethics. In the essay "Naming God," Ricoeur discusses the ways in which God's name acts as a "limit-expression" in a number of different discursive genres within scripture. For example, in the narrative of a confession, God is named as the one addressed, but this act ruptures the narrative of confession and brings it into a polyphonic relationship with the prophetic (and other) voices of the biblical text.[43] By carrying the different genres to their limits, God's name brings the various discourses into conjunction and conversation with one another, creating what Ricoeur terms an enriched and multivalent "poetic" reference.[44] The polyphonic naming of God creates possibilities within and for each genre that it did not contain in isolation, thereby expanding the imaginative possibilities for interpretive agency. As Mark Wallace writes, "Before God is defined in univocal terms as Being under the control of a particular metaphysical system, Ricoeur maintains that God is first "named"

---

41 Miskotte, *When the Gods Are Silent*, p. 19.

42 Miskotte's work presages the work of Kendall Soulen in its focus on the importance of the election of Israel and the Name in Christian theology. Soulen is both more careful and more emphatic in his focus on the connection between YHWH and the Trinity than Miskotte, whose argument is more exegetical than systematic. For Soulen's work, see *The God of Israel and Christian Theology* (Minneapolis: Augsburg Fortress, 1996) and "YHWH the Triune God," *Modern Theology* 15 (1999), pp. 25-54.

43 Ricoeur, "Naming God," pp. 225, 228-30.

44 Paul Ricoeur, *Figuring the Sacred*, ed. M. Wallace (Minneapolis: Fortress Press, 1995), pp. 221-3; for more on Ricoeur's understanding of reference in the hermeneutical sense, and his critique of analytic conceptions of reference, see his *Interpretation Theory: Discourse and the Surplus of Meaning* (Fort Worth: Texas Christian University Press, 1976).

polyphonically in the medley of diverse biblical genres ... Reflection alongside, not away from, this polyphony should be the presupposition and telos of all theological work."[45]

For Ricoeur, humanity discovers new ways of life in and through interpretation of this polyphonic and poetic reference. For Ricoeur, "reference" is not an ostensive relation of text to the thing named, but rather the opening of a world for the reader *through* the text. Ricoeur argues emphatically that this polyphonic discourse, in the restricted openness of its poetic indeterminacy, should not be equated with any distinct political program.[46] However, while not strictly political, naming God brings a superabundance of meaning to the imagination that creates new ethical and political possibilities. Again, naming God is closely related to how we act in the world; its symbolic "worlding" of the subject both precedes and makes possible any ethical intentionality. In their multivalence, divine names open an interpretive field constituting both poetic and political possibilities.

In arguing for the priority of ethics over hermeneutics, naming God is likewise of central importance to Emmanuel Levinas, one of the most prominent phenomenologists of the twentieth century. Levinas is best known for his practice of phenomenology in a way that leads to a sense of infinite responsibility that can neither be thematized nor recuperated by the intentionality of the subject. In the infinite responsibility of "ethics as first philosophy," Levinas argues that the primordial possibility of phenomenology rests upon a metaphysics that goes beyond being (*epekeina tes ousias*) to a responsibility to the Other. Only in responsibility to the other does the phenomenological cognition of the world become just and peaceful. In this responsibility, the intention of the subject is called by another prior to its own intention, held hostage to a duty and agency that it cannot escape, in a face-to-face encounter in which no one can take the subject's place.[47]

In Levinas' Talmudic commentaries, the Name calls the Jewish people to this unforeseen responsibility, the responsibility of election. For Levinas, the Name is an epiphany that breaks into the realm of consciousness and egoistic enjoyment, calling the subject to respond (as exemplified for Levinas by Abraham's response to God, "Here I am!"[48]). Since his work is closely related to that of Derrida, it will be discussed further in chapter 5, but he is worth mentioning here for two

---

45 Mark Wallace, introduction to Ricoeur, *Figuring the Sacred*, p. 26.

46 Ibid., pp. 232-5. Ricoeur elaborates on the relation between interpretation and politics in the essay "Love and Justice," later in the same volume. For more on naming God in Ricoeur, see James Fodor, *Christian Hermeneutics: Paul Ricoeur and the Refiguring of Theology* (Oxford: Oxford University Press, 1995).

47 For Levinas' phenomenology of the face, see *Totality and Infinity Totality*, trans. A. Lingis (Pittsburgh: Duquesne University Press, 1968); I address the parallels between his phenomenological discussion of the face and his Talmudic interpretation of the Name in chapter 5.

48 See, for example, Emmanuel Levinas, "God and Philosophy," trans. R. Cohen, in *Basic Philosophical Writings*, ed. A. Peperzak and R. Bernasconi (Bloomington: Indiana University Press, 1996).

reasons. First, in Levinas, the Name is deeply connected with a transformation of human responsibility and subjectivity, calling the ego to its ownmost possibility of dispossession by the other. Second, while this responsibility is often termed "ethics," there are religious terms that bring his discussion of infinite responsibility closer to that of friendship. The relation to the other is a personal relation in the deepest sense: it is a relation of *election* and singularity rather than a general or deontological duty, and it precedes the more general, communal relation of justice. The infinite responsibility for the other reveals both one's own singularity and that of the other, drawing each toward the other in a transcendent relation of proximity. In disrupting the intentionality of the subject, the Name signifies an alternative community and relation that goes beyond modern ethics. Thus, in both Levinas and Ricoeur, the relational dimension of reference in naming becomes more prominent, extending the trend toward pragmatics begun in Barth and Rosenzweig.

V. Deconstruction and the Politics of Orthodoxy

From Barth and Rosenzweig through Miskotte to Ricoeur and Levinas, a trajectory of recent continental thought on the name of God can be traced. This trajectory rejects the idealism and subjective focus of much of modern theology; while it could be described as intersubjective, it would be better described as focusing on the intersubjective dimensions of a linguistic, scriptural event. These thinkers see the semantic dimension of naming God as contextualized and shaped by its pragmatic, relational, and political dimensions. In brief, because of its semantic depth and poetic or symbolic significance, as well as being an event of revelation and prayer, naming God bears a rich surplus of meaning that unfolds into relationship and community.

These issues have been taken up recently in the work of Derrida, Jean-Luc Marion, and John Milbank, among others, and the debates between their positions constitute the field of inquiry for this essay. While Derrida's work will be the focus of chapter 5, it is worth noting several ways that his work extends and questions the trajectory of study described above. First, for Derrida as for Barth, the naming of God must be an address to the other, rather than a predicative description. However, where Barth sees Anselm as naming God through the thematic language of the proof, Derrida's work argues that the name makes address to the other both possible *and* impossible. This complicates the relation between prayer and praise, as Derrida and Marion examine and debate at length. Second, if thematic language necessarily renders impossible relation to the singular other, then this has implications for community as well. In particular, while Derrida would agree that the naming of God does found a community, he raises the possibility that the community founded on a theological naming of God is also constituted by violence and exclusion (or at least, by its possibility). Specifically, Derrida raises the question of whether or not the naming of God neutralizes sexual difference, in part by conceiving friendship on the basis of fraternity. In thinking of the limits of such community and friendship,

Derrida opens a new thought of friendship and community, in the register of the impossible, relating to the other both in and beyond the naming of God.

While this trajectory of reflection is enormously important on its own, several features of its development provide warrant for bringing the work of Thomas Aquinas into the conversation. Thomas' work provides alternative accounts of signification and friendship that can historicize and contextualize modern thought. In many ways, and largely due to contingent historical factors, the study of naming God in the twentieth century has proceeded through a focus on Christian and Jewish scriptures, largely neglecting the resources and richness of traditional interpretation. Of the thinkers discussed in the previous section, only Levinas draws upon the insights of Talmudic commentary and the Jewish tradition to enrich and develop his own position. Placing Aquinas' work in conversation with these contemporary conversations will enrich and reframe the discussion. Thomas' grammar, largely influenced by Aristotle, attends to the particular modes of signification in greater detail than the Saussurean notion of the sign. Moreover, Thomas' development of charity through an Aristotelian ethics of virtue stands at some distance from the more Kantian strands of the thinkers discussed above (with Milbank standing as an obvious exception to the rest). Indeed, as chapter 4 will demonstrate, Thomas' work on charity illustrates precisely how the naming of God, as found in sacred doctrine, reshapes pragmatic relations; by reading his discussion of virtue and charity as friendship with God in light of his commentary on the Gospel of John, it will become clear how Thomas adopts and theologically reshapes an Aristotelian ethics of virtue. In his account of naming God and friendship, Thomas' work can illuminate the contemporary debate by bringing it into conversation with the Christian tradition of commentary, and thereby move the debate forward in new directions.

Thomas' work is important in another way, as it provides a methodological model for charitable theological reflection in engaging the critical discourses of postmodernity. With the rise of postmodernity, theology seems to be faced with modes of knowledge and inquiry that are contrary to faith. The "hermeneutics of suspicion" of Marx, Freud, and Nietzsche, and their genealogical descendants such as Derrida, Lacan, and Foucault, often are taken as the foils for theological reflection. Even radical orthodoxy, which takes many of the issues of postmodernity as the starting point for theological reflection, nonetheless establishes its position through a rejection of postmodern reflection. Likewise, the reception of postmodern reflection often involves a knee-jerk rejection of more traditional theological discourses and practices. The relationship between contemporary theology and postmodernity, then, is best described as polemical.

Thomas' practice of theology, however, displays another approach to religious reflection. When Thomas "baptized" Aristotle, as is often said, Aristotle's philosophy was hardly seen as amenable to Christian reflection. On many points, Aristotle appears to be in direct conflict with Christian doctrine on the issues of the eternity of the world and the mortality of the soul. Throughout and after Thomas' life, Aristotle's status remained controversial within medieval theology. Given this apparent antinomy between Aristotelian philosophy and scriptural theology, the theological status of

Aristotle's work in Thomas' time was analogous to that of postmodern reflection today. Thomas' innovation, however was to integrate Aristotelian philosophy into the Christian faith. He showed how a science that appeared to contradict theology could actually contribute to it and enrich its discourse.[49] Central to Thomas' practice was a hermeneutics of charity that recognized the need for continuing deliberation regarding the relationship between theology and other sciences.[50]

One can debate the successes and costs of Thomas' work, but this essay takes it as a model for theological reflection in a postmodern era. While postmodernity should not set the terms of debate for theology in an *a priori* fashion, as a form of neo-liberal theology, one cannot simply ignore or reject the discourse and patterns of inquiry of postmodern thought. Studying the ways that Thomas adopts Aristotelian patterns of inquiry can establish a path for the theological appropriation of postmodern inquiry as well. One can be faithful to Thomas' practice, even as engagement with postmodernity may go beyond the limits of Thomas' own work. Thomas' work will historicize contemporary religious thought, but contemporary thought can also enrich, qualify, and develop Thomas' views on theological language and ethics in unforeseen ways. In particular, it will let us raise questions about the appropriateness of Aristotelian descriptions of friendship for the friendship that emerges from the naming of God, given the essentialism and elitism of Aristotle's explication of friendship in the *Nicomachean Ethics*. The wager, then, is that following Thomas' practice of interpretation can lead to a new understanding of naming God and of friendship that speaks to both Thomistic and postmodern concerns. The two traditions of reflection can transform one another in their mutual engagement. In working toward such mutual discovery and transformation, this essay practices a hermeneutics of friendship, seeking understanding and relation in the particularity of each approach, and opening onto further conversation through contemplation of their differences.

---

49 For a detailed analysis of Thomas' procedure, see Bruce Marshall, "Absorbing the World," in B. Marshall (ed.), *Theology and Dialogue: Essays in Conversation with George Lindbeck* (Notre Dame, IN: Notre Dame University Press, 1990), pp. 69-102.

50 For a recent application of this approach, see Eugene F. Rogers, Jr., "When Scripture and Science Conflict: Retrieving a Traditional Hermeneutics," in *Sexuality and the Christian Body: Their Way into the Triune God* (Oxford: Blackwell, 1999), pp. 127-39.

Chapter 2

Proper Names and the Logic of Friendship

As the introduction discussed, naming and friendship are modes of singularity. In this light, it becomes conceivable that for a particular philosophical position, there will be a correlation between the conceptions of naming and friendship. This chapter will move the argument forward by explicating the philosophical conceptions of naming, as singular reference, and friendship, as conceived on an analytic, Aristotelian basis. This is significant for this work, because Aristotle's work on both topics serves as the basis for Thomas Aquinas' theological reflections and undergirds the philosophical tradition which Derridean deconstruction interrogates.

To explore this Aristotelian logic, let us begin with two remarkably parallel puzzles that have deeply shaped the philosophical landscape. An individual subject is as fully self-sufficient as she can be when she is virtuous, since she has all internal goods, but insofar as humans are political animals, we cannot be truly flourishing unless we share our lives with others. The importance of sociality leads into questions regarding the type of equality found in friendships of character. For Aristotle, the equality of two friends of either pleasure or utility (the derivative types of friendship) is a contingent one; only so long as both parties receive benefit does the friendship last. But things get more complicated for friendships of character. Unlike friendships of pleasure or utility, friends of virtue are friends because of the principle of each other's activity—that is, the virtuous character that makes them who they are. There is, then, a deeper form of equality in friendships of character. As one loves one's own good, so one would seem to want to love the good of the other in the same way. That is, if a and b have the same virtue, then one can say that a=b. Friendships of character involve an equality between two essences, and Aristotle says these friendships are "permanent."[1] Yet how can two different beings be identical? A friend is, as Aristotle says, "another self," but am I equal to the friend in the same way I am identical to myself?

A similar problem is found in the famous essay "On *Sinn* and *Bedeutung*," where Gottlob Frege reflects upon relations of equality:

> Equality gives rise to challenging questions which are not altogether easy to answer. Is it a relation? A relation between objects, or between names or signs of objects? In my

---

1 Aristotle, *Nicomachean Ethics*, trans. D. Ross (Oxford: Oxford University Press, 1980), p. 197. See NE 1157b36, and below.

Begriffschrift I assumed the latter. The reasons which seem to favour this are the following: a=a and a=b are obviously statements of differing cognitive value [*Erkenntniswert*]; a = a holds *a priori* and, according to Kant, is to be labeled analytic, while statements of the form a=b often contain very valuable extensions of our knowledge and cannot always be established *a priori*.[2]

As Fege states, there are situations in which two things appear to be the same, as symbolized by the statement a=b. Frege takes this to be an equality between the names of things. The problem, in brief, is the following: a=a necessarily, and as an analytic statement is knowable *a priori*; by contrast, that a=b is not knowable *a priori*. The equality of a to itself and the equality of a and b are known differently. And yet, a=b would seem to have the same necessity, because if a=a necessarily and a=b, then by substitution a would equal b necessarily (It is necessary that a=a; if a=b, then by the process of substitution, it is necessary that a=b). How does one maintain equality while preserving the difference between a and b as represented by the differing cognitive values of these statements? This puzzle is the starting point for Frege's distinction between sense (*Sinn*) and reference (designation/*Bedeutung*). A and b refer to the same object, yet because they are known differently, they have different senses.

In both Aristotelian friendship and Fregean designation, problems arise regarding the relationship between self-identity and equality between different objects. The goal of this chapter is to explore these puzzles in detail, to see how these issues and their solutions parallel and illuminate one another. The specific problem is equality; to give a preliminary definition, two or more different things are equal if they share a property or an essence. They are equal necessarily, however, if they share a property essentially, so that we cannot think of the objects as not having the property they share.

Exploring Aristotle's account of friendship in the light of the notions of equality, necessity, and reference can help illuminate what is distinctive about friendships of character (*prote philia*). Focusing on analytical discussions of proper names will sharpen the discussion to issues of singular reference and singular relation. Saul Kripke's neo-Aristotelian analysis of the equality of proper names will provide the basis for our investigation of the equality of friendship. Kripke challenges Frege's account of sense and reference through his interpretation of proper names as *rigid designators*. Through the notion of rigid designation, Kripke argues that if a and b are proper names, and are equal (that is, share the same referent), they are identical *necessarily*.

Kripke's point is to show that necessary identity can be discovered *a posteriori*, when one is considering rigid designators.[3] For Kripke, the difference between

---

2 Frege, "On *Sinn* and *Bedeutung*," trans. M. Black, in M. Beaney (ed.), *The Frege Reader* (Oxford: Blackwell, 1997), pp. 151-71. Black notes that he uses "Equality" to translate *Identität*, and a=b should be understood as "a is the same as b."

3 Kripke indicates that these are "ordinary" proper names; he rejects Russell's distinction between "ordinary" proper names, which Russell argues actually function more

necessary and contingent equalities parallels the difference between rigid designators (i.e., proper names) and descriptions. Building on Kripke's work, my argument will show that *necessary* equality is a feature of Aristotelian friendships of character. Moreover, the necessary equality of friendship, like the equality of proper names, can only be discovered *a posteriori*. Contingent equality is a feature of Aristotle's accounts of virtue, justice, and friendships of pleasure, and thus is central to much of the *Nicomachean Ethics*. However, contingent equality cannot account for the strict equality found within friendships of character, because friendships of character are based on the property that makes two individuals who they really and truly are. As I will argue, reading the equality of friendship as a necessary one—in a sense, as rigidly designative—fits better with Aristotle's discussion of friendship's role in the moral life. In particular, by reading friendships of character as necessary equalities, Aristotle's claim that we can contemplate our own activity within friendship—and thereby achieve *eudaimonia*—is more readily comprehended. As a science of practical wisdom, in which we discover who we are, friendships of character mediate the practical and philosophical activities of the intellect and unify the human soul.

By comparing these issues, this chapter sets out the terminology and concepts prevalent in contemporary discussions of proper names and friendship, concepts that will be central to the theological and postmodern sections of this work. The new avenues of thought that these connections open—here, a different interpretation of Aristotelian friendship as a science of our action—will serve as a reference point for the ensuing discussion, as well as exemplifying the value of this correlation between names and friendship.

Consideration of these issues will shed light on oft-marginalized aspects of Aristotle's texts and call into question two tendencies in modern interpretations of Aristotle. The first is the tendency to conflate friendship and practical wisdom. The second is a related tendency to misread Aristotle regarding the relation of friendship to science (*episteme*) and contemplation. By exploring the logic of proper names, it may be possible to avoid these two tendencies and read Aristotelian friendship in a new light. In particular, it opens the possibility that it is in friendship that we really discover what actions are our own. Friendship, for Aristotle, would seem to be the source of knowledge (*episteme*) for the moral life.

I. Proper Names, Descriptions, and *a posteriori* Necessity: Kripke's Analysis of the Problem

Saul Kripke's discussion of proper names in *Naming and Necessity* departs radically from traditional theories of reference, as represented by what he terms the "Frege-Russell" Theory of Descriptions.[4] Kripke constructs his picture of how reference

---

like descriptions, and "genuine" proper names, which do necessarily designate a particular object.
  4 Saul A. Kripke, *Naming and Necessity* (Cambridge, MA: Harvard University Press, 1980), p. 27. Since Kripke's work, much work has been done to argue that for Frege, the sense

works largely on the basis of the difficulties of this traditional theory. Kripke's focus on the modal functioning of proper names leads to his inversion of the relationship between the description and ostension (designating an object through indication, like pointing to it). Description had traditionally been seen as underlying reference; ostension was treated as dependent upon description for its possibility.

By showing that ostension operates independently from description, Kripke stands this on its head: "Once we realize that the description used to fix the reference of a name is not synonymous with it, then the description theory can be regarded as presupposing the notion of naming or reference."[5] Kripke's crucial move is to treat proper names as rigid designators, such that a proper name designates the same object *in all possible worlds*. Through the rigid designation enforced by intending to use a name as others in the community have previously, we are able to refer in the first place. The key for Kripke is the way in which the name is used within the community, rather than the name's place within language; this makes reference possible without dependence upon description. To make this clearer, I shall briefly lay out Frege's views, treating them for the moment as a straw example of a descriptive theory of sense, as background for Kripke's theory.

Frege's views on the sense and reference of proper names are most famously articulated in his essay "On *Sinn* and *Bedeutung*," and other works flesh out the details of his approach. The view set forth in this essay can be summed up as follows: a proper name is a designation of a definite object by a word (or series of words, such as the Holy Roman Empire).[6] This is contrasted with a concept, such as "the man in the brown hat with the open zipper" whose designation may vary. A proper name, one could say, has a singular reference that does not change.

The sense of a proper name, on the other hand, is more difficult to articulate. Frege deems the sense of a proper name to be "grasped by everybody who is sufficiently familiar with the language or totality of designations to which it belongs."[7] Understanding the sense of a proper name involves grasping how it fits with other designations and descriptions within the language. One can contrast this with the sense of a concept, which consists in its placement within a sentence, since it is through the truth or falsity of the sentence as a whole that its reference takes place.[8] Moreover, Frege indicates that for proper names there is a one-to-one correspondence between the sign (i.e., the name itself), its sense, and the *Bedeutung*.[9] This correspondence will be important in terms of Kripke's analysis. By saying that there is a "one-to-one" correspondence of sense and reference, and treating the

---

of a proper name is not found via description. Thus, perhaps the view is primarily Russell's. Nonetheless, Frege has been read as holding this view, so for the purposes of simplicity I will follow Kripke's analysis of the problem, noting potential problems with his reading of Frege in footnotes.

5 Ibid., p. 97, n. 44.
6 Frege, "On *Sinn* and *Bedeutung*," pp. 152-3.
7 Ibid., p. 153.
8 See ibid., pp. 159-61.
9 Ibid., p. 153.

sense as familiarity with designations and descriptions, it sounds as though Frege is making a particular description the sense of the proper name, as it corresponds to the referent.[10] For example, "the man who taught Alexander the Great" would be the sense of the proper name "Aristotle."[11] If the description is the sense of the name, then it is synonymous with the name, and it is this point that Kripke rejects.

As seen above, the distinction between sense and reference becomes significant when there are questions regarding the equality or identity of two terms that have the same reference yet different senses. An example of this is Venus, which is named "Phosphorus" (or, descriptively, the Morning Star) and "Hesperus" (descriptively, the Evening Star). Frege's distinction between sense and reference is articulated in part to make comprehensible why one would name the star Hesperus in the morning and Phosphorus in the evening. Both have the same reference, but in our language, Phosphorus has the sense of the star as it is seen in the morning. To say, "Oh, there's Hesperus" at 7 a.m. would be wrong. Given that the names cannot be interchanged, much as the descriptions (Morning/Evening Star) cannot be interchanged, it does appear that names are synonymous with their descriptions, since both seem to function in the same manner.[12] Because proper names and descriptions seem to be synonymous in these contexts, along with Frege's comments regarding the correspondence between a proper name's sense and reference, Kripke reads Frege as treating the description as the sense of a name.[13]

---

10 Though Kripke does not explicitly say why he treats Frege as a description theorist, it would seem to be this conjunction of correspondence and Frege's definition of sense that leads him to this interpretation. However, if more than one description can be offered, then it would seem that description cannot be in a one-to-one correspondence with the referent, so that the sense would have to be something else. See note 13.

11 The description may fix the reference, so that one knows that this sign designates this particular object; perhaps Frege is better read in this way. In an article entitled "Reference and Sense: An Epitome," *Philosophical Quarterly* 34 (1984), pp. 369-72, David Bell argues that one should understand sense as the conditions or circumstances in which the name does designate a specific object (p. 369), which would not require that it is synonymous but may only fix the reference.

12 Leonard Linsky would disagree with this last point. See Linsky, *Names and Descriptions* (Chicago: University of Chicago Press, 1977), pp. 12-14, 42-3. "Frege held both that proper names have sense and that, in general, this sense is not the same as that of some definite description which denotes the same object as the name. From "Phosphorus= the morning star" and "Thales knows that Phosphorus=Phosphorus," it does not follow that "Thales knows that Phosphorus =the morning star." This just shows that Phosphorus and "The morning star" differ in sense. It does not show that "Phosphorus" does not have a sense" (p. 43). While this may mean that Kripke is wrong in his criticism of Frege on this point, it does not substantially undercut his position.

13 Recently, Wolfgang Carl has argued that Kripke and others have failed to appreciate Frege's views on sense and reference in part because they ignore his posthumous publications, particularly the *Logical Investigations*. He disputes that Frege equates the sense of a proper name with that of a description. Carl also seeks to show that if a proper name does not have a sense, it cannot have a reference—if one cannot understand how it fits into the totality of

Kripke's challenge to the theory of descriptions begins by considering differences between names and descriptions in modal logic. Whereas in the examples given by Frege and Russell, proper names (or for Russell, ordinary proper names) behave in the same fashion as descriptions, this is not the case in consideration of possible worlds—that is, worlds involving counterfactual situations.[14] Kripke takes the following case from Quine:

(1) 9= the number of planets revolving around our sun
(2) It is necessary that 9>7
(3) It is necessary that the number of planets revolving around our sun>7

In modal terms, a statement is necessary only if it is true in all possible worlds. (1) is a statement of fact. (2) is a necessary statement. But if this is the case, then by the substitution of equals given in (1), what follows in (3) would *also* seem to be necessary. Yet we can imagine (or stipulate) a possible world in which there might be seven planets or less. If one can imagine a possible world in which there were only seven planets, then in spite of the equality between the number "9" and the description "the number of planets" in (1), (3) would not be necessary. The metaphysical status of (2) and (3) differ in spite of the equivalence of "9" and "the number of planets" in (1). This is only a very obvious case in which numbers (as rigid designators) and descriptions operate differently, but already it raises a problem for a description theory of reference.[15]

Kripke's criticism works in a way similar to Quine's example, but using proper names instead of numbers. One cannot take a description to be synonymous with the name, because the description could be false yet the name could still refer. For example, Aristotle could have been "Aristotle" and yet not have been "the teacher of Alexander the Great." The description is clearly contingent. Someone might give "Aristotle" a different sense, such as "the greatest student of Plato."[16] In both cases,

---

language, it does not designate. Indeed, as Carl points out, Frege goes so far as to claim that a name may have a sense without a reference, but not a reference without a sense, precisely in the case of fictional characters such as Odysseus. See Wolfgang Carl, *Frege's Theory of Sense and Reference* (Cambridge: Cambridge University Press, 1994), pp. 179-81. For Frege's discussion of the issue see "On *Sinn* and *Bedeutung*," p. 157.

14 The distinction between logical and ordinary proper names for Russell arises because of the possibility of raising questions about the existence of an entity named by a proper name, such as, say, Moses or Aristotle.

15 See Kripke, *Naming and Necessity*, p. 40 for this example.

16 The possibility of different people giving different senses to a name is at the heart of Searle's view, which represents what Kripke calls the "cluster concept" of naming. See John Searle, "Proper Names," in Charles Caton (ed.), *Philosophy and Ordinary Language* (Urbana: University of Illinois Press, 1963), pp. 160-1. This view is rejected by Kripke as retaining the spirit of the traditional. Also, see Ludwig Wittgenstein, *Philosophical Investigations*, trans. E. Anscombe (Oxford: Blackwell, 1953), §79 for another discussion of the cluster view of names.

if the description is the sense of the name, and is therefore synonymous with the proper name, then the proper name only names Aristotle *contingently*. "The teacher of Alexander the Great" could have been someone else. But could Aristotle have been someone other than *Aristotle*? Given that "Aristotle" designates a certain person rigidly, so that the name identifies the same person in all possible worlds (in which the person exists), one cannot imagine that "Aristotle" refers to someone else.[17]

Kripke sees this as a frequent mistake in discussions of modal logic: by treating possible worlds as purely qualitative, we forget that when one asks whether or not it is contingent that Aristotle was the teacher of Alexander the Great, one is asking about *Aristotle* in this possible world. "Possible worlds are *stipulated*, not *discovered* by powerful telescopes. There is no reason why we cannot *stipulate* that, in talking about what would have happened to Nixon in a certain counterfactual situation, we are talking about what would have happened to *him*."[18] His work responds to the problem of transworld identification. By stipulating that in modal situations, one is talking about a specific individual, one is able to identify the individual across different possible worlds.

Kripke makes his argument for proper names as rigid designators based on such differences between the operation of proper names and descriptions in possible-world scenarios:

> One of the intuitive theses I will maintain in these talks is that names are rigid designators. ... a rigid designator rigidly designates a certain object if it designates that object wherever the object exists; if, in addition, the object is a necessary existent, the designator can be called *strongly rigid*.[19]

A rigid designator designates the same object in all possible worlds. We cannot imagine Aristotle being other than Aristotle in any possible world. He goes on to argue that it is precisely the rigidity of proper names that makes the whole project of possible worlds possible:

---

17 For the purposes of simplicity, Kripke (and most other name theorists) do not deal with the fact that a name can have more than one bearer. However, John McDowell has shown that in terms of defining the sense of a name, the multiplicity of potential bearers does cause problems for both a description theory and a causal theory of names (to be described below). See John McDowell, "On the Sense and Reference of a Proper Name," in *Meaning, Knowledge, and Reality* (Cambridge, MA: Harvard University Press, 1998).

18 Kripke, *Naming and Necessity*, p. 44. The example he uses involving Nixon works as follows: Nixon won the election in 1968; therefore, "Nixon" = "the man who won the election in 1968." Thus, when one stipulates a possible world regarding this case, one asks if it is possible that *Nixon* might not have won the election in 1968. Clearly, the answer is yes; even if his election in '72 seemed inevitable, it is a contingent fact that he won in both cases. But while we can ask whether Nixon might have lost, and we can ask "Could the man who won the election in 1968 have not won the election in 1968?"; however, we cannot ask if Nixon might not have been Nixon.

19 Ibid., pp. 48-9.

Those who have argued that to make sense of the notion of rigid designator, we must antecedently make sense of "criteria of transworld identity" have precisely reversed the cart and the horse; it is because we can refer (rigidly) to Nixon and stipulate that we are speaking of what might have happened to him (under certain circumstances), that "transworld identifications" are unproblematic in such cases.[20]

The rigid designation of proper names gets modal logic off of the ground by allowing for transworld identification. Kripke's argument shows that it is implausible that the sense of the description either equals or fixes the reference of a name.[21] Indeed, Kripke argues that in many cases, we use the names of people with either no description or a false description of who they are—yet we may nonetheless refer properly to the person named.[22] For example, I may see Sissy Spacek in the supermarket and say, "There's Sissy Spacek. She starred in *Sophie's Choice*." The description is clearly false—yet I may nonetheless be referring to her.

Kripke discusses several other contemporary theories of naming, all dependent on the theory of descriptions for their understanding of reference. The specifics need not concern us here; however, what he notices is that by and large these views treat it as a trivial fact that someone is *called* by a name—for example, that Socrates is called "Socrates." On Kripke's view, the importance of "calling" becomes evident precisely in those situations where no accurate description is available. If descriptions do not play a primary role in naming—neither as synonymous with names (and therefore sharing the same sense) nor fixing the reference when no description is given—then how can proper names refer? Kripke writes: "Obviously if the only descriptive senses of names we can think of are of the form 'the man called such and such' ... then whatever this relation of calling is is really what determines the reference and not any description like 'the man Socrates'."[23] "Calling" determines and enables reference even where the description is false (or absent). Insofar as one "calls" properly, the name retains its status as a rigid designator and can refer without description or sense.

For Kripke, "calling" involves intending to use the name precisely as others in one's community use the name. This works as follows: there is an "initial baptism" of an object, in which a name is given ostensively. The name is then passed on to others who refer to that object insofar as they use the name with the same intention

---

20 Ibid., p. 49.

21 To say that a description fixes the reference of a proper name is to say that the description serves as a criterion for letting others know what the reference is. So, for example, "The man with the champagne in his glass over there is Bob." "The man with the champagne in his glass" is a description. Hopefully, Bob does not *always* have champagne in his glass, so that the description does not designate him rigidly. Likewise, one may be mistaken about it being champagne in his glass, but he may still be Bob. The description, in cases like these, helps one to fix the reference by serving an epistemic function, telling someone before they meet Bob (*a priori*) who Bob is.

22 Kripke, *Naming and Necessity*, pp. 81-2, 91-2. His example is Richard Feynman.

23 Ibid., p. 70.

as those from whom they received it (and therefore, hopefully, the same intention as at the initial baptism).[24] If John introduces me to his friend Karen, then I will refer to her as Karen, intending to name her as John did. As Kripke writes: "In general our reference depends not just on what we think ourselves, but on other people in the community, the history of how the name reached one, and things like that. *It is by following such a history that one gets to the reference.*"[25] Since reference depends on shared intention, it can function independently of description.[26]

Kripke's discussion of the rigidity of proper names leads to two important points: first, one can know *a priori* contingent truths, and second, one can know *a posteriori* necessary truths. A brief explanation of how and why he makes these claims is important, because these will be important for the ensuing discussion of friendship, particularly with regard to the possibility of *a posteriori* necessary truths.

Kripke argues for distinguishing epistemology and metaphysics based upon cases which consider such rigid designators as proper names. To take the classical case, are Hesperus and Phosphorus necessarily identical? This case is particularly useful for Kripke's point because their identity is clearly not something you could know *a priori*. We have knowledge of their identity only on the basis of experience, yet Kripke argues that their identity *is* necessary. This is because in speaking of Hesperus or Phosphorus, one is speaking of *this particular star*—not a property of the star such as its location in the night sky. The star that we call Hesperus (or Phosphorus) would still be the same star, in all possible worlds and therefore necessarily.[27] The identity between these two is necessary, even though we only discovered it *a posteriori*; insofar as we speak of the proper names of this object, we regard them as rigid (and therefore necessary) designators of that object.

By contrast, we often identify Phosphorus as "the morning star," or "the star in position A in the morning." Likewise, Hesperus is identified as "the evening star." We may know that "the star in position A in the morning" is the same as "the star in position B in the evening." This would be knowable *a priori*. However, in a possible world, a different star could occupy the place in the heavens occupied by Hesperus. It is therefore *contingent* that the star fits these descriptions, and thus that "the star in position A in the morning" = "the star in position B in the evening." To summarize:

---

24 Ibid., pp. 91-6. The "initial baptism" and ostensive reference need not always be a specific event. Part of the importance of intending what others have meant by the name is to make this condition of reference noncircular—that is, it doesn't amount to "What I Willie call 'blue' refers to what I Willie call 'blue.'" If I refer to what Bob calls "blue," then it's not a circular condition of reference, and may therefore be valid. See also ibid., pp. 70-75.

25 Ibid., p. 95, my emphasis.

26 As Kripke points out, this also makes reference to mythical or fictional characters possible; ibid., pp. 163-4.

27 Ibid., p. 109.

Equivalence	Epistemological Status	Metaphysical Status
star in position a in the evening= star in position b in the morning (Description 1=Description 2)	*a priori*	contingent
Hesperus=Phosphorus (Rigid designator (name)1=R2)	*a posteriori*	necessary

One could know *a priori* that D1=D2. However, this identity is contingent, because it is possible that this would not be the case.[28] On the other hand, one would only discover the identity of Hesperus and Phosphorus by experience. This identity is necessary, because in talking about Hesperus or Phosphorus, you are talking about *this* planet.

According to Kripke, the equation of *a priori* knowledge with necessity, and *a posteriori* with the contingent is the result of a philosophical confusion of metaphysics (or ontology) and epistemology. The confusion between *a priori* and necessary as well as *a posteriori* and contingent leads to a misunderstanding about scientific discovery. He claims that it is precisely because names function as rigid designators that scientific knowledge is possible.[29] Because names rigidly designate, they enable the necessity constitutive of scientific knowledge. He writes: "So if this consideration is right, it tends to show us that such statements representing scientific discoveries about what this stuff *is* are not contingent truths but necessary truths in the strictest possible sense."[30] The rigid designation of proper names opens up new questions as to just what constitutes a science, and how we define scientific knowledge.

Kripke's theory leads to a philosophically controversial essentialism. A corollary of the necessity of identity between rigid designators is that certain properties of an object may be necessary features of that object. He takes the following example:

> This table is composed of molecules. Might it not have been composed of molecules? Certainly it was a scientific discovery of great moment that it was composed of molecules (or atoms). But could anything be this very object and not be composed of molecules? Certainly there is some feeling that the answer to that must be "no".[31]

---

28 The clearest cases of *a priori* contingent identity in Kripke are those descriptions which are presumed to be used to fix a reference. See especially his discussion of the "meter stick" and Wittgenstein's treatment of this problem, ibid., pp. 54-6.

29 This is behind his defense of the necessity of claims such as "heat is the motion of molecules," and other scientific truths. For his claims regarding "common names," see ibid., pp. 127-8.

30 Ibid., p. 125. See also Saul Kripke "Identity and Necessity," in S. Schwartz (ed.) *Naming, Necessity, and Natural Kinds* (Ithaca: Cornell University Press, 1977), pp. 87-9.

31 Kripke, *Naming and Necessity*, p. 47.

Likewise, Kripke takes it to be a necessary property of Nixon that he was human. To attempt to imagine that Nixon—the rigidly designated bearer of the name—was not human, or to stipulate such a possible world, is inconceivable on Kripke's view. When one imagines Nixon as an inanimate object, one is no longer using the proper name in accord with the chain of reference through which one received the name. Failing to use the name in accord with the use intended by others is to fail to refer with it—the very idea of a possible world becomes senseless, since it is no longer clear what one is talking about (since the criterion for transworld identification would be lost). For an essentialist, it is a necessary condition of *this* object's existence that it have certain properties; failing to have them, it would be a different object.[32]

While an object has essential properties, these may not be the properties by which we identify the object. We do not identify Nixon by saying he was human, nor a table as "the thing over there with the molecules." Those properties by which we identify an object may be contingent and simply fix the reference. However, essential properties *do* come into play when we attempt to consider the equality or identity between objects. Take, for example, twins. Why do we say that they are twins—because they look the same? Not necessarily; George W. Bush and Alfred E. Newman look alike, but we don't call them twins. We may use the contingent fact that twins look the same to fix the reference of the term "twins." However, there are clearly examples of twins (i.e., fraternal twins) who do not look the same. It would seem to be a different property, then, perhaps one of origin that would establish their identity. They could not be twins if born to different parents or on different days. In a case where two objects did not have the same essential property, or if one had it only contingently (i.e., not as an essential property), we could not say they were identical.[33] Thus, in some way, we are able to discover the identity between objects because they possess certain properties necessarily.

In Kripke's work, we see that the establishment of necessary identity via rigid designation is required for scientific knowledge. Bearing in mind the role essential properties play in considerations of equality between objects, and how scientific knowledge grows from this equality, we now can turn to Aristotle's discussion of friendship.

---

32 See his discussion of cats, ibid., pp. 125-6.
33 See Michael Della Rocca, "Essentialists and Essentialism," *Journal of Philosophy* 93 (1996), pp. 186-202, for the significance of essential properties with regard to relations of equality from a Kripkean viewpoint. The technical formulation of this essentialist position in terms of the equality between two objects would, I believe, be the following:

If x=y, then if x has property F necessarily, then y must have property F necessarily as well.

II. The Necessity of Friendship: From Practical Wisdom to Science in the *Nicomachean Ethics*

The remainder of this chapter will explore the relevance of Kripke's work on necessary equality for understanding Aristotle's conception of friendship. First and foremost, Kripke's analysis of the rigid designation of proper names, and their ensuing necessary equality, is useful in discussing the notion of equality put forth in Aristotle's discussion of complete friendship. In terms of the necessity of true friendship and the manner in which we know this *a posteriori*, friendship parallels the metaphysical and epistemic status of proper names. I will argue for the validity of such an interpretation by demonstrating how it accounts for a broad range of features of Aristotle's *Nicomachean Ethics*.[34] Viewing *philia* as an *a posteriori* necessary equality is helpful in wrestling with several problems in interpretations of Aristotle: the self-sufficiency of *eudaimonia*, the relation between practical and philosophical wisdom, and how one wishes goods for one's friend. Finally, given the similarities between Aristotle's discussion of friendship and Kripke's discussion of names as rigid designators, it is not surprising that Aristotle's discussion of friendship contains a number of essentialist features. The problems associated with such an essentialist approach to friendship—especially its exclusivity—will be addressed in the concluding section of the chapter.

There are a number of *prima facie* reasons to think that friendship should not be considered a necessary equality according to Aristotle's ethics. For many commentators, this is not an issue. For most, this is because of Aristotle's argument in book v of the *Ethics* for a nonscientific view of moral philosophy. Practical wisdom (*sophrosune*) is clearly distinct from philosophical wisdom; they are distinguished not only by method but by differences in the subject matter as well:

> Practical wisdom on the other hand is concerned with things human and things about which it is possible to deliberate; for we say this is above all the work of the man of practical wisdom, to deliberate well, but no one deliberates about things invariable, or about things which have not an end which is a good that can be brought about by action ... Nor is practical wisdom concerned with universals only—it must also recognize the particulars; for it is practical, and practice is concerned with particulars.[35]

Among recent interpreters, Martha Nussbaum is particularly clear and emphatic about this distinction. Aristotle associates practical wisdom with mutability, indeterminacy, and particularity, all three of which distinguish it from the necessity of scientific knowledge proceeding from first principles.[36] Moreover, the actions constitutive of practical wisdom proceed from *orexis*—movements of the will; they are forms of

---

34 Unless noted, *Ethics* refers to the *Nicomachean Ethics* (NE in the footnotes).
35 Aristotle, NE, vi.7, p. 146.
36 Martha Nussbaum, *The Fragility of Goodness: Luck and Ethics in Greek Tragedy and Philosophy* (Cambridge: Cambridge University Press, 1977), p. 302.

motion distinct from cognition (*noesis*).³⁷ Insofar as the *Ethics* deals with practical rather than philosophical wisdom, it seems unconcerned with metaphysical issues such as necessary equality.

This emphasis on particularity in the *Ethics* has been central to recent attempts to understand our passionate nature as integral to Aristotle's account of character. It has made possible an accompanying refusal to treat moral philosophy as simply or primarily an intellectualist endeavor. Perhaps most important among these efforts is Nancy Sherman's book *The Fabric of Character*, in which it becomes evident that Aristotle does not see virtuous action as simply intellectually rational; rather, virtuous action is virtuous through its integration and ordering of passionate responses in accord with the mean.³⁸ In what follows, I will build on Sherman's argument regarding the nature of virtuous character.³⁹ Her challenge to modern intellectualist conceptions of ethics opens the possibility of an Aristotelian intellectualism that includes the passions as a form of "proto-thinking" whose rationality is developed and articulated through character.⁴⁰

My caution, however, would be that Sherman and Nussbaum, as two recent proponents of this view, may treat friendship as *too* much like character, while Aristotle clearly recognizes some differences between friendship and virtue. Friendship is not simply virtuous activity or practical wisdom. Given its permanence, as contrasted with the contingency and particularity addressed by virtue, it is at least possible that friendship is closer to scientific or philosophical wisdom than to practical wisdom and character. The differences become clear if we contrast friendship with Aristotle's account of justice.

Justice is representative of Aristotle's account of character and virtue in several important ways. It is, as he writes, the complete and "actual exercise of virtue": "It is complete because he who possesses it can exercise his virtue not only in himself but toward his neighbor also; for many men can exercise virtue in their own affairs, but not in their relations to their neighbor."⁴¹ Justice is an other-regarding activity,

---

37 Ibid., ch. 9. Aristotle's distinction between the matter of practical wisdom and philosophical wisdom is the subject of NE vi.

38 Sherman makes it exceptionally clear that action "in accord with the mean" is hardly tepid or suppressive of emotional responses. Rather, it is to be angry when one should be angry, and to feel pleasure in a way that is good for oneself as well, and to an appropriate extent. The inappropriateness of the direction of the passions, rather than their strength *per se*, is at the root of *akrasia*. See Nancy Sherman, *The Fabric of Character: Aristotle's Theory of Virtue* (Oxford: Clarendon Press, 1989), pp. 34-5, 37.

39 It should be clear, then, that like Sherman, I am not in agreement with John Cooper's primarily intellectual understanding of Aristotle's moral theory as set forth in *Reason and Human Good in Aristotle*. The noticeable absence of the passions and character from his account of practical deliberation is, I think, a flaw that is corrected by Sherman's reading.

40 I take the term "proto-thinking" from Jonathan Lear's *Love and Its Place in Nature: A Philosophical Interpretation of Freudian Psychoanalysis* (New York: Noonday Press, 1990).

41 NE, v.1, p. 108.

exemplifying the role of character in Aristotle's moral theory. The virtue of justice arises from voluntarily just actions that proceed from one's character:

> Men think that acting unjustly is in their power, and therefore that being just is easy. But it is not; to lie with one's neighbor's wife, to wound another, to deliver a bribe, is easy and in our power, but to do these things as a result of a certain state of character is neither easy nor in our power ... to play the coward or to act unjustly consists not in doing these things, except incidentally, but in doing them as the result of a certain state of character, just as to practice medicine and healing consists not in applying or not applying the knife, in using or not using medicines, but in doing so in a certain way.[42]

For Aristotle, an act itself is clearly not enough make one just or unjust. It is via character that one acts in a *voluntary* manner, and therefore can be either praised for justice or despised for injustice.[43]

Sherman's discussion of *prohairesis* is helpful for understanding how character makes acts into voluntary actions. *Prohairesis* is a higher-order desire connected with projection and expansive, long-term intentions. It is a more rational desire than *boulesis*, which proceeds directly from the passions (both fall under *orexis*—desire or action that proceeds from the will). Through the deliberation of *prohairesis*, one's actions become ordered and take on the shape of a planned or intended life representative of character. As Sherman writes: "One consequence of the above connection of *prohairesis* and *boulesis* is that a *prohairesis* cannot promote the ends of lower desires, such as appetite or emotion, unless these ends themselves fall under a more general conception of good living definitive of some character."[44] One develops and demonstrates the character of a just person through the integration of bouletic desires into consistent, planned (prohairetic) acts of justice. As Aristotle writes with regard to virtue in general: "Virtue, then, is a state of character concerned with choice, lying in a mean, i.e. the mean relative to us, this being determined by a rational principle, and by that principle by which the man of practical wisdom would determine it."[45] The examined pattern of chosen goodness demonstrates the acquisition of virtue.

A just person exemplifies virtue because her prohairetic action integrates a series of particular actions into a comprehensive sequence. In seeing how these actions fit together one establishes a pattern representative of the agent's character; the establishment of a habit involves the determination of one's action towards a specific good. By giving respect and honor appropriately to one's parents, elders, and community leaders through a series of actions, one can be said to be a just person. By contrast, someone who reserves all of their adoration and honor for a professional athlete (who gives them two hours of pleasure every week) to the point

---

42 Ibid., v.9, pp. 131-2.
43 Ibid., v.8, p. 127.
44 Sherman, *The Fabric of Character*, p. 81.
45 NE, ii.6, p. 39.

of neglecting other community relations may be said to act unjustly, and if this is a pattern they may even be said to *be* unjust.

Several important features of justice strongly parallel Aristotle's discussion of friendship. As already mentioned, justice is enacted toward the neighbor. Justice is concerned with proportion, equality and reciprocity; one should give and take in accord with one's merit and the merit of others. Strictly speaking, Aristotle discusses two forms of justice, distributive and commutative (also called rectificatory, in Ross' translation). Commutative justice is only discussed by Aristotle as applying to states of injury, in which a wrong needs to be corrected. Commutative and distributive justice differ in terms of the equality they exhibit. While commutative justice judges on the basis of parties already deemed to be equal, distributive justice equalizes parties who are different through proportionate equality. Aristotle therefore terms the equality of commutative justice quantitative, by contrast with the proportionality of distributive justice.

In its proportionality, distributive justice allows the *polis* to function. Aristotle argues that reciprocity based upon proportion can be just, while strict reciprocity is not just in most cases. He dismisses the idea of an official who wounds someone being himself wounded as strict reciprocity would have it.[46] He then shows how proportional reciprocity does hold: "But in associations for exchange this sort of justice does hold men together—reciprocity in accordance with a proportion and not on the basis of precisely equal return. *For it is by proportional requital that the city holds together*."[47] The problem with strict reciprocity is that it would not help the *polis* to function; exchanging tomatoes from my backyard for tomatoes from yours would leave us right where we started. "For it is not two doctors that associate for exchange, but a doctor and a farmer, or in general people who are different and unequal; but these must be equated."[48] The proportional equality of justice, then, serves to equalize those who are *different*. Equalizing those who are different requires attention to the particulars of a situation through the planning and projection of practical wisdom.

A just exchange can occur between people of different skills when they share an interest in the other's work. Through mutual need, a commensurability of value can be established that allows them to be treated equally. Money often serves this commensurating function: "This is why all goods must have a price set on them; for then there will always be exchange, and if so, association of man with man."[49] Learning to be just in these situations, then, is learning to give appropriate value to each good that one seeks, and thereby to the person who provides it. To give appropriately to others contributes to the community as a whole. One's actions with regard to such

---

46 Would it be just for the police officers in the Abner Louima case to be as brutally beaten as they beat their victim?
47 NE, v.5, pp. 117-18, my emphasis.
48 Ibid., v.5, pp. 118-19.
49 Ibid., v.5, p. 120.

deliberations are based on one's character and ability to judge of particulars, and one is just when one acts appropriately as a member of the community.

In many ways, the shared interest and equity in Aristotle's discussions of distributive justice are very close to friendship (*philia*) of the derivative sort—friendship of utility, or perhaps even of pleasure. In both of these sorts of friendship, shared interest creates the equality or proportion that leads to friendship—both parties seek either pleasure or something of use from the other, which they cannot provide themselves. Aristotle refers to the *philia* between dissimilars as one of proportion, in which (like justice) a common measure for friendship is provided in the form of money.[50] Where this likeness of intention is not found or does not last, friendships are said to be transient and collapse:

> If these be the objects of the friendship it is dissolved when they do not get the things that formed the motives of their love; for each did not love the other person himself but the qualities he had, and these were not enduring; that is why the friendships also are transient. *But the love of characters, as has been said, endures because it is self-dependent.*[51]

Because these friendships are proportional, between those who are different, they resemble the equality of justice.[52]

However, *friendship* determines the extent of justice, and not vice versa; this will be the first key step towards distinguishing them. Aristotle makes this point twice: "when men are friends they have no need of justice, while when they are just they need friendship as well, and the truest form of justice is thought to be a friendly quality."[53] And again: "And the demands of justice also seem to increase with the intensity of the friendship, which implies that friendship and justice exist between the same persons and have an equal extension."[54] While friendship and justice have "equal extension," it is clear from the context of these quotations that friendship motivates the extension and heightens the demands of justice. This becomes significant if we shift to complete friendships, or friendships of character, which surpass justice and reshape equality.

While friendship and justice are related forms of equality, justice is a derivative type of equality and relation. Whereas the equality of distributive justice is qualitative and proportional, Aristotle rejects such a notion of equality for friendships of character:

> But equality does not seem to take the same form in acts of justice and in friendship; for in acts of justice what is equal in the primary sense is that which is in proportion to merit,

---

50 Ibid., ix.1, p. 220.

51 Ibid. My italics. The parallel between derivative friendships and justice is further confirmed by the fact that a friend who has been misled as to the nature of the relationship cannot expect recompense unless a written contract exists between the friends, such that derivative friendships are tantamount to economic exchange.

52 Ibid., viii.9, pp. 207-8.

53 Ibid., viii.1, p. 193.

54 Ibid., viii.9, p. 208.

while quantitative equality is secondary, but in friendship quantitative equality is primary and proportion to merit secondary. This becomes clear if there is a great interval in respect of virtue or vice or wealth or anything else between the parties; for then they are no longer friends, and do not even expect to be so. And this is most manifest in the case of the gods; for they surpass us most decisively in all good things ... In such cases it is not possible to define exactly up to what point friends can remain friends; for much can be taken away and friendship remain, but when one party is removed to a great distance, as God is, the possibility of friendship ceases.[55]

This difference in types of equality between justice and friendship is telling. What does "quantitative equality" (*iso poson*) mean? It means the following: the equality between two such friends is not based simply on the qualities of the two which are shared, but rather the claim that *these two* are equal.[56] Quantitative equality is a stricter form of equality than the qualitative equality found in justice.[57] Quantitative equality means that one returns like for like. Where there is difference, the possibilities for friendships based on strict equality are diminished or even denied.

Using Kripke's discussion of equality, we could say the following: whereas the equality of proportion in justice and derivative sorts of friendship is contingent and *descriptive* (or, in Aristotle's terms, based on qualitative properties), the equality found in friendships of character *denotes* the two individuals, and therefore is a necessary one. Since it is precisely an equality between the characters of *these two* individuals, and character as "second nature"[58] is the essence of their voluntary

---

55 Ibid., viii.7, p. 204.

56 Aristotle's fullest discussion of quantitative equality is in *Physics* vii.4. W. von Leyden notes that this equality is different from the proportionate equality discussed in relation to distributive justice, and that quantitative equality should be considered in relation to Aristotle's political theory, given the importance of the link between equality and justice. However, he does not mention the connection between quantitative equality and friendship, which is a surprising limitation of his study. Quantitative equality is important to Aristotle's political theory, and consideration of this topic should be related to his understanding of friendship and its place in his political theory, as well as the quantitative equality of rectificatory justice; obviously, such considerations go beyond the scope of this work. See W. von Leyden, *Aristotle on Equality and Justice: His Political Argument* (New York: St. Martin's Press, 1985), especially chs 1, 2, and Conclusion.

57 That quantitative equality is found here as well as in justice is important in light of attempts to read Aristotle in relation to modern democratic concerns. In particular, Pierre Aubenque's discussion of equality in justice limits Aristotle's discussion by locating quantitative equality only in commutative justice rather than friendship. This becomes more problematic when one considers the connections between friendship and democracy on Aristotle's view. See Pierre Aubenque, "The twofold natural foundation of justice according to Aristotle,", trans. Robert Heinaman, in R. Heinaman (ed.), *Aristotle and Moral Realism* (London: UCL Press, 1995), pp. 35-47.

58 For a discussion of character as "second nature," see John McDowell, "Two Sorts of Naturalism," in *Mind, Value and Reality* (Cambridge, MA: Harvard University Press, 1998), pp. 167-97.

action, a friendship of character indicates the equality of two rigid designators and names the individuals as who they are.

This sounds like a strange claim, since if friendship designates rigidly it would have a necessity more in tune with philosophical than practical wisdom. Yet this is precisely the case. Aristotle describes friendships of character as requiring time to develop, and clearly places friendship in the realm of *a posteriori* relations.[59] As we saw before, friends of character develop through "eating salt together," such that they are able to perceive how the other acts with some certainty based upon the constancy of past experience. One can make a straightforward case for friendship having the *a posteriori* status of rigid designators. But is the equality of friendship metaphysically necessary?

The best indication of necessity in friendships of character is Aristotle's discussion of their *permanence*. First, as we have already seen, friendships of the derivative, participatory sort are contingent and short-lived. The interests of the parties being shared only incidentally, there is no reason for these relations to be lasting.[60] In contrast, as we have seen, Aristotle refers to friendships of character as "enduring." In the following passage, he explicitly addresses their permanence in articulating the activity specific to friendships of character:

> Perfect friendship is the friendship of men who are good, and alike in virtue; for these wish well alike to each other *qua* good, and they are good in themselves. Now those who wish well to their friends for their sake are most truly friends; for they do this by reason of their own nature and not incidentally; therefore their friendship lasts as long as they are good—*and goodness is an enduring thing*. And each is good without qualification and to his friend, for the good are both good without qualification and useful to each other ... And such a friendship is, as might be expected, *permanent*, since there meet in it all the qualities that friends should have.[61]

Friendships of character can endure because these friends wish well to each other on the basis of goodness of character rather than usefulness. They depend upon nothing

---

59 NE, viii.3, p. 197.

60 In his essay "Aristotle on Friendship" John Cooper argues that in all three types of friendship, one wishes one's *philos* well for his or her own sake, yet with a difference in scope depending on the type of friendship. Thus, one wishes one's *philos* of pleasure well insofar as the *philos* is pleasurable (pp. 304-5). Cooper uses this to argue that there could be different levels of well-wishing within each type of friendship as well as distinctions between the three types. This point is especially important to him with regard to friendships of character, since he argues that this reading makes these friendships more common than they would otherwise seem to be. I think he is right with regard to derivative sorts of friendship, since the intensity and extent of the shared interest would be precisely what allowed a friendship to continue for a longer period. But I do not see how friendships of character could be more or less permanent, as a difference in scope with regard to well-wishing would seem to imply. See John Cooper, "Aristotle on Friendship," in A. Rorty (ed.), *Essays on Aristotle's Ethics* (Berkeley: University of California Press, 1980), pp. 301-40.

61 NE, viii.3, p. 196, my emphasis.

outside of themselves; nothing could lead them to act against it. Acting well through choice based on character,[62] their activity perpetuates itself:

> Now equality and likeness are friendship, and especially the likeness of those who are like in virtue; for being steadfast in themselves they hold fast to each other ... for it is characteristic of good men neither to go wrong themselves nor to let their friends do so.[63]

Good action, as good without qualification, leads to continued good activity; it binds the two together to their goal and to the good in a stronger manner than when by themselves.

Since their nature is their shared interest, it extends itself in a way not found in derivative sorts of friendship. Friendships of character differ from friendships based on accidental pleasure or utility in a manner similar to the difference between necessary and contingent relations.[64] Friends of character would be friends in any possible world. The equality of these friendships is the necessary equality between two essences, and it therefore seems plausible to read Aristotle as claiming that the identity of these friends is necessary.

The necessary and unchanging equality of friendship is further supported by Aristotle's consideration of a friend as "another self," particularly when one takes into account his reflections on the nature of self-love. Self-love is the paradigm for how one should love a friend.[65] "Each of these (features of friendship) seems to belong to the good person by virtue of his relation to himself, and he relates to his friend as he does to himself, for the friend is another self."[66] Aristotle recognizes a problem: if one is of good character, one should love oneself. Yet popular belief, as represented in common parlance, regards self-love as a bad thing—Athens speaks of self-love as egoism and selfishness.[67] The disparagement of self-love by Athenians is no small matter for Aristotle. As G.E.L. Owen argues in a classic article, an Aristotelian approach to moral science cannot exclude what is commonly said about the moral life.[68] To disregard common parlance would be to develop a theory that did not accord with the facts. For Aristotle, ordinary perception tells us something

---

62 Ibid., viii.5, pp. 200-1.

63 Ibid., viii.8, p. 206.

64 For Nussbaum's discussion of the incidental character of derivative friendships, see *The Fragility of Goodness*, p. 356.

65 Julia Annas, "Self-Love in Aristotle," *The Southern Journal of Philosophy* 27 (1988, Supplement), p. 1.

66 NE, ix.4, p. 227.

67 Ibid., ix.8, p. 235.

68 G.E.L. Owen, "Tithenai ta Phenomena," in S. Mansion (ed.), *Aristote et les Problèmes de Methode* (Louvain: Publications Universitaires, 1961), pp. 83-103. Annas argues that Aristotle's discussion of self-love is not a standard conflict between different beliefs (*endoxa*) or belief and theory, such that it would not fit Owen's formulation. However, I would disagree with her on the location of the conflict between the facts and what is commonly said. Annas argues that the conflict comes about because of the premise that one ought to love most one's

about the world rather than leading us astray.[69] Yet, here we have a case in which the phenomena and what moral philosophy demands would seem to be in direct contradiction.

Aristotle resolves this problem by distinguishing two sorts of self-love, based upon whether or not this self is of good character. The self-love of the bad person is a self-love without constancy, based upon love of a particular interest or in search of a particular pleasure; such a self-love is constantly in flux. "They [attributes of *philia*] hardly belong even to inferior people, for they are at variance with themselves, and have appetites for some things and rational desires for others."[70] While incontinent people may have rational desires, they do not behave as they think they should. Since they do not act in accord with what they believe to be right, one can hardly call their actions their own; they are selves only in the minimal sense. "And having nothing lovable in them they have no feeling of love to themselves."[71] For evil men, the search for friends is an effort to hide from oneself, repressing the bad deeds one has done and is likely to do again. The self-love of the bad character ignores his or her rational capacity.[72] Self-love in this sense is focused only on those features of oneself that are contingent, accidental, and subject to change—lower-order desires operative without the ordering function of *prohairesis* that would give them continuity and harmony.

By establishing a view of the self-love of bad characters that agrees with the common criticism of self-love as egoism, Aristotle opens the possibility for self-love in the *good* sense to fit his account of the moral life. Self-love, as practiced by one who is good, contrasts most strongly with the bad form of self-love in that it is self-love in accord with a rational principle. Aristotle emphasizes this aspect because such self-love is love of that which is *most* one's own—the ability to choose one's actions and appreciate good action for its own sake: "Besides, a man is said to have or not to have self-control according as his reason has or has not the control, on the assumption *that this is the man himself*; and the things men have done on a rational principle are thought *most properly their own acts* and voluntary acts."[73] Without

---

best friend. Rather, it seems to me that the conflict lies precisely in the factual discovery that one's best friend is oneself; it is at this later stage in the argument that the conflict arises.

69 In *The Fragility of Goodness*, Martha Nussbaum has extended this argument, in an attempt to show that it is not simply with regard to moral philosophy that the "appearances" (*phenomena*) of popular belief are important, but with regard to other sciences as well. See ibid., pp. 243-5. I agree with her, but would also like to emphasize a different point: the recognition is consistent with the passions and emotions telling us something about the world as well. While neither beliefs nor passions are *phenomena* which give scientific understanding, an Aristotelian account of science cannot do without either.

70 NE, ix.4, p. 229. Next quote, same page.
71 Ibid., vii.3, p. 166.
72 Ibid., ix.8, p. 236.
73 Ibid., my emphasis.

this self-love, one is almost not a self.[74] Moreover, in this self-love one recognizes *a posteriori* the necessity of one's being a *rational* animal; one discovers that this is who one truly is, and that without this one would not be fully human.[75]

Julia Annas discusses the importance of reason to this conception of self-love, in relation to the practical activity of the intellect.[76] She assumes that in self-love one is identified only with the practical aspect of the intellect, noting that this sets up a conflict with book x's identification of an individual with the theoretical activity of her intellect (i.e., philosophical wisdom).[77] Likewise, Nussbaum argues that *philia* is connected with particularity and therefore with practical wisdom rather than contemplation.[78] Clearly, both are correct that practical reasoning is involved in this identification of oneself with a rational principle; as Aristotle writes connecting self-love with the practical wisdom, "Whence it follows that he is most truly a lover of self, of another type than that which is a matter of reproach, and as different from that as living according to a rational principle is from living as passion dictates, and desiring what is noble from desiring what seems advantageous."[79] However, the text does not support the exclusion of theoretical wisdom from this identification. A virtuous person loves himself because he can contemplate his virtuous activity:

> For existence is good to the virtuous man, and each man wishes himself what is good, while no one chooses to possess the whole world if he has first to become someone else; he wishes for this only on condition of being whatever he is; and the element that thinks would seem to be the individual man, or to be so more than any other element in him. And such a man wishes to live with himself; for he does so with pleasure, since the memories of his past acts are delightful and his hopes for the future are good and therefore pleasant. *His mind is well stored too with subjects of contemplation.*[80]

The constancy of virtuous self-love contrasts sharply with the self-forgetting, alienation and regret of the irrational person. The activity of the virtuous person is more essentially her own than the wicked one, as are her desires for friendship. Secondly, the "element that thinks" of the virtuous person, while clearly involving practical reason, *exists for the sake of contemplation*. By having good character, so

---

74 I am indebted here to Jonathan Lear's discussion of individuation in *Love and Its Place In Nature*. Without the self-love developed through psychoanalysis, the alternative—which would be very close to what Aristotle terms the self-love of the bad character—would be, in our modern society, an "individualism without individuals" (p. 19), in which no one makes their action truly their own through reflection. See ibid., pp. 183-222, especially 218-22 on the mindfulness of love.

75 In *Aristotle and Logical Theory*, Lear notes the possibility (as developed by Kripke) of recognizing a truth *a posteriori* which is often known *a priori*. See Lear, *Aristotle and Logical Theory* (New York: Cambridge University Press, 1980), pp. 77-9.

76 Annas, "Self-Love in Aristotle," p. 3.

77 Ibid., pp. 3-4.

78 Nussbaum, *The Fragility of Goodness*, pp. 364-5.

79 NE, ix.8, p. 236.

80 Ibid., ix.4, p. 228, my emphasis.

that one can see more clearly the principle of one's own activity as it is exercised in the world, one can discover and contemplate who one really is. The constancy and permanence of the virtuous person's self make contemplation (*theorein*) of past actions and plans for the future possible in a way that involves philosophical as well as practical wisdom.[81]

Much as self-love enables contemplation, integrating reason and virtue, so too complete friendship in its constancy does likewise. Aristotle notes that one's own actions are not as intelligible to oneself as those of one's neighbor:

> We can contemplate our neighbors better than ourselves and their actions better than our own, and if the actions of virtuous men who are their friends are pleasant to good men (since these have both the attributes that are naturally pleasant)—if this be so, the supremely happy man will need friends of this sort, since his purpose is to contemplate worthy actions and actions that are his own, and the actions of a good man who is his friend have both these qualities.[82]

Thus, it would seem that friendship makes a more complete incorporation of intellectual and philosophical wisdom possible.

A number of features of Aristotelian friendship, then, are intelligible according to the logic of rigid designators discussed by Kripke. First, arising over time and through the building of trust, friendship is an equality which is discovered *a posteriori*. Second, as a quantitative equality, and one which is permanent, it is a necessary equality that holds as long as both parties are alive.[83] Complete *philia* is unchanging since it is grounded in the natures of the two parties rather than being a contingent relation sought for pleasure or utility. Finally, insofar as friendships of character involve a rational principle, they seem to involve both the practical and theoretical parts of the intellect. Friendship and self-love make possible contemplation of good activity and knowledge of one's character. *Philia* is a process of discovery of the principle of one's virtuous activity, and thus of what makes us human. Moreover, this rational principle is that which *properly* belongs to the individual involved; it is what designates the individual himself or herself, in a way that particular actions or exhibited features do not. In these ways, then, the equality found in Aristotelian friendships of character fits the equality of rigid designators, as an *a posteriori* necessary identity similar to that of proper names.

---

[81] Aristotle is here consistent with his earlier statements regarding the relation between practical and philosophical wisdom as analogous to the relation between medicine and health; practical wisdom would seem to exist for the sake of philosophical wisdom. See NE, vi.13, p. 158.

[82] Ibid., ix.9, p. 239.

[83] The fact that friends die need not be seen as a barrier to necessity as described by Kripke. For it is only given the existence of the object that the equality is necessary; "true in all possible worlds" does not extend to worlds in which one or both parties do not exist.

III. Between Bovinity and Divinity: The Goal of Human Friendship

> If one takes the idea of such a science [of subjectivity] to heart, one cannot just start with the category of science and ask whether psychoanalysis fits into it; the very category of science must be re-evaluated.[84]

To show that Aristotle conceives of friendships of character as *a posteriori* and necessary equalities may seem an intriguing enough proposal. Yet, it may likewise strike the reader as anachronistic; that Aristotelian friendship is scientific on Kripke's view says nothing about whether or not it would be a science (*episteme*) according to Aristotelian criteria. Moreover, its import for such issues as the need for friendship, Aristotle's anthropology, and his view of *eudaimonia*, as well as the place of friendship in the *Nicomachean Ethics* as a whole, remains unaddressed. It is incumbent upon this reading of *philia* to show how it fits with Aristotle's moral philosophy as a whole if Kripkean logic is to prove helpful. I will indicate how the argument to this point affects interpretations of Aristotle's moral philosophy by focusing on Aristotle's discussion of our need for friends, and build from that into a discussion of the other topics. The following discussion depends on the notion of friendship as a necessary identity, which helps to connect it with scientific knowledge.

Aristotle's discussion of a virtuous person's need for friends is one of the most convoluted arguments found in the *Nicomachean Ethics*. The discussion centers on the problematic topic of self-sufficiency: if a virtuous person is self-sufficient, then in what sense can she be said to need friends? Such a need would seem to imply a lack contradicting this individual's self-sufficiency. Aristotle solves the problem through the notion of external goods, which are outside of the control of the acting subject. They are identified earlier in the text with "goods of fortune."[85] These goods, he argues, are necessary ingredients for the human good life; someone who is virtuous but constantly encounters misfortune would not be deemed as happy as those who are both virtuous *and* fortunate. External goods play a crucial role in Nussbaum's analysis of the contingency of *eudaimonia* in Aristotle's philosophy, since it is clear (as in Greek tragedy) that human flourishing is not simply within our power, but requires an element of fortune (*tukhe*).[86]

Friends, Aristotle writes, are commonly thought to be the greatest of external goods.[87] You cannot make others your friends, even by paying them. One is fortunate to discover a friend who shares one's character. As an external good, one needs this good in order to live a life that is truly *eudaimon*; yet this good is out of one's control and requires a bit of luck (*tukhe*). As Sherman writes, "For human beings, then, the self-sufficient life is a life larger than that of one individual."[88] She therefore

---

84 Lear, *Love and Its Place in Nature*, pp. 217-18.

85 NE, vii.13, p. 188.

86 The centrality of fortune to Aristotle's conception of *eudaimonia* is most fully discussed by Nussbaum in *The Fragility of Goodness*.

87 NE, ix.9, p. 238.

88 Sherman, *The Fabric of Character*, p. 128.

argues for a relational definition of self-sufficiency: humans are basically political and relational creatures, so that we would not be acting according to our nature were we to live purely solitary lives. Aristotle makes this clear when he writes, "Surely it is strange, too, to make the supremely happy man a solitary; for no one would choose the whole world on condition of being alone, since man is a political creature and one whose nature is to live with others."[89] One person on a deserted island cannot be self-sufficient. Nussbaum uses this argument to claim that the books viii and ix of the *Nicomachean Ethics* put forward a communal view of *eudaimonia*, which then conflicts with book x, where contemplation is privileged instead of practical wisdom, in an apparent lapse into Platonism.

This is a significant point in interpretation of the *Nicomachean Ethics*. For, to say that humans need friends because we are political animals, and that therefore contemplation cannot be our goal, confuses *how* we act with that for which we act. That we are political animals tells us that we need friends in order to accomplish our proper end, but it does not tell us what that end is.[90] Happiness, as Aristotle states, is an activity of contemplation, and as humans we carry it out *in a political manner through friendships*. Aristotle gives two arguments for his view.

Aristotle lays out a three-step argument for how the activity of happiness is carried out relationally in friendship. First, the activity of the person of good character is virtuous and pleasant in itself. Second, for a thing to be one's own makes it pleasant. Third, as mentioned above, we can *contemplate* the activity of our neighbors better than our own. From these premises, Aristotle arrives at the following conclusion: "if this be so, the supremely happy man will need friends of this sort, since his purpose is to contemplate worthy actions *and actions that are his own*, and the actions of a good man who is his friend have both these qualities."[91] It is precisely in view of this purpose that the political nature of humans becomes central: friends are necessary so that we can contemplate our own action, which is (for Aristotle) the activity of happiness.

Both of these qualities—that the actions are one's own, and that they are worthy—are central to this argument. Anthony Kenny discounts the "ownness" of the actions as impossible: "If it was the ownership, rather than the consciousness of goodness which made life pleasant, then there would be no argument to the benefits of friendship; because one cannot in the same way *own* one's friends' goodness."[92] This is, I think, a mistake. Because of the necessary equality between friends, one's

---

89 NE, ix.9, p. 238.

90 McDowell, "Two Sorts of Naturalism," p. 172. McDowell's argument seeks to free moral theory from the nature studied in scientific discourse, and challenges naturalism to rethink its limits in light of character as a "second nature" with internal justification. It also means that we must what we seek and how we seek it.

91 NE, ix.9, 239, my emphasis.

92 Anthony Kenny, *Aristotle on the Perfect Life* (Oxford: Clarendon Press, 1992), p. 46. Kenny's argument regarding contemplation as social in the *Eudemian Ethics* is excellent; see pp. 48-52. Where we differ, I think, is in our views on the contemplation of friends (and its implications) in the NE, ix.9.

own actions *are* present in one's friends—in seeing them, one knows that one would act in the same way. Thus, as Cooper argues, one gains *self*-knowledge through friendship.[93] As political animals, we contemplate our actions through and with others.

The second, longer argument given by Aristotle works in much the same way as the first. Perception and thought are pleasurable, and the awareness that one lives and exists is even more so. In that one's friend is "another self," to be aware of the existence of another self is as desirable as one's own existence. Consciousness of a friend is thus part of happiness:

> He needs, therefore, to be conscious of the existence of his friend as well, and this will be realized in their living together and sharing in discussion and thought; for this is what living together would seem to mean in the case of man, and not, as in the case of cattle, feeding in the same place.[94]

Contemplation occurs through the political, relational life of friendship.[95] By contemplating the actions of another, our nature is properly actualized; political activity becomes *human* political activity in the exercise of rationality. There is no contradiction in the *Ethics*; books viii and ix establish the conditions for contemplation, leading to the eudaimonism of book x.

To emphasize both the ownness and the worthiness of one's friends' actions produces two significant results. First, the argument in ix.9, in conjunction with Aristotle's statements regarding the endurance of character friendship and its quantitative equality, permits one to read friendships of character as fulfilling the Aristotelian criteria for a science (*episteme*). While several recent commentators have emphasized that friendship allows for self-knowledge,[96] they have not considered at length the possibility that friendship is a science. This is worth considering, then, since it may help us to understand how Aristotle sees the practical and philosophical activities of humanity fitting together.

For knowledge to be constitutive of *episteme*, it must be knowledge of an unchanging form, since the first principles of a science are unchanging, necessary, and self-dependent. There are several ways in which we can know and understand scientifically the form—the principle of activity or change—of an operation. First,

---

93 Cooper, "Aristotle on Friendship."

94 NE, ix.9, p. 241.

95 That friendships are contingent in how or when they arise, so that our knowledge of activity (and the equality between friends) depends upon living together as well as staying alive, does not undercut the necessity of the knowledge thereby gained, any more than the necessity of cell biology would not be undercut were all microscopes, along with the instructions for building them, to vanish from the face of the earth.

96 See Cooper, "Aristotle on Friendship," and Paul Schollmeier, *Other Selves: Aristotle on Personal and Political Friendship* (Albany: State University of New York Press, 1994), pp. 53-73. The work of Suzanne Stern-Gillet (*Aristotle's Philosophy of Friendship* (Albany: State University of New York Press, 1995)) does point more toward a union of *theoria* and friendship.

the form can be perceived when we focus on the matter, the stuff of which it is made (material causality). Second, it can be understood in terms of the form when we understand what the principle of activity itself is (formal causality). The form (*logos*) which makes a thing what it is is present both in the world and in the mind that understands it. Third, the cause can be specified as the *primary source of a change*: Lear describes this as properly understood as the actualization of potential (efficient causality). Finally, a cause or form can be understood with regard to the end (*telos*), that for which the form is active (final causality).[97] This need not be conceived as an end outside of the activity; Aristotle often writes of "what pertains to the end" in ways that do not require us to think of the *telos* along the lines of a means/end distinction. The end is often integral to the activity itself.[98] All four of these are different ways of considering the same event.[99]

Given Aristotle's discussion of why friends are necessary for self-sufficiency, we can see how friendship fits the description of scientific knowledge. First, matter. The matter of friendship is the virtuous action itself of the persons towards each other, acts of virtue (e.g., justice) which can be perceived, yet which cannot of themselves make human activity intelligible. Recognition of this point preserves the important emphasis on practical wisdom as concerned with particularity and passions. Without virtuous activity and attention to particulars, there would be nothing for the friends to contemplate. Virtue is a material cause of friendship; it is a *sine qua non* for contemplation to occur. Second, one can consider the form of friendship. When one contemplates a friend's action, the principle of activity is in the world—in the action of the friend—*and* in the mind of the one contemplating. Given their equality, it is the *same* form, since they are of the same character; this explains why Aristotle says a friend's action is one's *own* action. In contemplating a friend, the form in the mind is adequate to the form in the world. Friendship is a realistic science of human action.

Third, in friendship human activity is the primary source of a change. Because the action is rational and ownable by the actor, in friendship one can identify the person herself as the source of the change or efficient cause. This efficient causality is represented by the high degree of praise or blame attributed to the agent. Finally, friendship can be considered in terms of final causality: as we have seen, in friendship one acts for the friend's own sake. Good human activity seeks its own perpetuation. When these causal features of friendship are combined with its permanence, it becomes intelligible to conceive of friendship as the locus for necessary, scientific knowledge of our own activity.[100]

---

97 Jonathan Lear, *Aristotle: The Desire to Understand* (Cambridge: Cambridge University Press, 1988), pp. 28-36.

98 See Nussbaum, *The Fragility of Goodness*, p. 297.

99 See Aristotle, *Metaphysics* 1013a24-1013b4.

100 This is in accord with how we understand in a *receptive* manner, as contrasted with the active understanding of God. See Lear, *The Desire to Understand*, p. 301.

Focusing on contemplation in friendship allows us to compare human happiness with the self-contemplation proper to divinity that Aristotle describes as perfect happiness. This can help to clarify two issues of interpretation regarding the relationship between human flourishing and divine life in Aristotle. The first regards the goods which one wishes for one's friend—in particular, whether or not one wishes for a friend to become a god. As we saw in the previous section, when one is a god and the other human, the distance is such that friendship is no longer possible. Aristotle continues:

> This is in fact the origin of the question whether friends really wish for their friends the greatest goods, e.g. that of being gods; since in that case their friends will no longer be friends to them, and therefore will not be good things for them (for friends are good things). The answer is that if we were right in saying that friend wishes good to friend for his sake, his friend must remain the sort of being he is, whatever that may be; therefore it is for him only so long as he remains a man that he will wish the greatest goods. But perhaps not all the greatest goods; for it is for himself most of all that each man wishes what is good. [101]

This passage has been extensively debated by commentators. Initially, it was interpreted in egoistic terms: because one would lose one's own goods if a friend became a god, one would not wish the friend to be a god. However, this is clearly in conflict with wishing a friend well for her own sake. An alternative interpretation has therefore arisen: because the *friend* would lose one's friendship, one would not wish the friend to be a god.[102] Yet the fact that one wishes the greatest goods "most of all for oneself" renders such a reading problematic.

When we realize that what is lost is the opportunity to participate in the divine life of contemplation *as* friends, the loss becomes clearer. Through friendship, one is able to contemplate one's own human activity, seeing it enacted in one's friend and knowing it to be one's own. This is very close to the activity of a god, who thinks thought, contemplating its own activity continually and in an unchanging manner. As a god, however, one would no longer be contemplating *human* activity. As Aristotle says, gods do not make transactions, nor act justly, bravely, nor liberally.[103] Friendship, on the other hand, allows one to exercise the reason that is most one's own, and to live a fully human life in the exercise of both reason and virtue.

As the activity that is most one's own, friendship is rigidly designative of who one is; wishing for another sort of happiness is to wish to no longer be this very individual. As Aristotle writes, "It would be strange, then, if one were to choose not the life of himself, but that of something else."[104] In this quote, Aristotle is speaking of the life of reason, but the same could be said of *philia* as well: in *philia* one

---

101 NE, viii.7, p. 204.
102 Jens Timmerman, "Why We Cannot Wish Our Friends to Be Gods," *Phronesis* 40: 2 (1995), 209-15.
103 NE, x.8, p. 267.
104 Ibid., x.7, p. 265.

discovers and contemplates the life that is truly one's own. Through friendship one can wish the best good—i.e., the divine life—for one's friend *as* one's friend and as human, and for oneself as oneself:

> But we must not follow those who advise us, being men, to think of human things, and, being mortal, of mortal things, but must, so far as we can, make ourselves immortal, and strain every nerve to live in accordance with the best thing in us; for even if it be small in bulk, much more does it in power and worth surpass everything.[105]

Through friendship, contemplation can be integrated into the human life as a whole, as the element in which human (as opposed to bovine) friendship finds its true end and happiness. To wish one to become a god, then, is to wish the end of human happiness for both the friend and oneself, whereas wishing the best *within* friendship allows for some participation in divine activity—in short, to make ourselves immortal as far as possible insofar as we are human. Through friendship, one wishes goods for one's friend (and oneself) as the specific persons involved; it is, in a sense, to wish goods for another in a rigidly designative fashion, as *this one* who is a friend.[106]

If the life of the gods is available to us as humans through friendship, then the relationship between Aristotle's view of *eudaimonia* in book x of the *Nicomachean Ethics* and the rest of the work needs to be reconsidered. While the practical life is treated throughout the first nine books as good in itself, and as the happiness appropriate to humans, book x argues for contemplation as a more perfect form of *eudaimonia*. He argues that gods are happy beyond all other beings, yet gods do not enter into contracts or deliberate about moral considerations, nor hunt or do other animal activities. The only activity open to them is contemplation; thus, since they are supremely happy, contemplation and happiness must go together. Aristotle goes on to strengthen the claim with regard to human happiness as well:

> This is indicated, too, by the fact that the other animals have no share in happiness, being completely deprived of such activity. For while the whole life of the gods is blessed, and that of men too in so far as some likeness of such activity belongs to them, none of the other animals is happy, since they in no way share in contemplation. Happiness extends, then, just so far as contemplation does, and those to whom contemplation more fully belongs are more truly happy, not as a mere concomitant but in virtue of the contemplation; for this is in itself precious. Happiness, therefore, must be some form of contemplation.[107]

This equation of happiness and contemplation seems to throw the inherent goodness of the practical life into disarray. This is all the more true, Aristotle claims, in that the self-sufficiency of the philosopher surpasses that of the practically virtuous person, precisely in that it is closest to the life of the gods.[108] He even states that the practical

---

105 Ibid.
106 Much of the argument of this section is in agreement with Stern-Gillet, *Aristotle's Philosophy of Friendship*, especially pp. 123-45.
107 NE, x.8, p. 268.
108 Ibid., x.7, p. 264. See also Lear, *The Desire to Understand*, p. 316.

life is good, but "in a secondary degree."[109] Based on such passages, one is left wondering just how good the good life of virtue really is.

Two approaches have predominated in recent interpretations of the relation between the intellectual *eudaimonia* of book x and the *eudaimonia* of virtue in the preceding books. These approaches have been termed "inclusive" and "dominant." The inclusive view sees *eudaimonia* as "an end consisting of a plurality of independent goods, goods constituting the objects of various desires or interests of a given agent."[110] On the inclusivist view, then, *eudaimonia* would allow for a plurality of goods, such that contemplation may be a constitutive part, but the goods of the practical life need not be excluded from consideration.[111]

Whatever break may remain between the practical and theoretical aspects of the human good on the inclusive view, the gap between them is far more pronounced in the "dominant" interpretation. Martha Nussbaum and Jonathan Lear are two recent proponents of this view. Nussbaum reads x.6-8 in a highly critical manner, arguing that it represents a departure from the earlier emphasis in the *Ethics* on the contingency, communal *eudaimonia*, and concern for particulars constitutive of the virtuous life. Seeing a lapse into the Platonism against which Aristotle had struggled, Nussbaum goes so far as to suggest that x.6-8 may not even be an original part of the *Ethics*. On her view, the tension between these views remains a problem and an open question for Aristotle's philosophy.[112]

Where Nussbaum views the split between communal, practical *eudaimonia* and the life of the intellect as a tragic one, Lear embraces it strongly. He writes:

---

109 NE, x.7, p. 266.

110 Timothy D. Roche, "The Perfect Happiness," *The Southern Journal of Philosophy* 27 (1988, Supplement), p. 103.

111 A proponent of this view is J.L. Ackrill, who argues that *eudaimonia*, not contemplation, is final and self-sufficient. On Ackrill's view, final ends may be sought for their own sake, or for the sake of something else; the practical life, then, may be sought for its own sake *and* for the sake of contemplation and still be considered a final end. Ackrill takes contemplation to be the "most final" in that it is never sought for the sake of another end; since other final ends may be sought in conjunction with it, however, he argues that *eudaimonia* may be inclusive. Roche, however, notes that there are several problems with this view—most important being that Aristotle does not discuss *eudaimonia* as simply encompassing a number of different ends. Rather, Roche argues that intrinsic goods (i.e., final ends) as well as some instrumental ones may be included because they are constitutive elements of *eudaimonia*. This is a modified version of the inclusive view, which sees what is included as determined by the final end and what is required for its human achievement. However, the choice to "go beyond" moral virtue and its happiness to that of theoretical activity remains, on Roche's view, a break; there is no connection between practical and philosophical wisdom at this crucial point.

112 Nussbaum, *The Fragility of Goodness*, pp. 375-6. See also her essay "Transcending Humanity" in *Love's Knowledge: Essays on Philosophy and Literature* (Oxford: Oxford University Press, 1992), pp. 365-90, for a clear and emphatic description of her preference for the practical, communal concern of the first nine books of the *Ethics*.

> Now, man is able to express his personality and character in the ethical life. And he is able to live a flourishing, happy life within the arena of the ethical. But, by contrast to the life of contemplation, the ethical life is second best ... But, then, what is "all too human" about the ethical life, such that, in transcending it, the contemplative life brings us to the highest realization of the human? ... the philosopher comes to see that "the merely human perspective" is *merely* human. He comes to see the existence of *metaphysical* virtues: excellences, so to speak, from the point of view of the universe ... By studying the world man finds his highest place by occupying mind's place. By realizing what is best in him man transcends his own nature: he no longer lives the life that it is best *for man* to live; he simply lives the life that is best.[113]

Humanity is, on Lear's view, "radically divided" between these two sorts of life. While human life remains enmattered to an extent, Lear's account does limit the importance of practical wisdom and virtue.

These views are broadly representative of the different lines of interpretation currently at work on Aristotle's view of *eudaimonia*. On both sides, there ends up being a split between the moral and intellectual life; they are seen as in conflict, so that the accommodation of one becomes a limitation of the other. The choice is always an either-or: either the moral life or the theoretical one takes precedence. It is no coincidence, in my view, that these interpretations either barely mention friendship or ignore its connection with contemplation. Through friendship, one can hypothesize that the view of *eudaimonia* in book x is consistent with the emphasis on practical wisdom and character earlier in the *Ethics*. It is precisely through the development of character that friendship becomes possible, and through this friendship a form of *communal*, embodied contemplation—neither Platonist nor rejecting the practical virtues.

Moreover, an emphasis on friendship as a locus of virtue and contemplation is consistent with Aristotle's description of practical wisdom as related to philosophical wisdom as medicine is related to health. "But again it [i.e., practical wisdom] is not *supreme* over philosophic wisdom, i.e. over the superior part of us, any more than the art of medicine is over health; for it does not use it but provides for its coming into being; it issues orders, then, for its sake, but not to it."[114] Through the practice of virtue and the development of friendship, one can discover a deeper sense of human flourishing. If contemplation arises within friendship, then it means that intellectual and practical virtue can be combined in one life, so that it is through being *fully* human that one transcends human life, participating in the divine life of contemplating (*theorein*) one's own practical activity. One can see here that humanity is not the measure of all things; yet, at the same time, one also sees that humanity is one's nature. Through the perfection of one's activity in *philia*, meta-physics—going beyond one's nature—becomes possible. Friendship thus makes a richer inclusivism possible than recent approaches have discussed. This does not make

---

113 Lear, *The Desire to Understand*, p. 318.
114 NE, vi.13, p. 158.

human flourishing easier, since friendship in the best sense is, on Aristotle's view, rare. But, it indicates that a fully human form of *eudaimonia* is at least possible.

If, as I have argued, one can read friendships of character as necessary equalities along the lines of equality between Kripkean rigid designators, then one is faced here as well with the problem of essentialism. Essentialism has long been acknowledged as a feature of Aristotle's scientific works, but is not often discussed in relation to the *Ethics*. Yet there are points of contact between Aristotle's essentialist arguments and his discussion of friendship, most notably on the importance of rational capacity to one's humanity.[115] Rationality is an essential property of being human. Insofar as people have this property, and have it necessarily, they are able to be friends with another—i.e., to enter into the relationship of equality between friends of character. Insofar as friendships of character require quantitative equality, and deal with these two specific individuals rather than a contingent proportionate equality, it does seem that an essential equality is demanded.

There is a corollary to the above statement: if one does not have the above property, or does not have it necessarily, then one cannot be equal to a person of character, and in lacking this equality one cannot be such a friend. As Kripke says, without certain properties, one could not be a certain individual. This claim is found in Aristotle, particularly with regard to slaves but also with regard to women. The case of slaves is more straightforward and demonstrates this logic quite well: the slave is a "living tool," such that the slave only has a purpose or rationality insofar as it is used by another; its rationality does not belong to it necessarily. "*Qua* slave, then, one cannot be friends with him."[116] In the relation between master and slave (or tyrant and subject) the benefit is all on one side, not shared; without such a sharing, no friendship can exist at all. One can, Aristotle says, be friends with a slave as human, yet clearly not to the same extent as with one who is self-ruling. As Lear points out, it was precisely based upon belief that there were natural slaves that Aristotle justified slavery: the belief that slaves could not rule themselves was based on their origin, and so in some sense on a property (or the lack of a property) from birth.[117] Here, then, we begin to find the limits of who can be friends in the primary sense.

The case of women is more complex, yet Aristotle's discussion shares the fundamental premise with slavery that one's origin is an essential property. He draws the parallel between aristocracy, in which rule is based upon merit, and the friendship between husband and wife. Thus, the friendship here is defined as one of proportion; while there is a fuller version of friendship and justice than is possible with slaves, the proportion between men and women is defined via different functions given

---

115 See Michael V. Wedin, "Singular Statements and Essentialism in Aristotle," in F.J. Pelletier and J. King-Farlow (eds), *New Essays on Aristotle* (Guelph, Ontario: Canadian Association for Publishing in Philosophy, 1984), pp. 67-98.
116 NE, viii.11, p. 212.
117 Lear, *The Desire to Understand*, p. 225.

naturally.[118] Friendship of virtue is possible here in a derivative manner: "But this friendship may be based also on virtue, if the parties are good; for each has its own virtue and they will delight in the fact."[119] However, this is not friendship between equals in the strict sense, but rather again seems to be between unequals in proportion to their relative goodness.

The issue of male–female friendship is complicated by several other factors. First, as Sherman notes, Aristotle discusses women as deficient with regard to practical wisdom. Yet they are charged with the upbringing and education of children, at least to a certain point. They clearly must have some participation in virtue in order to thus teach.[120] Second, and in a likewise important manner, mothers are often deemed exemplars of the activity of *philia*—particularly its disinterested elements (i.e., wishing the other well for his or her own sake)—in relation to their children.[121]

Unlike slaves, then, women can have some participation in friendship, though Aristotle uses biology to limit this participation as well. The connection between friendship and biology becomes all the clearer when one considers the way in which brothers—who share parental origin and upbringing—seem to Aristotle to exemplify the equality of friendship in the best manner: "Brothers love each other as being born of the same parents; for their identity with them makes them identical with each other ... They are, therefore, *in a sense the same thing, though in separate individuals*."[122] The Kripkean resonances (in terms of necessary equality) of fraternal friendship are striking. For Aristotle, origin is an essential property, and two who do not share the same origin cannot be considered equal in the strict sense required for friendships of character. Furthermore, two who do not share the same origin in a manner which allows for equal exercise of practical virtues cannot be friends of character. On Aristotle's view, biological origin as an essential property both makes possible (i.e., for brothers) *and* limits in scope (for women and slaves) the equality found in friendships of character. Given the connection we have found between friendship and the contemplative self-discovery found therein, this likewise enables and limits the science of human action, and *eudaimonia*, in terms of who can participate.

The correlation between the rigid designation of names, and the necessary identity of friendships of character, lays a philosophical foundation for the rest of this work. The influence of Aristotle's discourse on friendship, as well as the denotative theory of reference, have both deeply shaped the philosophical and theological landscapes. From Kripke's work on names, and Aristotle's work on friendship, we can take our bearings for exploring both Thomas' and Derrida's work. The relationships between friendship, knowledge and the essentialist limitations of friendship will likewise be central issues through the philosophical tradition. Thus,

---

118 NE, viii.12, p. 214.
119 Ibid.
120 Sherman, *The Fabric of Character*, pp. 154-5.
121 See, for example, NE, ix.4; mothers seem to exhibit the qualities of friendship at least as much as self-love does.
122 Ibid., viii.12, p. 214, my emphasis.

looking at these issues together, and how an Aristotelian logic risks limiting the range of friendship, provides an initial illustration of how friendship is the pragmatic or political correlate to a particular logic of naming. To see how this correlation is inflected by the particularity of theological language, we will now turn to Aquinas on naming God and friendship.

Chapter 3

Names and Proofs

Modes of Signification in Aquinas' *Summa Theologiae*

> In the case of some terms, people might have doubts as to whether they're names or descriptions; like "God"—does it describe God as the unique divine being or is it a name of God?[1]

I. Introduction

As discussed in the preceding chapter, Kripke's work links proper names closely to the possibility of singular reference, as names can refer independently of description. While descriptions are epistemically useful for fixing the reference, the differing truth-values in modal contexts between a name and a description indicate that the name permits the description to refer, rather than the reverse. While not directly a theological argument, the work of theorists such as Kripke and Putnam reshapes the problem of reference in religious language. In philosophy of religion, religious language is frequently presumed to be anthropomorphic in its attempts to describe God or delineate God's attributes. This reduces God to the level of things in the world—something known by us; it thus remains in tension with the religious claim that God transcends the world that we know. However, if reference is not circumscribed by description, then it is possible that one could name God without describing God. By naming God without description, one can refer without reducing God's transcendence. The Kripkean inversion of the relation between names and descriptions may suggest that *naming* God makes theological realism possible, to the extent that it elides description.

Of course, Kripke's work says little specifically about how one could name God. Moreover, when one extrapolates from his theory, the problem of properly speaking about God is not so easily resolved. For, if we refer to things in the world by rigid designation, then naming God would still be similar to how we refer to things in the world. Insofar as naming grounds referential possibilities *within* the world, it cannot properly reflect God's transcendence *of* that world. If reference to God and the world work in the same way—whether by naming or description—then a recognition of God's transcendence remains doubtful. If God is unique—as St. Thomas Aquinas

---

[1] Kripke, *Naming and Necessity*, pp. 26-7.

says, neither a member of a genus nor of a species—then our naming of God should reflect this uniqueness. This reshapes the problem of religious language: it is not simply a tension between description and transcendence, as Janet Martin Soskice has described "naive" theological realism, but rather a tension between God's transcendence and reference itself.[2] How, then, can we name God in a way that both refers transcendently and is comprehensible?

Thomas' discussion of naming God in the *Summa Theologiae* provides guidance for a theological response to this problem. Thomas frames the problem primarily in terms of the relationship between God and creation. As rational animals within the world, our linguistic and intellectual capacities are primarily directed to understanding things within creation—"complex" entities composed of form and matter. However, because God is simple, with God's essence and existence being one and the same, God is radically different from creation. Thus, as shall be discussed further below, we are not able to properly know or refer to God by natural reason.[3] To name God properly, we must signify God's existence differently from how we name other beings, so that we grasp what David Burrell calls "the distinction"—that God exists otherwise than creation. However, any reference that bypassed our intellectual and linguistic faculties would remain virtually unintelligible for us; our naming of God must be both different from and the same as the way we name creatures.[4] These two apparently irreconcilable demands regarding divine ontology and human psychology guide Thomas' account of how one names God in sacred doctrine, which must speak principally of God, and yet must perfect—not destroy—the language constitutive of human nature.

Thomas answers this double bind of reference and transcendence by proposing that we need not think about reference in univocal terms. Rather, while there remains a family resemblance between reference to God and to creatures, one sort of naming need not rigorously determine the other. To name God in this life can only be an act of faith, such that knowledge of God (*scientia Dei*) is only available to us after death in the light of glory.[5] The naming of God in faith preserves our mental relation to the world even while surpassing it—allowing for human participation in the divine

---

2 See Janet Martin Soskice, *Metaphor and Religious Language* (Oxford: Oxford University Press, 1985), chs 6-7. What follows is, I believe, one attempt to articulate a "reflective realism" consistent with her proposal in ch. 8.

3 For the uniqueness and difficulties of such attempted reference, see Victor Preller, *Divine Science and the Science of God: A Reformulation of Thomas Aquinas* (Princeton: Princeton University Press, 1967), pp. 4-37.

4 An example of such meaninglessness "for us" is Aquinas' discussion of mystical visions and beatitude. Aquinas argues that such beatitude has no value for how we live as humans since it so radically surpasses human intelligibility, remaining inaccessible and linguistically indescribable. As Preller writes, "Since only the beati possess the Science of God in intelligible form [i.e., it is intelligible only to them], it must be viewed as a radically eschatological concept," ibid., p. 233.

5 *Scientia Dei* is God's thinking God's own activity. Following Preller, *Divine Science*, p. 233: "*Scientia dei*, which is the knowledge communicated in Sacred Doctrine, is primarily

life without destroying natural reason. It is the distinctive *way* of naming God that navigates the narrow straits between anthropomorphism and unintelligibility.

For Thomas, such naming begins with God's revelation, as set forth in scripture. Based on God's revelation of who God is—God's giving of God's name *to* us—we can refer to God in a way that was unavailable via our natural modes of denomination. Because God has revealed God's self in Jesus Christ, and in the scriptural history of Israel, and conveyed this to us through scripture and the sacraments, reference to God becomes possible. At once appropriate to the thing spoken of (the *res significata*, thing signified) and yet taking on our modes of signification (*modi significandi*), sacred doctrine enables uniquely divine reference. As the Incarnation takes up human nature and directs it towards its supernatural end, so too God's revelation is God's gracious turning of human language toward the divine. Reshaping our understanding of singularity, we signify God's simplicity in a way that surpasses what we could do through reason alone.

Already, it should be clear that the issue of naming God impinges upon many of the central issues in Thomas' theological corpus: the relation of God to creation, divine simplicity, faith and natural reason, and the necessity or fittingness of the Incarnation. Thomas' understanding of naming God brings these issues into relation to one another, and sheds new light on several problematic issues, particularly regarding the importance of modes of signification in Thomas' thought. The trajectory of this chapter follows the path that Thomas lays out in the *prima pars* of the *Summa*, in which faith perfects natural reason. The first section therefore explores how God is named via philosophical reason, especially the "five ways" often described as cosmological proofs. The focus here, however, will be the deficiencies of the five ways with regard to their modes of signification, and the ensuing vagueness of their reference to God. As represented by these proofs, natural reason does not properly refer to God because it cannot name God *singularly*. The next section considers how the mode of signification known as *suppositum* lets us speak about God's simplicity in a mode appropriate to faith. Building on these points, Thomas appropriates Dionysius' work on divine names for his doctrine of analogy.

While the opening section of the *Summa* (commonly called *de Deo uno*) discusses what one must do in order to name God properly, Thomas does not yet say how one names God, in Christian faith. This, as will become clear, is the burden of his doctrine of the Trinity. The argument integrates Thomas' speculative and grammatical explanations in an investigation of the five notions of the Trinity. In question I.32, these five notions perfect the inadequate reference to God found in the five ways, primarily through a transformed, personalized mode of signification. In the doctrine of the Trinity, Thomas conceives of singular reference to God as the one who has freely and lovingly created the world. His doctrine of the Trinity, then, puts into practice his views on naming God, and helps to clarify the importance of the proofs, modes of signification, and the Dionysian doctrine of divine names in the

---

and radically God's own eternal act of knowing, both as possessed immanently by God, and as directly and intrinsically participated in by the *beati* through the *visio dei*."

early questions of the *Summa*. This suggests a closer intimacy between the treatment *de Deo uno* and *de Deo trino* than is frequently perceived in Thomas.[6] Thomas places the discursive knowledge of philosophy in the service of theology, refracting its language in the light of faith. This enrichment of linguistic possibility exemplifies the way that theology perfects philosophy in turning its water into wine.[7]

Building on this chapter's focus on naming God, the next chapter will consider further the importance of how naming God, as a transformation and redirection of our referential capacities (namely, God as the object of faith), reshapes our capacity for friendship. There is a strong connection between naming God and friendship with God in Thomas' work. God's giving of God's name in the Incarnation and in revelation is an act of charity—an act of divine friendship. It is at once God's gift to humanity, and an event that opens the possibility of human participation *in* charity as well. Since the Incarnation reshapes our signifying and grammatical practices, we can act *voluntarily* toward God in a new way; God gives to humanity in a way that simultaneously enables human reciprocation. Through God's teaching in sacred doctrine, which enables rational participation in the divine life, God calls us to friendship (John 15:15). Sacred doctrine functions as the "communication" between God and humans that constitutes charity. Charity, as we will see, develops the pragmatic significance of naming God, moving us toward beatitude.

There is, then, an internal fittingness to the topics of naming God and friendship in Thomas' work. To name is a cognitive act, expressed through words, and to be friends is an act of will, that proceeds through knowledge. Naming God and friendship, as acts of intellect and will, are thus analogous to the Trinitarian processions of the Son and the Holy Spirit, as Thomas takes up the psychological analogy for the Trinity developed by Augustine.[8] The significance, here, is that naming God and friendship thus represent two activities through which humanity is taken up into the divine life. They signify the embodied ways that we come to participate in the divine life—or,

---

[6] For an extended discussion of this issue, and how Thomas' treatment relates to contemporary Trinitarian theology, see Matthew Levering, *Scripture and Metaphysics: Aquinas and the Renewal of Trinitarian Theology* (Oxford: Blackwell, 2004), pp. 1-74. For the connection of this structure with Dionysius, see Wayne Hankey, *God in Himself: Aquinas' Doctrine of God as Expounded in the Summa Theologiae* (Oxford: Oxford University Press, 1987), p. 12.

[7] St. Thomas Aquinas, *Faith, Reason, and Theology: Questions I-IV of His Commentary on Boethius' De Trinitate*, trans. A. Maurer (Toronto: Pontifical Institute of Medieval Studies, 1987), 2.3 ad 5: "So those who use the works of the philosophers in sacred doctrine, by bringing them into the service of faith, do not mix water with wine, but rather change water into wine."

[8] One may question the suitability of the analogy, but Thomas sees these categories of human activity as modes of participation in divine being. For a defense of Thomas' use of the psychological analogy, see Levering, *Scripture and Metaphysics*, pp. 144-64.

as Anna Williams has shown, how we become divinized.⁹ They are the linguistic and pragmatic dimensions of our wayfaring journey toward beatitude.

To argue, as this chapter does, that Thomas sees theological reference as exceeding our natural capacities and transcending philosophical understanding, is to enter a morass of secondary material debating the relationship between theology and philosophy in Thomas' work. The debate is complex, in part because (as Michel Corbin has argued) Thomas may have been developing a new understanding of the relationship between theology and philosophy in the *Summa Theologiae*. The crux of the argument frequently turns on how one understands the relationship between questions 1 and 2 of the *Summa*, as question 1 argues for the necessity and primacy of sacred doctrine over other sciences, and question 2 demonstrates the existence of God through the arguments of natural reason. Question 2 does argue that people name God (*nominant Deus*) through the demonstrations of the five ways, but unless read in light of the differences between sacred doctrine and natural reason, this naming of God is easily misunderstood. Question 1's clarification of sacred doctrine's status as a science thus helps us to understand how the naming of God in faith relates to the linguistic practices of natural reason.

In the first two articles of the *Summa*, Thomas asks whether a cognition of God other than philosophical study is necessary, and if so, whether sacred doctrine (*sacra doctrina*, this other mode of cognition)¹⁰ is a science (*scientia*). By the end of question 1, the answer is affirmative on both counts. There are two reasons sacred doctrine would not be considered a science: first, we do not have certain knowledge of its principles, and second, it deals with singulars whereas sciences consider universals. As several recent commentators have noted, Thomas resolves each objection in due order. Sacred doctrine is a science because it is our mode of participation in *scientia Dei*—the science of God, knowledge of God's own self possessed by God and the blessed.¹¹ As God's knowledge is most certain in itself, and *scientia Dei* is the *highest* of sciences, then even if our participation through faith is less certain than those sciences we know by natural reason, sacred doctrine remains the highest of human sciences. Furthermore, God's knowledge of the singular events dealt with

---

9 A.N. Williams, *The Ground of Union: Deification in Aquinas and Palamas* (New York: Oxford University Press, 1999), pp. 76-80. As Williams notes, and as shall be discussed in more detail in chapter 4, Thomas' adoption of the language of friendship is an enrichment of the doctrine of deification.

10 Sacred doctrine for Aquinas is: God's revelatory communication to humanity as found in a) scripture and b) the patristic tradition and church doctrine. As Thomas writes, "Doctrine is the action of someone making something known (*Nam doctrina est actio eius qui aliquid cognoscere facit*)." Saint Thomas Aquinas, *Summa Theologiae* (Madrid: Biblioteca de Autores Cristianos, 1951), ST II-II.189.1 ad 4; all references to the *Summa* will be by part number (*secunda secundae*), question number (189) and article (1), with the objection (ob) or reply number (ad 4) if relevant.

11 ST I.1.2. See Eugene F. Rogers, Jr., *Thomas Aquinas and Karl Barth: Sacred Doctrine and the Natural Knowledge of God* (Notre Dame, IN: University of Notre Dame Press, 1995), pp. 19-20.

by sacred doctrine unifies them, superceding their contingency and diversity. While we know such events uncertainly, singular events serve as examples through which we discover a moral science, leading to a deeper (albeit noncognitive) participation in God's knowledge of the world.[12] In sacred doctrine, through faith, one participates in a higher knowledge than one can demonstrate or understand.

The formal object of sacred doctrine is God. Sacred doctrine studies God and creatures in light of God's activity of revelation: "For therefore Sacred Scripture considers things according to how they are divinely revealed, as has been said above, and all things as they are divinely revealable, share in reason's one formal object of this science."[13] God's revelation permits other things (events, individuals, singulars) to be considered in the light of faith; insofar as these are divinely revealable, they comprise the *material* object of the science of sacred doctrine: "[To the first objection] it can be said that sacred doctrine does not treat God and creatures equally: but principally of God, and of creatures as they are referred to God as to a principle or an end."[14] Because it has *one* formal, principal object—God—and treats other things in light of this formal object, sacred doctrine is a unified science; only in terms of its material object is its subject matter diverse. Where God is the material object of metaphysical theology, God as revealed is the formal object of sacred doctrine.

By contrast, the formal object of metaphysical theology is *not* God, but the natural light of the intellect. More exactly, the object of metaphysical theology is to understand the world. In metaphysical theology, one studies God as part of a study of how everything in the world fits together. As natural reason is the formal object of this science, it is a study of God that is taught through philosophy. Metaphysical theology appears more unified than sacred doctrine because it appears to study only one thing, but this is only an apparent unity because metaphysical theology has one material object. This science studies God in light of the same principles and

---

12 ST I.1.2 ad 2.

13 ST I.1.3, translation modified: "Quia igitur sacra Scriptura considerat aliqua secundum quod sunt divinitus revelata, secundum quod dictum est (ST I.1.2), omnia quaecumque sunt divinitus revelabilia, communicant in una ratione formali obiecti huius scientiae." Thomas does not say that sacred doctrine treats of all things that are divinely *revealed*, but as they are divinely *revealable*, thus opening the field more widely for what can be studied within sacred doctrine.

14 ST I.1.3. Things considered in the light of God as the formal object of sacred doctrine are considered as *revelabilia*—revealable. See Rogers, *Thomas Aquinas and Karl Barth*, pp. 26-7, but also and especially p. 49: "*Revelabilia* are things trans*formed*—that was the point of the thought-experiment about a new form—things that not only could have been revealed, but things that contain within themselves the form of revealability. They possess an intrinsic under-God-ness, they enjoy natural citizenship in the world that revelation depicts, they already belong to and comprise that world, quite apart from whether scripture comes to mention them or not. They are revealable as God-created and God-ordered. And that under-God-ness is theirs and ours and the whole world's patient of discovery, just as the Aristotelian forms of natural things remain their own apart from study." See also Michel Corbin, *Le Chemin de la Théologie chez Thomas d'Aquin* (Paris: Beauchesne, 1974), pp. 737-43.

arguments through which it studies the world; one could say, then, that metaphysical theology primarily studies the world, and only studies God in a secondary sense.

The contrast between these two sciences is now apparent. As God is the formal object of the science of sacred doctrine, with other things considered insofar as God is their beginning or end, sacred doctrine differs from philosophical wisdom. As Thomas writes:

> [But] sacred doctrine essentially treats of God viewed as the highest cause—not only so far as He can be known through creatures just as philosophers knew Him—"That which is known of God is manifest in them" (Rom. 1.19)—but also so far as He is known to Himself alone and revealed to others. Hence sacred doctrine is *especially* called wisdom. (ST I.1.6, my emphasis)[15]

This "especially" (*maxime*) offers a clue to how Thomas relates *scientia Dei* and *divina scientia* in the *Summa*. Sacred doctrine draws upon the science of God (*scientia Dei*), which is most perfect and certain; because God is its principle, sacred doctrine surpasses human wisdom. It is the highest science due to the necessity and certainty of the principles from which it proceeds. As Michel Corbin writes:

> Une science n'est donc pas réelle parce qu'en elle jouent les catégories, jugements, et syllogismes ... Une science est réelle parce qu'un objet se montre, parce qu'une source réelle de lumière se donne, parce que des principes vrais sont appréhendés: son premier regard est si bien dirigé sur une réalité qui devient objet que l'aspect logique demeure toujours second, réflexion seconde.[16]

Insofar as *scientia Dei* deals with a thing *most* certain in itself, and sacred doctrine proceeds subalternately[17] from these most certain principles, *scientia Dei* and sacred doctrine are the noblest sciences. Sacred doctrine's subalternative relation to *scientia*

---

15 See also ST I.1.7 for God as the principal subject (*subiectum principiorum*) of sacred doctrine, as sacred doctrine is either about God (*ipse Deus*) or something ordered to God as beginning and end (*quia habent ordinem ad Deum, ut ad principium et finem*).

16 Corbin, *Le Chemin*, p. 717: Corbin makes this argument to show that Aquinas' position changed over time on what constitutes a science, and that the *Summa* reflects his reengagement with Aristotle's *Posterior Analytics* and *Peri Hermeneias*. See also Rogers, *Thomas Aquinas and Karl Barth*, pp. 26-31.

17 "Subalternation" is a technical Thomistic term for the relationship between various sciences. Two sciences are said to be subalternate when one takes its principles from another—in short, when it logically depends upon another. For instance, music depends logically upon mathematics, even if musicians don't prove mathematical formulae and graph overtones and harmonies themselves.

Likewise, sacred doctrine is said to be "subalternate" to *scientia Dei*, because it proceeds from God's knowledge without demonstrating that knowledge itself. The point of contention within Thomism is how this subalternation relates to other forms of subalternation between sciences. For a discussion of these issues, see M.D. Chenu, *La théologie comme science au XIIIème siécle*, 3rd edn (Paris: J. Vrin, 1957), pp. 71-81, and John Jenkins, *Knowledge and Faith in Thomas Aquinas* (Cambridge: Cambridge University Press, 1997), pp. 56-76.

Dei is the *proper* form of subalternation from which others then derive.[18] Thomas' use of the Aristotelian conception of science is "self-relativizing"; even as Aristotelian science directs us towards the proper understanding of *scientia Dei*, its inadequacy in the face of sacred doctrine's divine subject matter becomes apparent.[19] In short, Aristotelian philosophy can tell us what a science *is* (describing it), but cannot tell us *what* is a science (denoting it). The pre-eminence of sacred doctrine's formal object more than makes up for our deficient cognition, locating it at the pinnacle of the scientific hierarchy.

To summarize, then, metaphysical theology studies God in light of the world, while sacred doctrine studies the world in light of God, and the transcendence of its object leads it to surpass other sciences (ST I.1.5). Moreover, whereas metaphysical theology proceeds through the light of natural reason, sacred doctrine reasons on the basis of scripture and the articles of faith. Because the formal objects of these sciences differ, what we can know through them differs as well. Since natural reason only knows God through the light of the intellect, it is unable to cognize God as the end of human action; moreover, what it grasps is both vague and prone to error (ST I.1.1). Without knowledge of the *telos* of our action, we cannot act for the good,[20] such that the goodness of human action is in a perilous state without the presence of sacred doctrine.[21] Sacred doctrine enables better comprehension of humanity's final end as salvation and beatitude, an end that cannot be known by natural reason, and in directing us toward this end it acquires its necessity. The highest of the speculative sciences is thus practical, reshaping human agency while reshaping our view of the world (ST I.1.4).

The above discussion sheds light on several central principles in Thomas' theology. First, he sees sacred doctrine as scriptural and christocentric in its principles and mode of argument. Second, this means that natural reason adopts a secondary, limited role within sacred doctrine. Third, sacred doctrine directs us toward a participation in divine life that transcends what one can achieve through natural

---

18 Corbin, *Le Chemin*, pp. 716-27, and 202-5; Rogers, *Thomas Aquinas and Karl Barth*, p. 26.

19 "Self-relativizing" is Corbin's term: "La théorie aristotélicienne sert à mettre en évidence un fondement qui ne dépend pas d'elle ... l'usage d'Aristote est relativisé dans son exercice même" (*Le Chemin*, p. 720). For Corbin, Aristotelian philosophy (or whatever other philosophy takes its place) is relativized *in* its use; natural reason cannot simply be dispensed with, but rather leads beyond itself through itself—in an almost Kierkegaardian manner willing its own downfall. This fits with Thomas' claim in ST I.1.5 ad 2: "This science can in a sense receive (*accipere*) from the philosophical sciences, not as though it stood in need of them, but only in order to make its teaching clearer."

20 ST I.1.1: "But the end must first be known by human beings who are to direct their thoughts and actions to the end."

21 Sacred doctrine also deals with some things that could be known by natural reason, but which as revealed can be believed more readily, and by a wider audience—these are revealed "in order that the salvation of men might be brought about more fitly and more surely" (ST I.1.1).

reason. Sacred doctrine is scriptural contemplation—drawing on philosophy for its explication, but reshaping philosophy and metaphysics in the process as well.[22] In light of this approach, Thomas' account of naming God can now be examined more directly. In sacred doctrine, Thomas practices a Dionysian, christocentric approach that renders the philosophical naming of God secondary. This will be illustrated below by an alternative reading of the five ways, and how they do not name God properly. Through sacred doctrine's scriptural interpretation, the language of natural reason is reordered to take on a mode of signification that directs it to its proper end. This will be confirmed by the five notions of the Trinity in ST I.32, which adopt the content of the five ways while radically altering their mode of signification via the light of faith. Examining questions 2 and 3 of the *Summa*'s *prima pars* will advance the argument by showing the centrality of modes of signification in sacred doctrine, and by laying out the terminology central to both Thomas' understanding of divine names and the doctrine of the Trinity.

II. Names and Proofs: A Reading of Question 2

Question 2 of the first part of the *Summa* has occasioned volumes of philosophical and theological debate. Both Thomas' supporters and his critics have often read this question as the focal point of a "natural theology" proceeding solely on the basis of natural reason. The focus on the proofs has frequently led to their being read in abstraction from the preceding question on sacred doctrine. However, a close examination of Thomas' argument demonstrates that Thomas actually rejects "natural theology" in his discussion of the five ways, which illustrate Thomas' central claim that we only know what God is not. Given the dominant readings of the proofs, this appears counterintuitive; however, reading question 2 in this way fits better in the context of the *prima pars* as a whole. First, it clarifies Thomas' rejection of Anselm's ontological argument; second, it attends more carefully to *how* the five ways name God. The criticisms of the proofs that follow should be read as criticisms of how people frequently *read* the proofs—as demonstrating the existence of the unique, transcendent God of sacred doctrine. This is not a criticism of Thomas himself, but rather is intended to open the field for an alternative interpretation of the five ways. By reading the five ways as telling us what God is not, we can see them as *apophatic* moments in a Dionysian discourse, finding their proper signification in the doctrine of the Trinity's eminent naming of God.

In ST I.2.1, Thomas discusses and rejects Anselm's ontological argument as part of an argument regarding the self-evidence of God's existence. Thomas reads Anselm

---

22 As Levering argues, metaphysical contemplation is required, for Thomas, as a way of remotion (as he puts it, "metaphysical ascesis") that avoids idolatry. Without philosophical reflection, we would not know what God is not. See Levering, *Scripture and Metaphysics*, pp. 45-6. While I agree with Levering that Thomas' Trinitarian theology is fruitfully read in this way, his work understates the way that such scriptural contemplation not only challenges contemporary Trinitarian theology, but reshapes metaphysical inquiry itself as well.

(perhaps wrongly) as saying that the word "God" signifies "that than which nothing greater can be conceived," so that the very idea of God self-evidently includes God's existence. In order for a proposition or term to be self-evident, its essence (predicate) must be knowable immediately from the subject. In itself, God's existence is self-evident, because God knows that God's essence is to exist. However, God's existence is *not* self-evident to us, since scripture suggests that we can conceive the opposite: "The fool said in his heart, 'There is no God'" (Ps. 52:1). This leads to a distinction between the self-evidence of God's existence in itself (*secundum se*) and its evidence for us (*quoad nos*). God's essence is incomprehensible for the finite intellect of a creature. As Thomas writes:

> I say therefore that this proposition, "God is," considered in itself, is self-evident (*per se nota*): the predicate is the same as the subject: since God is his essence, as will be laid out below (ST I.3.4). But as we do not know (*scire*) God's essence, it is not self-evident for us: but requires to be demonstrated by those things which are more evident to us, and less evident according to their nature, and so by effects.[23]

God's existence, then, is not self-evident to us. We can learn by demonstration that God exists, but we cannot know this truth immediately. In response to Anselm, the five ways are the demonstrations by which we know that God exists. From the start, however, Thomas clearly states that in knowing God by the things evident to us, we see through a glass darkly, since the effects conceal God's essence even in revealing God's existence.

The self-evidence of God's existence opens up the difference between *scientia Dei* on the one hand and the knowledge of human reason on the other. We do not know God as God knows God; natural reason's knowledge of God can never become *scientia Dei*. Thomas emphasizes the limitations of natural reason in his reply to the first objection:

> To know that God exists in a general and confused way [*in aliquo communi, sub quadam confusione*] is implanted in us by nature, inasmuch as God is man's beatitude. For man naturally desires happiness, and what is naturally desired by man must be naturally known to him. This, however, is not to know absolutely that God exists; *just as to know that someone is approaching is not the same as to know that Peter is approaching, even though it is Peter who is approaching*; for many there are who imagine that man's perfect good which is happiness, consists in riches, and others in pleasure, and others in something else. (ST I.2.1, ad 1, my emphasis)

This passage is significant, as it connects the "general and confused" natural knowledge of God with the inability to name God properly. Our "general and confused" natural knowledge of God does not tell us *who* God is, but rather what God is in relation to the world. Natural reason tells us that God is an individual ("someone"), but not which individual, nor the individual's nature. As ST I.1.1 states, God is the goal of human existence, yet we only know this goal imperfectly and

---

23 ST I.2.1.

vaguely. As shall be discussed further below, this knowledge is what Thomas terms a "vague individual," where the distinctive person is not specified. This difference between "someone" and a proper name (e.g., "Peter") provides a clue for how to read the five ways: they tell us something about God via God's effects, but they do not *properly* name God.

The deficient character of natural reason's knowledge of God becomes even more apparent in the ensuing articles of question 2. From God's effects, we can know *that* God exists, but neither *who* God is, nor what God is *essentially*—only what God is in relation to us. In demonstrations from the effects known to us, the effect is substituted for the essence. Since natural reason cannot relate to God's essence (ST I.2.2), its findings should be read as contingent truths. In Kripkean terms, natural reason and philosophy *describe* God by God's effects. Proofs for the existence of God cannot rigidly designate or properly name God.[24]

While each of the five ways will be discussed in more detail in conjunction with the five notions of the Trinity, their status as *descriptions* of God can be demonstrated briefly. Let us take the second way's argument as an example:

> The second way is by reason of efficient causality. We encounter an order of efficient causes in sensible things. Nevertheless it does not happen, nor is it possible, that something is its own efficient cause. For this would make it prior to itself, which is impossible. Nor, however, is it possible to proceed to infinity in efficient causes: For in the order of all efficient causality, the first is the cause of the mediate, and the mediate is cause of the last, whether the mediate is one or many. However, removing the cause removes the effect: therefore, if there were not a first efficient cause, there would not be ultimate nor mediate. But if one proceeded infinitely in efficient causality, there would be neither ultimate effect nor a mediate efficient cause, which is clearly false. Therefore it is necessary to suppose some first efficient cause: this all call [name] God.[25]

An efficient cause makes something actual, bringing a form or activity to fruition from a state of potential. If I shape a mound of snow into a snowman, I am the efficient cause of the snowperson's form, bringing the snow's potential for "snowhumanity" to fruition. Likewise, Aristotle terms a father (or, we could now say, the parents) to be the efficient cause of a child, as its progenitor.[26] Thus, something acts as an efficient cause when it reduces something else's potential to actuality. Since things

---

24 J. William Forgie has argued that it is by taking the phrase "God exists" as an *a posteriori* truth, in which God rigidly designates (or acts as a proper name) in a Kripkean sense, that one can make sense of several key tenets in Thomas' work. Forgie makes this claim in an effort to defend Thomas from Kant's claim that the cosmological arguments depend on the ontological argument, and to challenge Alvin Plantinga's reading of Thomas.

Forgie's claim is interesting, but Thomas' remark that our knowledge of God from natural reason is general and confused poses problems for his reading. See Forgie, "The Cosmological and Ontological Arguments: How St. Thomas Solved the Kantian Problem," *Religious Studies* 31 (1995), pp. 89-101.

25 ST I.2.3.

26 Aristotle, *Metaphysics* 1013a30.

in the world cannot be their own efficient causes, they are best understood as *mediate* efficient causes occurring within a series.

Thomas does not arrive at the idea of a first efficient cause by limiting the series of mediate causes. Within the series, there could be as many mediate causes as one wishes—even an infinite number. Nonetheless, for there to be a series *at all*, something must bring the series itself into actuality. Without something from which the series began, the causes within the series could not be active. It may be helpful, here, to think of old-fashioned strings of electric lights, where the current flowed from light to light. One can have one string, and when one plugs it into the wall, the whole string lights up; the socket is the efficient cause of the activity of the whole series, and makes the whole string of lights active. Likewise, one could attach three strings together (or more), so that the number of lights was greater. Again, however, the string would light up only when plugged into the socket. Without a first efficient cause, the whole series could not get started. A first efficient cause, then, may best be understood as an efficient cause that is *not* within a series.[27] And people called this first cause of efficient causality "God."

There is thus an equivocation between "mediate" efficient causes, which we experience, and the "first" efficient cause that one presupposes, without experiencing it. In our experience of the world, we encounter one mediate cause affecting another, and we need not look outside of the series to see how they interact. There is no reason to conceive of anything we experience as a "first" efficient cause; an electrical socket only works because it is hooked to a power grid. The idea that something must bring the whole series into actuality is not something we encounter in the world, but rather is necessary for conceiving the possibility of the series itself. Thus, when Thomas says it is impossible for the series of mediate causes to go to infinity, he means that this idea generates a logical impossibility (since that would mean that only "mediate" causes would exist).[28] This logical impossibility can only be countered by supposing that there is a first efficient cause—that is, a cause of the series itself that is therefore not within the series. The idea of a first efficient cause is therefore a need of reason, not something that we experience. It is therefore, in my opinion, appropriate to term it an *a priori* statement, since it is an idea of reason that helps us to make sense of our world.[29] Likewise, one can argue that the other four ways are also *a priori* arguments, since they are features of how we understand the world rather than derived from experience.

In light of these aspects of efficient causality, one can examine the metaphysical status of the proof's reference. The five ways "name" (*nominant*) God, but do they

---

27 I am indebted to Jamie Ferreira for helping me to clarify this understanding of first efficient cause.

28 The second way, then, employs a "*per impossibile*" syllogism.

29 Louis Mackey suggests that the five ways be read as ontological proofs. While I disagree with much of his argument (see below), I do think that his assertion that the five ways are known *a priori* is correct. Louis Mackey, "Entreatments of God," in *Peregrinations of the Word: Essays in Medieval Philosophy* (Ann Arbor, MI: University of Michigan Press, 1997), p. 118.

refer to God necessarily? While people call the first efficient cause "God," do they thereby refer to God as God? The answer on Thomas' terms is clearly no. There is nothing in the proof that binds the idea of "first efficient cause" to the God of Abraham, Isaac, and Jacob (or Brahman or Allah, for that matter). As Anthony Kenny has noted with respect to the prime mover, the world itself could fit the bill of "unmoved mover" just as well as an omnipotent, eternal being.[30] The same holds true for the idea of a first efficient cause; there is no reason to think that this refers only to God, because all we know is that it is the cause of efficient causality. Therefore, in light of Kenny's skepticism, if "first efficient cause" does refer to God, then one must admit that its reference is *contingent*.[31] At this point, we are left with five ways of knowing that God exists, but they are ways that are both *a priori* and contingent in their reference. Recall from the previous chapter that, according to Kripke, *a priori* contingent statements are not names, but descriptions. This, then, is the status of the five ways. They represent our general and confused knowledge, telling us that "some god" is there. Natural reason does not name God properly, or refer necessarily to God.

While descriptive, the five ways nonetheless occupy a peculiar status. As exemplified by the idea of a first efficient cause, which tells us that God is "an efficient cause that is not in a series," the five ways tell us more what God is *not* than what God is, emphasizing how God differs from things we know. They do not show God's essence; rather, they deny the adequacy of our language and the things we see in our world (such as mediate efficient causality) to properly name God. They are, one could say, *apophatic* descriptions. The five ways, then, do not lead to natural theology: they lead to *negative* theology, an act of remotion that conceives of God as a being unlike the world we know, and through which we discover God—and thus, one to whom we cannot refer.

These referential deficiencies of our natural knowledge of God become even clearer in light of Thomas' explanation of scientific understanding. For Aquinas, as for Aristotle, there are two modes of scientific demonstration or argument—*propter quid* (on account of which) and *quia* (why). Only *propter quid* demonstrations result in scientific knowledge in the strict sense (*scientia*), while *quia* demonstrations provide less certain cognition. A *propter quid* demonstration proceeds from something's essence to its effects: beginning with knowledge of what the cause itself is, one can say how it actively leads to its effect. A *quia* demonstration, on the other hand, proceeds from effect to cause. If I attempt to reason from the effects to the cause—for example, from a car's spinning wheels to what makes them turn—my knowledge would be deficient. In short, from the effect, I cannot discern the operative principle

---

30 Anthony Kenny, *The Five Ways: St. Thomas Aquinas' Proofs of God's Existence* (New York: Schocken Books, 1969), pp. 31-3. As descriptions, they can be *a priori and* contingent. There are theological reasons, as well, for agreeing with Kenny. Because Thomas' concern in sacred doctrine is theological, the five ways need not bear the burden so many philosophers wish them to carry.

31 See also Preller, *Divine Science*, pp. 146-50.

of activity.³² While an effect can tell us that it *has* a cause, it cannot tell us its principle of activity on account of which (*propter quid*) the cause operates.³³

When the five ways demonstrate God's existence in ST I.2.3, they clearly function as *quia* demonstrations. The five ways give us descriptions of God's activity towards the world; we know that something called God is there as prime mover, first efficient cause, necessary being, most real being, and that which governs and directs nature to its end. However, the five ways demonstrate that God exists by arguing from the world *to* the existence of God; they are *quia* demonstrations that name God by God's effects. As *quia* demonstrations, these demonstrations by natural reason cannot give us *scientia*; we do not know God's essence, and cannot proceed to it from certain first principles. Again, as *quia* demonstrations, the five ways only result in a "general and confused" knowledge of God.

As noted in the discussion of "someone" in article 2, the deficiency of these *quia* demonstrations is partly due to their inability to signify God's singularity. As is well known, Thomas defined God as one whose essence is to exist.³⁴ Yet the five ways clearly fall short. We can know that there is some agent at work in the world, because there is change, but since we only know of the agent from its effects, our knowledge remains contingent and indeterminate. The five ways function more like a personal advertisement—a description of one knows not whom, looking for someone who fits the description:

> MMP (Monastic Medieval Philosopher) ISO prime mover, first cause, being necessary of itself, maximum being. Governance of the world necessary. Looking for extended contemplation; solution to problem of evil a plus. I like demonstrations from first principles, fourfold interpretation of scripture, and Platonic dialogues. I know you're out there—let's get together!

Thus, the deficiency of natural reason is twofold: first, since it does not know God's essence, it cannot give a *propter quid* demonstration, so that what we know of God is unscientific. Also, it thereby has a deficiency in its mode of signification, since natural reason can only tell us "someone" is coming without properly signifying the determinate individual. We may know by natural reason that God is one; but we

---

32 Mackey argues that *quia* demonstrations can have the same necessity as *propter quid* demonstrations ("Entreatments of God," p. 118). I do not see any textual support for this claim in Thomas' work; as previously stated, *quia* demonstrations may be *a priori*, but they are clearly deficient in terms of necessity and certainty when compared with *propter quid* demonstrations.

33 Thomas' discussion of *scientia* and demonstrations is heavily indebted to his commentary on and analysis of Aristotle's *Posterior Analytics*. For a helpful discussion of how the *Posterior Analytics* shape Aquinas' understanding of *scientia*, see Jenkins, *Knowledge and Faith in Thomas Aquinas*, pp. 1-77. In that the form in things and the form in the mind are the same, on the Aristotelian view, a focus on epistemology does not get Thomas exactly right. For the *propter quid/quia* distinction, see also Preller, *Divine Science*, pp. 88-90.

34 St. Thomas Aquinas, *On Being and Essence*, trans. A. Maurer (Toronto: The Pontifical Institute of Mediaeval Studies, 1968) pp. 51-9, esp. 54.

cannot properly *signify* God's singularity by natural reason. As Victor Preller notes, this deficiency of signification may be the most crucial failure in natural reason's inability to refer to God: "The *modus significandi* of a referential term may in certain contexts be more relevant to the determination of the truth of a belief-statement than the actual nature of the *res significata*."[35]

If the five ways were all we had, necessary, rigid designation of God would be impossible. However, the scriptural and interpretive contexts of the proofs come into play at this point. The real basis for Thomas' claim that God exists, of course, is none of the five ways. In the *sed contra* of ST I.2.3 is Exodus 3:14: "It is said in the person (*ex persona*) of God: 'I am who I am' (*Ego sum qui sum*)."[36] Within sacred doctrine, God's name, as given by God in Exodus, serves as scriptural warrant for the claim that God exists. The Lord's ways (the Name) are not our (five) ways. Revelation, rather than natural reason, takes priority because it signifies God's personhood in a way that natural reason cannot.[37] Based on God's communication, sacred doctrine can consider God as God knows God's self—i.e., by God's name. Through revelation participation in *scientia Dei* becomes possible.[38] Of course, we may not understand the nature signified by the name, but it does let one signify God personally.

It is important to note that question 2 gives *both* God's name *and* the proofs as "demonstrations" of God's existence. In light of the Name, as the *fons et origo* of sacred doctrine, the five ways take on religious import. The proofs do demonstrate that "God" exists, even if they do not tell us who this God is. It is by putting the work of natural reason in the context of sacred doctrine that one comes to understand who God is, beginning with an affirmation of God's revelation in faith. As Aquinas states in ST I.2.2, the relation of faith to natural reason is one of presupposition—that "perfection supposes something that can be perfected." This reading, then, is not designed to show that the five ways are invalid or unimportant. They clearly occupy a prominent place in the *Summa*. However, the referential deficiencies of natural reason indicate that the five ways may play a different role than is commonly understood. To flesh out this claim requires development and articulation of how one names God in sacred doctrine, particularly with regard to how its mode of signification differs from natural reason.

---

35 Preller, *Divine Science*, p. 142.

36 Ibid., pp. 22-3.

37 This difference is by and large missed by Gilson, as is the accompanying difference between the modes of signification of faith and natural reason. See Etienne Gilson, *The Christian Philosophy of St. Thomas Aquinas*, trans. H. Shook (New York: Random House, 1956), ch. 2.

38 This need not mean that God is known as "necessary existence." Rather, as discussed in the introduction, it could also mean that God is known in sacred doctrine as the one who is faithfully committed to Israel in the covenant at Mount Sinai. Of course, this is not Thomas' interpretation, but it would nonetheless be consistent with his theological method.

III. Modes of Signification: The Turn to *Supposita*

The giving of God's name in the *sed contra* of ST I.2.3 exemplifies our participation in *scientia Dei* through sacred doctrine. It therefore provides an initial clue as to how sacred doctrine differs from the uses of language that occur within natural reason. God's name, as given in scripture, is an *effect*, given through divine activity. It is something which we come to know *a posteriori*, and by it we still do not know God's essence. However, in faith our intelligence is turned towards a new understanding by proceeding from different principles—in this case, from effects of *grace*. As Thomas writes:

> Although we cannot know in what consists the essence of God, nevertheless in this science [*sacra doctrina*] we make use of His effects, either of nature or grace, in place of a definition, in regard to whatever is treated of in this science concerning God; even as in some philosophical sciences we demonstrate something about a cause from its effect [*sicut et in aliquibus scientiis philosophicis demonstratur aliquid de causa per effetum*], by taking the effect in place of a definition of the cause. (ST I.1.7 ad 1)

Exodus 3:14 is how God names God, rather than how we name God by natural reason. As an effect of grace, it tells us that God exists, but it also signifies the unique *mode* of God's existence in a way that natural reason cannot. As Thomas proceeds through the opening section of the *Summa*, modes of signification become central to delineating the respective spheres of activity of faith and natural reason.

In the name given in Exodus 3:14, we learn that God is the one who *is*. More exactly, the name given in I.2.3—*ego sum qui sum*, "I am who I am"—indicates that God must be thought of as a subject, and therefore that God is singular. Here—and not in the five ways that follow—we find an approach appropriate to the one whose essence is to exist. As David Burrell writes, we can know that God's essence is "to be," which means that God must always be thought of as an individual.[39] Through the name, we may know God differently through scripture than we know God from the world.

In suggesting that we know God "differently" through effects of grace, one risks saying that one knows more about God through sacred doctrine than through metaphysics. This would be a problematic claim, not least because Thomas thinks that one knows God's essence in neither science. Yet the mode of signification in scripture is helpful in seeing how Thomas resolves this issue, as it signifies God's essential individuality. Because of what we discover about God through the name, we know that we must think of God as individualized—as a *who*, and not just as a what. And yet, because this tests the limits of our knowledge, when we know God through sacred doctrine, the new mode of signification *deepens* our awareness of divine mystery, revealing God to be one unknown.

---

39 David Burrell, *Aquinas: God and Action* (Notre Dame, IN: University of Notre Dame Press, 1979), pp. 7-9, 42-54. What follows is indebted to his analysis of Aquinas' "doctrine of God" as rules for theological grammar.

We cannot know God singularly because we cannot *know* individuals. Here, Thomas' use of Aristotelian psychology guards divine transcendence. Our cognitive faculties are oriented towards the world of composite beings in which matter instantiates and individualizes universal forms. We know the forms of things by abstracting them from the material (sensible) individuation through which they present themselves to us. Insofar as we know the universal forms of things, we do not know the things singularly. Grasping the form that gives an individual a particular nature, we never know the individual as such. Therefore, if God can only be thought as an individual, we cannot know God. Thomas spells out this intensified mystery of the language of faith in the ensuing questions, as exemplified by his discussion of God's simplicity in question I.3.

In his analysis of Thomas' "doctrine of God," Burrell argues that Thomas' primary concern is articulating prescriptive rules for how we speak of God, again by stating what God is not. Thomas contrasts the complex nature of creatures—which we understand, as described above—with God's simplicity. Having shown in ST I.3.1 that God cannot have a body, Thomas argues God is not composed of matter and form, yet that God's immaterial form as immaterial is *self-individualizing*. To say that God is simple indicates that God is neither composite nor material, but exists altogether differently from the way that things exist in the world. Thus, if God is properly conceived as an individual without materiality, then one cannot know God's individuality or God's essence—divine simplicity remains a mystery.[40] As Thomas writes later in the *Summa*, "to know simple things defectively is not to know them at all" (ST II-II.2.2 ad 3). By the name, which indicates God's simplicity, we signify that God is one who is unknowable for us by existing differently than the material creatures through whom we acquire knowledge.

In this light, one can develop Burrell's argument: questions 3-11 serve as grammatical rules for how we speak of God, such that we understand and signify that God is mysteriously simple. How we signify this mystery becomes a central issue. In ST I.3.3, Thomas explains how our mode of signifying applies to divine simplicity. As discussed above, we know the forms of things by abstracting from material things encountered in the world; these subsistent individuals that inhere in the abstract natures are *supposita*.[41] *Supposita*, for Thomas, are both ontological and

---

40 See Burrell, *Aquinas*, especially pp. 52-4. That existence is not a predicate, or something we can know, leads to the striking conclusion that the statement that God is *ipsum esse* is a way for us to say what God is *not:* God is not knowable for us, because we cannot predicate anything of God. Burrell reads questions 3, 5, 7, 9, 11 as telling us what God is not. God's simplicity is a *prescriptive* rule for theological discourse, not a description of God's essence. Since our focus is on the mode of signification of divine names, I will focus solely on question 3. See *Aquinas*, pp. 26-41 for this intriguing discussion. The question one is left with after Burrell's discussion is what role scripture plays in Aquinas' God-talk. I would propose that as these rules are clearing away what God is not, they allow us to speak of *who* God is, by reminding us that God is not a what.

41 See P.T. Geach, *Reference and Generality: An Examination of Some Medieval and Modern Theories* (Ithaca: Cornell University Press, 1980), ch. 3. My analysis will

grammatical. First, they are the individual, existent things in the world. In grammatical contexts, *supposita* are those types of signs that signify *supposita* in the world. In *Christ the "Name" of God*, Henk Schoot defines a [grammatical] *suppositum* as "the signification of something as subsistent (*significatio alicuius ut subsistentis*)," and he argues that a similar definition is operative throughout Thomas' work.[42]

A *suppositum* differs from other modes of signification in that it signifies an individual's subsistence rather than the individual's nature.[43] For example, in Socrates, we see the form of humanity (a rational animal) at work, but there is also the material body that individuates him. When we say, "Socrates is a human," we signify his nature. When we say, "Socrates is this person," we signify his individual subsistence (a person being a *suppositum* of a rational nature). As an entity whose material body individuates the form of humanity, Socrates is a *suppositum* of humanity. For Thomas, in material being a *suppositum* is never the universal form itself:

> Now individual matter, with all the individualizing accidents, is not included in the definition of the species ... Therefore this flesh, these bones, and the accidental qualities distinguishing this particular matter, are not included in humanity; and yet they are included in that which is a human. (ST I.3.3)

Indeed, as Thomas writes, "In created things the *suppositum* is not the same as its nature: for 'the man' is not the same as his humanity" (ST I.3.3 ob 2). We signify that a form is individualized—or singularized—in the mode of signification of *supposita*. We can distinguish between "humanity" and "this human" (the supposit of human nature). Ralph McInerny describes this quite clearly:

> Because there is a difference between form and the subject of the form in the material things to which our mind is proportioned, we have one mode or way of signifying the composite of form and matter and another way of signifying the form as such. Thomas calls these the concrete and abstract modes of signification. Names that signify forms do not signify them as subsisting; *it is the composite that has the form that subsists*.[44]

The individual stands under (*sup-ponere*, sup-posit) the universal form; the universal form stands outside itself (*existentia*) in the concrete individual.[45]

---

be of determinate *supposita*, though indeterminate ones are possible as well. Determinate supposition is the mode of signification proper to the divine nature.

42 Henk Schoot, *Christ the "Name" of God: Thomas Aquinas on Naming Christ* (Leuven: Peeters, 1993), p. 52. Schoot adopts his definition from the work of William of Sherwood. Since our focus in this text is on names of God, we will concentrate our attention on *suppositum* as a mode of signification rather than a mode of being.

43 Ibid., pp. 60-64.

44 Ralph McInerny, *Aquinas and Analogy* (Washington, DC: The Catholic University of America Press, 1996), pp. 76-7, my emphasis.

45 Ibid., p. 84: "The species is 'supposed for' by the genus; it is directly placed under (*sup-ponere*) it. And the species supposes for the individuals, which are thus called *supposita*, suppposits."

This distinction between a nature and the individual who subsists therein is a decisive move. It permits a distinction between *id quod* (that which) and *id a quo* (that from which), and renders intelligible a realist ontology. The *id quod/id a quo* distinction, which parallels the *esse/essentia* distinction, is central to Thomas' understanding of the individuation of forms. While the nature that is active (*id a quo*) is the agency of an action, the agent who effects the action (*id quod*) is an individual participant in the nature. *Suppositum* helps to signify the distinction between individuals and natures, enabling the realist claim that individuals inhere in natures. Thus, Thomas renders the *esse/essentia* distinction intelligible by clarifying a parallel distinction between linguistic modes of signification.[46]

What we have said to this point—that supposits are distinct from natures—is true for material, composite beings. God's simplicity complicates this point. For God, for whom the form and the individualization are inseparable, the nature *is* the *suppositum*. "Since God then is not composed of matter and form, He must be His own Godhead, His own Life, and whatever else is thus predicated of Him" (ST I.3.3). By establishing a distinction between the form and the individual within creation, Thomas opens a way to signify God's transcendence, as the distinction collapses in divine simplicity. The ensuing articles confirm God's uniqueness, as Thomas denies that God is contained in either a species or a genus. Our grammatical categories of subject and predicate break down; as God is the one who is ("I am who I am"), our discursive understanding fails before God's radical subsistence. As Thomas summarizes his discussion of simplicity in ST I.3.7:

> First, from the previous articles of this question. For there is neither composition of quantitative parts in God, since He is not a body; nor composition of matter and form; *nor does His nature differ from His "suppositum"*; nor His essence from His existence; neither is there in Him composition of genus and difference, nor of subject and accident. Therefore, it is clear that God is nowise composite, but is altogether simple. (ST I.3.7, my emphasis)

To say that God's nature does not differ from God's *suppositum* indicates the inadequacy of our language to God's mode of being. However, it also suggests that it is possible for us to signify God's essence through names and *supposita*, even though this intellectual activity is least connected with how we know things. By signifying that God's nature is God's *suppositum*, we can name God in a way that surpasses all understanding, subverting comprehension through material and embodied linguistic signification.

To summarize, in his discussion of divine simplicity, Thomas thus articulates an important distinction between God and creation. However, given that our language and understanding are ordered to creation, this distinction carries with it the implication that our language must be reordered in order for it to refer to God.

---

46 The *id quod/id a quo* distinction is discussed at some length by A. Malet, *Personne et amour dans la theologie trinitaire de Saint Thomas d'Aquin* (Paris: Librairie Philosophique J. Vrin, 1956), pp. 32-6, 88-105.

Neither the language of forms nor the language of subsistence is adequate for naming God. As he writes:

> We can speak of simple things only as though they were like the composite things from which we derive our knowledge. Therefore, in speaking of God, we use concrete nouns to signify His subsistence, because with us only those things subsist which are composite; and we use abstract nouns to signify His simplicity. (ST I.3.3 ad 1)

In mentioning "concrete" and "abstract" nouns, and the necessity of both, Thomas foreshadows the discussion of divine names in question 13, and his appropriation of the Dionysian *triplex via* in terms of modes of signification. Question 3 explains why concrete and abstract terms are necessary, in light of God's simplicity. In question 13, we learn how to use concrete and abstract terms in light of Thomas' rule of divine simplicity. It is to this question that we now turn.

IV. Names of God: Question 13

If questions 3-11 provide rules for what we should say about God, apophatically gesturing to divine perfection, then question 13 gives Thomas' analysis of how we can speak of God, and how far our reference extends. While he recognizes that our complex language is not appropriate for God, he does not think this means we should remain silent. Rather, in making the transition to question 13, he argues that through grace one can have a knowledge of God that exceeds that of natural reason in this life (ST I.12.12). The crucial question, then, is how sacred doctrine's gracious gift allows one to say more than one can in natural reason, and thereby order one's mind and heart to God in a new way. This enabling of speech, which orders our language to God, reflects Thomas' study of Dionysius and his influential treatises on divine names, and it is in question 13 that we see Thomas drawing upon Dionysius' scriptural neoplatonism.

Dionysius is often described as an apophatic, negative theologian, whose mysticism would be at a complete remove from Thomas' philosophical and systematic study. However, like many medieval thinkers, Thomas was deeply influenced by the Areopagite, even writing an extensive commentary on *The Divine Names*—to which he accords a high degree of authority throughout the *Summa*. Moreover, while Dionysius is often read as a negative theologian, this only represents one aspect of his work. Dionysius' mystical theology is better understood as a "triple way" (*triplex via*) to speak about God. The triple way proceeds through three steps: affirmative, negative and eminent discourses. Because any one mode of speaking remains insufficient for the task, all three modes of discourse are closely interrelated. The best formulation of the *triplex via* in Dionysius's remaining work is from *The Mystical Theology*:

> Since it is the Cause of all beings, we should posit and ascribe to it all the affirmations we make in regard to beings, and, more appropriately, we should negate all these affirmations,

since it surpasses all being. Now we should not conclude that the negations are simply the opposites of the affirmations, but rather that the cause of all is considerably prior to this, beyond privations, beyond every denial, beyond every assertion.[47]

As this citation shows, both affirmative and negative theologies are required, as a way of recognizing God's transcendence of our language, much as Thomas sees God's simplicity as transcending creation.[48] As Fran O'Rourke puts it, there is a priority to the negative way, precisely so as to affirm the hyper-goodness of God beyond predication.[49]

While this very general similarity is itself important, the more technical features of Dionysius' work illuminate his influence on Thomas. For Dionysius, the proper practice of affirmation and negation requires recognizing the different types of names that one can give to God. He defines two broad categories of names: perceptual (or symbolic) and conceptual names. Perceptual names are those names we give to God based upon things we sense, or see, within creation. These include names such as lion, rock, hair, feet, and other names for material things. Conceptual names, on the other hand, are names we give to God based upon our understanding—being, good, beautiful, and other names that praise God as the cause of all things. In distinguishing these names, Dionysius places them in a neoplatonic hierarchy, as the conceptual names represent those aspects of creation which more fully and directly participate in the divine life, while perceptual names, which are more connected with materiality, participate indirectly. This hierarchy of names is significant for understanding the movement of affirmative and negative theology, and lays the groundwork for Thomas' own approach to divine names.[50]

The affirmative mode of discourse begins the sequence by praising God on account of what we know from creation. As Michel Corbin writes, "Affirmation is a thesis within the language which names God according to the names taken from the universe of beings, and is linked to God's causality in the work of creation."[51] We affirm these names of God because all things, as created by God, are in some way similar to God and thereby unified with one another. As Dionysius writes:

---

47 Dionysius, "The Mystical Theology," in *Dionysius: The Complete Works*, ed. C. Luibheid (New York: Paulist Press, 1987), p. 136.

48 For a general introduction to Dionysius, see Bernard McGinn, *The Foundations of Mysticism*, vol. 1 of *The Presence of God* (New York: Crossroad, 1991), pp. 157-82.

49 Fran O'Rourke, *Pseudo-Dionysius and the Metaphysics of Aquinas* (Leiden: E.J. Brill, 1992), pp. 16-20.

50 McGinn, *The Foundations of Mysticism*, p. 163; O'Rourke, *Pseudo-Dionysius and the Metaphsyics of Aquinas*, pp. 29, 34-5.

51 Michel Corbin, "Négation et transcendance chez Denys," *Recherches des Sciences philosophiques et theologiques* 69 (1985), p. 52.

> He is in fact the Cause of this (i.e., similarity) in all that have the quality of similarity. He is the subsistence of absolute similarity, and all the similarity in the world is similar to a trace of the divine similarity so that all creation is thereby made a unity.[52]

The affirmative theology begins with conceptual names, which are most like God, and proceeds into perceptual names, which are less similar, thereby drawing all of creation together in its varied similarity to God. Thus, for example, in *The Divine Names*, Dionysius discusses how conceptual names such as "Being," "Good," and "Life" apply to God,[53] and at the conclusion says he will next discuss perceptual names in *The Symbolic Theology*.[54] By moving through both categories of names, Dionysius shows both the similarity and dissimilarity of creatures to God; cataphatic discourse is the reflective likeness of the whole of creation to God's infinite, multiple perfections.

However, while things are like God, God is not like things. Mystical theology therefore requires a second moment that negates affirmative speech and moves beyond its limits. This transcendence by negation acts as a corrective against excessive emphasis on similarity between God and creation. As Dionysius continues:

> But surely there is no need to dwell on this point, for scripture itself asserts that God is dissimilar and that he is not to be compared with anything, that he is different from everything and, stranger yet, that there is none at all like him. Nevertheless words of this sort do not contradict the similarity of things to him, for the very same things are both similar and dissimilar to God. They are similar to him to the extent that they share what cannot be shared. They are dissimilar to him in that as effects they fall so very far short of their Cause and are infinitely and incomparably subordinate to him.[55]

Apophasis prevents us from treating the likeness between created being and God's being as exhaustive or univocal.[56] In negation, as described in *The Mystical Theology*, one reverses the cataphatic path, beginning with perceptual names, since these are most dissimilar from God, and then negating conceptual names, as "we have to start by denying those qualities which differ most from the goal we hope to attain."[57]

Eminent discourse negates the negative moment, resulting in a complex, qualified discourse. For the eminent moment, both the affirmative and negative predications are necessary; as stated above, things are "both similar and dissimilar to God." Eminent discourse, in short, refuses to take either affirmation or negation

---

52 Dionysius, "The Divine Names," in *Dionysius: The Complete Works*, p. 118 (913D-916A).

53 Ibid., p. 57.

54 Ibid., p. 131. See also "The Mystical Theology," in *The Complete Works*, p. 139.

55 Dionysius, "The Divine Names," p. 118 (916 A).

56 Corbin reads this moment in Dionysius as preserving the pre-eminence of how God is named in scripture—i.e, that God's naming of God (as the Tetragrammaton, or as Jesus) is more proper than any name that we ascribe. See Dionysius, "The Divine Names," 585 B-588 A; Corbin, "Négation et transcendance," pp. 54-6.

57 Dionysius, "The Mystical Theology," p. 140.

as an absolute or final discourse. The eminent way, then, should not be understood as a third way that is distinct from affirmation and negation, but rather as the proper ordering of affirmative and negative statements. As Corbin writes:

> There is no third biblical register that is possible above the polyonymy and anonymity [i.e., cataphatic and apophatic discourse]. There exist only two registers and the third does not add any content, but only a certain hermeneutical manner of reading the register of negation in order that it coheres with that of affirmation, or, at least, in order that this concordance—concordance of truth, as St. Anselm could say—would be said without being confused with the most elemental logic.[58]

Thus, the "triple way" is just a proper ordering of the two moments of affirmation and negation, the two types of predicative speech available to us. In its inclusion of both affirmative and negative language, involving both perceptual and conceptual names, it is clearly irreducible to either, opening a new register of naming in an effort to transcend worldly language in an eminently divine discourse. Indeed, the eminent way reflects the descent and return, in a neoplatonic *exitus/reditus* scheme, of God's overflowing generosity toward creation and drawing of creation back to the one from whom it proceeds.[59]

While deeply influenced by Dionysius' work, Thomas does not directly appropriate the affirmation/negation/eminence path of naming God. Rather, it remains implicit within his discussion of divine names. Thomas does begin his discussion by agreeing with Dionysius that, in a sense, God transcends all affirmations and negations; as our words signify created beings, none of them are proper to God. This is why, Thomas argues, Dionysius deems God to be "above any name (*supra nominationem*)" (ST I.13.1).[60] However, like Dionysius, he argues that the creaturely signification of names is not exhaustive, and thus that names can speak of God, in much the same way as Dionysius conceives of an eminent sense of language. The parallel between the eminent sense and Thomas' own understanding will emerge in light of Thomas' discussion of concrete and abstract modes of signification.

As we already saw in ST I.3.3, abstract and concrete significations are both necessary for naming God because neither our abstract language, which signifies universals, nor our concrete language, which signifies individuals, is adequate for speech about the simple God. If God is simple *and* existent, then clearly neither our abstract language nor our concrete language is appropriate by itself. As Thomas writes:

> Now God is both simple, like the form, and subsistent, like the concrete thing, and so we sometimes refer to him by abstract nouns to indicate his simplicity and sometimes by concrete nouns to indicate his subsistence and completeness; though neither way of speaking measures up to his way of being, for in this life we do not know him as he is in himself. (ST I.13.1 ad 2)

---

58 Corbin, "Négation et transcendance," p. 57.
59 O'Rourke, *Pseudo-Dionysius*, pp. 217-20.
60 Dionysius, "The Divine Names," p. 54.

We must use both abstract and concrete predication in order to refer to God, since only thereby can we signify the coinherence in God of these disparate modes of creaturely being. The parallel with Dionysius' discussion of perceptual and conceptual names is striking: concrete nouns, like perceptual names, signify material subsistence, while abstract nouns, like conceptual names, signify immaterial forms that share more fully in God's perfection.

Thomas not only distinguishes two categories of names in a way close to Dionysius; his discussion of how the names apply to God likewise parallels Dionysius' reflection. First, with abstract terms, Thomas argues that these terms can be said substantially, or properly, of God. As Thomas writes in the introduction to his commentary on *The Divine Names*, "We suppose, therefore, one principle which is itself essential goodness and unity and being; we call this God and all other good or unity or being is said by derivation from this first principle."[61] These terms signify the divine nature—divine goodness, life, etc. Because God is not just the cause of these qualities, but also *is* these qualities, albeit in a way different from creatures, what the terms signify is proper to God, even as the mode of signification is deficient (ST I.13.2).[62] Furthermore, as abstract nouns that signify form, the names do not in and of themselves signify materiality or creaturely subsistence. As Thomas writes:

> As to the names applied to God, there are two things to be considered—viz., the perfections which they signify, such as goodness, life, and the like, and their mode of signification. As regards what is signified by these names, they belong properly to God, and more properly than they belong to creatures, and are applied primarily to Him. But as regards their mode of signification, they do not properly and strictly apply to God; for their mode of signification applies to creatures. (ST I.13.2)[63]

Because the quality signified is essentially and properly in God—God being, for example, goodness itself [64]—Thomas says that these names apply properly to God (ST I.13.3), and to creatures by participation, or secondarily (ST I.13.5). "Certain words truly mean these absolute perfections but without enclosing the mode of participation in their meaning, as being, good, life, and such words. And these can be said properly of God" (ST I.13.3). The mode of subsistence is indeterminate in our words for perfections; since God is *simply* good, goodness, being, and like abstract names can be affirmatively spoken of God. However, since our use of these terms derives from creatures, it is deficient with respect to how the quality subsists in God.

---

61 "Ponebant, enim, unum primum quod est ipsa essentia bonitatis et unitatis et esse, quod dicimus Deum et quod omnia alia dicuntur bona vel una vel entia per derivationem ab illo primo." St. Thomas Aquinas, *In Librum Beati Dionysii De Divnis Nominibus* (Rome: Marietti, 1950), p. 2.

62 See also O'Rourke, *Pseudo-Dionysius*, pp. 34-5.

63 See also, Mark Jordan, "The Names of God and the Being of Names," in A. Freddoso (ed.) *The Existence and Nature of God* (Notre Dame, IN: University of Notre Dame Press, 1983), p. 167.

64 Both Dionysius and Aquinas draw on the scripture that none is good but God alone (Luke 18:19) in making this point. See O'Rourke, *Pseudo-Dionysius*, p. 65.

These names are deficient with respect to the mode of signification, even as the qualities themselves are proper to God.

Like Dionysius, Thomas understands concrete names to be at a greater distance from God than the abstract ones. As he says, these names apply to God metaphorically, since their primary or proper signification is creaturely. As discussed above, we use these names to signify divine subsistence—God's existence. We need to use concrete names because the abstract nouns, taken on their own, do not signify subsistence, according to how we understand them. Thus, we affirm the concrete nouns, such as "rock," as names of God, because they remind us that God's nature is different from that of creatures, such that the divine nature is self-subsisting.

While the subsistence signified by concrete names is appropriate to God, the mode of subsistence is still deficient. A rock or lion subsists through matter, and God is not material. Furthermore, this materiality is part of the meaning of the term "rock" or "lion"; whereas abstract names that signify forms do not necessarily signify creaturely being. Concrete names can only refer to God by extension, or in a metaphorical sense, to indicate God's subsistence, because their meaning is intrinsically distant from God's nonmaterial simplicity. Thus, when Thomas says that concrete nouns apply metaphorically, he is establishing a hierarchy in which abstract, conceptual terms more fully represent or name God, while concrete terms connected with materiality only signify God by extension. In this hierarchy, we see Thomas adopting and rephrasing Dionysius' hierarchy of being as varied degrees of participation in the good.

In exploring Thomas' discussion of both concrete and abstract names, it is clear that he sees both affirmative and negative moments as necessary in understanding them. Insofar as abstract terms signify the divine essence, albeit in diverse ways (ST I.13.4), they represent how these qualities are similar to God. Concrete terms, moreover, affirm that creation is like God in its subsistence. However, both sets of terms also require negation, as the universal, non-subsistence of abstract terms must be negated, while the materiality of subsisting concrete terms must be denied. Thus, both sets of terms must be affirmed and denied, and it is in this movement of affirmation and negation that the names can apply to God in an eminent sense. With the abstract names, which can apply properly to God, negating their ordinary mode of signification is a way of recognizing that these names are appropriate to the thing signified (*res significata*) while deficient in terms of our mode of signification (*modus significandi*) and our mode of understanding (*modus intelligendi*). By negating our understanding of these perfections, we can eminently signify God's subsistence as beyond our worldly modes of predication.[65]

---

65 See Schoot, *Christ the "Name" of God*, p. 96; Jordan, "The Names of God and the Being of Names," pp. 161-90. This role of material predication is also consistent with Aquinas' understanding of the role of metaphors and less noble descriptions, since these make it clear that our descriptions of God are not literal (ST I.1.9), and thereby tell us what God is not.

The *triplex via* of modes of signification is crucial to understanding Thomas as an analogical thinker. By distinguishing words spoken primarily of God from the same words spoken of creatures through the mode of signification rather than by their meaning, Thomas can affirm that such abstract terms are spoken analogically rather than equivocally (ST I.13.5).[66] That is, "goodness" in God and in creatures is the same thing, but its modes of existence are different. Because the names (Being, life, good, etc.) subsist properly and essentially in God and secondarily in things, the difference in modes of signification allows us to signify the difference between God and creation, and our words may apply properly to God and to creatures by participation.[67]

The need for a *triplex via* for our speech to be appropriate to God indicates an inverse relationship between the sense of theological language and its reference. Our understanding and our language begin with the order of things in the world; they are thus the *inverse* of the order of creation, in which all things proceed from God. As Ralph McInerny writes:

> This process makes it clear that, from the point of view of understanding the application of the term to God, we must invoke its creaturely use. But God's wisdom is not dependent on there being any creatures; rather the wisdom of creatures is dependent upon God. So we

---

[66] Because he distinguishes modes of signification in this manner, Aquinas is able to consider properties of God more fully than Maimonides. For example, when Aquinas discusses Maimonides' position in ST I.13.2, he attributes to Maimonides the position that God does not have properties; any affirmative statements should be read as denials of the existent limitations of created being. "God is living" would function as a negation of the privative statement "God is inanimate," rather than actually saying something about what is proper to God.

This captures at least a surface reading of Maimonides, for whom the simplicity of God means that given our language we cannot properly predicate anything of God. For Maimonides, all names given to God (except for the Tetragrammaton, given by God) are "appellatives" derived from creation, and thus only describing God's actions towards the world; to treat them as proper to God thus risks introducing composition into divinity. See Moses ben Maimonides, *Guide for the Perplexed*, trans. M. Friedländer (London: Routledge, 1928), chs LXI-LXII. However, it is important to note that Maimonides' refusal to predicate attributes of God is closely connected with his *not* distinguishing between the mode of signification and the thing signified. Maimonides is not denying goodness, etc. to God, but rather our ability to properly speak of these. And, if one considers the way that one who desires a knowledge of God's essential name must be trained in the virtues, the way to *scientia Dei* for both Maimonides and Aquinas may not be that different. For more on Maimonides, see Burrell, *Knowing the Unknowable God: Ibn-Sina, Maimonides, and Aquinas* (Notre Dame: University of Notre Dame Press, 1986), pp. 51-70. For a cautionary note on how one reads Maimonides, see Jordan, "Names," pp. 174-5.

[67] Hilary Putnam has questioned whether or not Aquinas' view actually differs from Maimonides' "attributes of action" in any meaningful way. The distinction between modes of signification and the thing signified allows us to speak where Maimonides would ask that we be silent. But the difference, I think, is on our part as speakers; Aquinas and Maimonides both agree on the character and simplicity of the divine nature. See Hilary Putnam, "Thoughts to an Analytical Thomist," *The Monist* 80 (1997), pp. 487-99.

want to say that there is an order *per prius et posterius secundum impositionem nominis* that does not express the order *secundum esse*.

In short, in names analogously common to God and creature, the creature is the *per prius* and the *ratio propria*, since we must make reference to the creaturely meaning to fashion its meaning as applicable to God. At the same time, we are aware that what we last name is what is ontologically first ... The *ordo rerum* in this case is exactly the opposite of the *ordo nominis*.[68]

Through the negations of Dionysian discourse, one expresses an awareness that that which one names last is ontologically first. The order of naming establishes an ascending remotion from creatures to God, reflecting the descent of God's being and goodness into creation. Only through attention to the limits of our modes of signification can we become aware of an analogy between God and creatures.

Thomas' appropriation of Dionysian affirmations and negations of divine names not only helps him to classify the categories of names and clarify how they enable reference to God. The Dionysian influence is also apparent in his discussion of which names are most proper to God. A word used to signify an individual, properly speaking, cannot be communicable (that is, shareable); God's most proper name, then, must be incommunicable. Moreover, as Thomas writes in his commentary on *Peri Hermeneias*, in order for a name to be proper, it must name *both* a determinate nature and a determinate individual. In question 13 of the *Summa*, there are three nominees for God's "most proper name": "God," "He Who Is" (*qui est*), and the Tetragrammaton. Each has some claim to propriety, and Thomas changed his views on the relationship between these names over the course of his intellectual career. In the *Summa* he argues that the Tetragrammaton is God's most proper name because of its incommunicability both in terms of the thing signified and its mode of signification, and this builds on the Dionysian approach just described.

Thomas' understanding of the name "God" remained consistent throughout his writings. The name "God" signifies the divine nature, whose essence is to exist and who is therefore *singular* (ST I.11.3); God is always and only an individual. On the part of the thing signified (*res significata*) the name "God" is therefore incommunicable. However, since our words for natures signify abstract universals, which can be principles of activity for multiple individuals, the words are not incommunicable. On the part of our mode of signification (*modus significandi*) or *opinion*, the word "God" is therefore communicable, and cannot be God's most proper name. Insofar as other things are able to participate in the divine life (e.g., Psalm 81: "I say you shall be gods"), the name "God" is communicable (ST I.13.9). As a side note, this confirms what we have seen earlier—that when people call "God" (*nominant Deus*, I.2.3) the first efficient cause or the other four proofs, they are not naming God as an individual.

---

68 McInerny, *Aquinas and Analogy*, pp. 160-61.

Throughout many of his earlier writings, Thomas argued that "*qui est*" was God's most proper name, as the name signifying being.[69] "*Qui est*" is the Latin translation for the name God gave to Moses to share with the Israelites (Ex. 3:14). It is most proper, in these arguments, because it signifies that God *is*, signifying God's subsistence rather than God's form (and thus, signifying a determinate individual). Furthermore, it is also proper because of its indeterminacy, which affirms that God remains unknowable for us; "For other names determined the mode of substance of a thing: but this name '*qui est*' determines no mode of being, but has itself an indeterminacy of all" (ST I.13.11). By this name, as Maurer writes, God "is praised primarily as existing, for existence is the most valuable gift God makes to creatures."[70] On this point, Thomas is close to Dionysius, and this appears to be the most appropriate name for God.

However, while it expresses our relation to God, Thomas revises his position in the *Summa*, arguing that "*qui est*" cannot be God's proper name. As just mentioned, it does not signify God's nature. If "God" was indeterminate with regard to signifying a particular individual, "*qui est*" does not properly signify a nature, and therefore does not truly signify a singular individual. He shifts his position, then, to say that "*qui est*" is most proper *for us*, on account of its signification.

In the *Summa*, Thomas considers the Tetragrammaton to be God's most proper name. As he writes:

> If, however, a name were given to God, not as signifying his nature but referring to him as this thing, regarding him as an individual, (*non ex parte naturæ, sed ex parte suppositi secundum quod consideratur ut hoc aliquid*) such a proper name would be altogether incommunicable and in no way applicable to others—perhaps the Hebrew name of God, the Tetragrammaton was used in this way: it would be as though someone were to use the word 'Sun' as a proper name designating this individual. (ST I.13.9)[71]

Singular reference to God can only be accomplished in the absence of communicability. The Tetragrammaton, because it is a name without an accompanying description, refers to God as "this one" such that nothing else can share in God's existence; moreover, it signifies the divine nature—that is, God is this one who exists purely as subject or as pure act.[72] Thomas confirms the propriety of the Tetragrammaton a

---

69 Armand Maurer, "St. Thomas on the Sacred Name 'Tetragammaton'," *Mediaeval Studies* 34 (1972), pp. 275-7.

70 Ibid., p. 277.

71 One might ask how the Tetragrammaton signifies a nature as well as existence. Thomas does not spell this out. However, his use of "Sun" as an example may be telling; the sun is the image Dionysius uses to symbolize the Good, in its self-communication. Thus, my hypothesis at this point is that the Tetragrammaton, for Thomas, signifies both God's existence (Being) and God's goodness. This would move Thomas' position closer to that of Dionysius on this issue than some scholars, such as O'Rourke, would perceive him to be. Still, this is admittedly conjecture.

72 Likewise, Maimonides describes the meaning of the Name as "absolute existence."

couple of articles later because it integrates the existence signified by "*qui est*" with the nature signified by "God." Thomas thus orders the names as follows:

> To the first objection it can be said that this name "*qui est*" is a more proper name of God than this name "God," according to how it is imposed, on account of being, and according to the mode of signification and consignification, as was said above. But according to that on account of which the name is imposed this name "God" is more proper, as it is imposed to signify the divine nature. And thus more proper is the Tetragrammaton, which is imposed to signify the incommunicable substance of God, and, as in this place, singularly. (ST I.13.11 ad 1)

Nonetheless, because the Tetragrammaton incommunicably and properly signifies both God's nature itself and God's individuality, it is the most proper name of God. Moreover, in ordering these three names, Thomas develops an eminent sense of naming through the interplay of concrete and abstract signification—the subsistence of "*qui est*" and the abstract nature of "*Deus*" are both incorporated and transcended by the Tetragrammaton.

In his commentary on Isaiah and elsewhere, Aquinas appropriates the name "*qui est*" to the Son.[73] Reading Exodus allegorically, Thomas reads this name of God as prefiguring the Son's Incarnation, as a *suppositum* of the divine nature assuming human nature in the person of Jesus Christ. Both "*qui est*" and Jesus allow us to identify God as a determinate individual. Yet neither name, of itself, signifies the divine nature. This raises an intriguing question: if Christ parallels "*qui est*," is there a name that acts as a parallel to the Tetragrammaton? What name, for Christianity, is God's most proper name, naming God in an eminent sense?

The answer to this question is really not surprising. For Thomas, God is properly named as the Trinity. The Trinity parallels the Tetragrammaton in the propriety and incommunicability of its reference. Yet while this answer may not be surprising, readings of the *Summa* do not often consider how Thomas' understanding of divine names relates to his doctrine of the Trinity. As the next section demonstrates, Thomas' doctrine of the Trinity puts into practice his doctrine of divine names and enacts the rules for speaking about God. What *is* surprising, still, is that the doctrine of the Trinity demonstrates a theological rationale for the five ways of question 2, perfecting natural reason through the signification of sacred doctrine.

V. The Notions of the Trinity and the Perfection of Natural Reason

For Thomas, naming God is best conceived as the traversal of a path that proceeds through the concrete and abstract aspects of our language, both affirmatively and apophatically. His explication of the Trinity synthesizes the various points of his analysis, and brings our composite language to refer to the one simple God. As three persons of one essence, the doctrine of the Trinity incorporates both God's personal,

---

73 Schoot, *Christ the "Name" of God*, p. 157. Aquinas does so as well in ST I.39.8.

individual subsistence and abstract nature. Thomas explains how this integrates and eminently transcends our diverse, deficient cognitions of God.

Thomas' doctrine of the Trinity affirms the goodness of God's relation to the world while maintaining God's freedom in the act of creation—a gift-like, gratuitous act of love. God's relation to the world proceeds from God's essence without relation to the world itself being essential. To signify this free relation, he draws upon Augustine's analogy of the Trinity to the mind, in which the Father is the intellect, the Son as understanding, and the Holy Spirit the loving will that proceeds from the agent's knowledge. As with Augustine, this analogy is illuminating on two counts: first, it depicts the internal conditions necessary for exterior agency, and second, it signifies distinctive acts that unite to produce one combined activity (ST I.27.1). Insofar as the external act presupposes the interior act, the internal act is more proper to a conception of agency than the external act, and thus an appropriate analogy for conceiving divine activity.

Since thought and will are proper to internal action, Thomas determines that there are two actions internal to God: the word as intellectual conception (the Son) and love as the internal act of will (Holy Spirit). Any other effects of divine activity, insofar as they proceed *ad extra*, should be differentiated from these processions, and therefore are termed inessential relations (ST I.27.4). While this could appear to trivialize God's relationship to the world, it is rather a first step toward conceiving the distinctive shape of God's relation to the world. For Thomas, the acts that distinguish the divine persons, as relational acts, are also conditions for God's relation to the world; triune activity is a condition for relation to creation. It is because Father, Son, and Holy Spirit really relate to one another that God freely loves the world.[74]

Since they constitute agency, Thomas terms the relations of Father, Son, and Holy Spirit *real* relations. All other relations (e.g., *ad extra*) are *rational*. A relation, for Aquinas, implies regard of one to another (*respectus unius ad alterum*). The real relations comprise the persons because they are relations of opposition that can only be conceived by distinction of persons. Whereas relation for creatures is accidental, since the other is external to the essence of the one relating, in God the relations are essential, since one divine person regards an other of the same essence. As Aquinas

---

[74] Aquinas terms the relation of the Son to the Father one of intellectual emanation (*emanationem intellectus*) (ST I.27, I.34.2). It may have been in an effort to distinguish the immanent Trinity from the economic Trinity (God's relation to the world) that Aquinas thus undertook his criticism of Avicenna's understanding of creation as emanation. Maintaining the divine life as a realm of emanating relations while making the creation of the world a free and contingent event may have been central to Aquinas' efforts to retain the Aristotelian elements contained in a doctrine of emanation, while likewise affirming the article of faith regarding God's freedom in the creation of the world. For Aquinas' criticisms of Avicenna (Ibn-Sina), see David Burrell, *Knowing the Unknowable God*, pp. 19-34. While Aquinas' criticisms of Ibn-Sina and emanation are well known, the presence of emanation within his work is not. His incorporation of this element into his doctrine of the Trinity, admittedly in a manner that is probably unacceptable to Islamic thought, may be a starting point for further dialogue and intratraditional reasoning, and it is towards that end that I raise this point here.

notes, real relations are thus very close to relations of identity (ST I.28.1 ad 2); the persons are only distinguished by their respective activities, as all three share the one divine essence.

In some respects, Thomas' analysis of the relations goes further than many Christian thinkers before him, as he uses the idea of relation to emphasize that the persons of the Trinity are the agents of divine activity. As represented in the first objection of ST I.28.2, both Western and Eastern Christianity had for the most part accepted a distinction between the relations of the persons and the divine essence (though the emphasis on the essence apart from the persons is a frequent criticism of Augustinian theology by Orthodox theologians).[75] As Thomas quotes Augustine, "For it [relation] is said of some things, as Father and Son; but this is not said according to the divine substance." Augustine is well in line with the tendency to distinguish God's essence from the persons of the Trinity. This distinction is often thought to be necessary in order to affirm God's incomprehensibility—while we may know the divine persons, we do not know their essence. This emphasis on the divine essence, however, often treats the essence as both principle of activity and as agent. As A. Malet writes of Augustine:

> Like the Greek fathers, Saint Augustine distinguishes poorly the role of the person and that of the nature in the act of procession. Is it the person who engenders the person or the essence which engenders the essence? The answer is often ambiguous ... For Augustine, the expression "The Father begets" signifies also "The essence begets."[76]

According to Malet, this ambiguity leads to an "ontologism" and essentialism that diminishes the focus on the persons. When one treats the essence as agential, the persons become secondary or derivative. Two effects follow from this essentialism. First, if the persons themselves are not the agents, it becomes difficult to tell how the processions really differ from one another: if the same essence is at work in the processions of the Son and the Spirit, then how can one distinguish the procession of the Spirit from the begetting of the Son? Second, on Thomas' own terms, this distinction would seem to imply that we could not truly name God properly, since by the Trinity we would only name determinate persons, without naming the divine essence. Thomas therefore makes a subtle break with the patristic naming of the Trinity, reshaping it toward a more personalized doctrine.

Adapting Gilbert de la Porrée's notion of the relations as distinct from the essence, Thomas makes a distinction: the relations are that which God is, so that the persons really do constitute who God is, while the divine essence is that *by which* God is who God is. The persons are the agents of divine activity; a divine person is the one who (*id quod*, that which) begets, is begotten, or proceeds. God's essence is that by which (*id a quo*) God is. God's essence is the principle of divine activity, and is common to all the agents; yet the persons themselves, as constituted by their

---

75 See, for example, Levering's discussion of Zizioulas, *Scripture and Metaphysics*, pp. 202-12.

76 Malet, *Personne et amour*, p. 24.

relations, are the agents to whom we ascribe the activity. To speak of the essence or of the relations, then, is to speak in two modes of the same thing, for while the relations are nonessential, on account of God's simplicity they are not accidental. Divine simplicity—the identity of person and essence—for Thomas, makes it conceivable that things that we distinguish for the purpose of understanding are really one and the same in reality.

Thomas therefore sees it as possible to treat the relations as different from the essence from the standpoint of our language and understanding. Yet, intriguingly, he does so in order to draw them closer ontologically. Because God is simple, unlike creatures, the persons can be the real agents of divine activity, without making them accidental to the divine essence. "What has accidental being in created things, according as it is transferred to God, has substantial being ... it therefore follows that in God some thing is not essential being and another relational being, but that they are one and the same" (ST I.28.2). By distinguishing how we speak about the persons and the essence, Thomas actually draws them closer together than an Augustinian approach; for Thomas: God's essence is God's *supposita*, the Father, Son, and Holy Spirit.

Having established the difference between real and rational relations, Thomas articulates the propriety of thinking of the Father, Son, and Holy Spirit as persons. In questions 29 and 30 of the *prima pars*, which define how the term "person" applies to the Trinity, the notion of *suppositum* returns to the fore. "Person" is a proper term for God because "person" is a "*suppositum* for rational individuals" (ST I.29.1). Thomas determines that the term "person" is proper to the Trinity, and to all three members, because of its relation to what is termed "first substance." First substance makes something a singular, determinate and concrete instantiation of an essence or nature. "Person" is therefore a term signifying the "first substance" of rational beings, and thus signifying immaterial individuality. "I respond to the objection that "person" signifies that which is most perfect in all nature, clearly subsisting in a rational nature. As a perfection, it is attributable to God" (ST I.29.3). By referring to Father, Son, and Holy Spirit as persons, one attributes the proper mode of signification to them, signifying that God's essence is to exist—or, as Thomas later, that the essence is the same as the *suppositum* (ST I.39.1). Thus, insofar as "person" has the mode of signification proper to individuals, distinguishing them by their relation and individuating them in their community, "person" applies *suppositum* as a mode of signification to God's inner life.

However, while "person" is appropriate as a mode of signification, it inadequately expresses God's activity since it only refers indirectly to the relations that constitute the persons. To say that God is "three persons of one substance" says how to refer to God, but it does not name the relations that individuate the persons. As Thomas describes it, "person" functions as a "vague individual" name; it signifies individuality, without properly signifying the individuals themselves; and

> it is also said in human things that this name "person" is common to the rational community, not as genus or species, but as vague individuals [*individuum vagum*]. For names of a

genus or species, such as "human" or "animal," are imposed to signify a common nature itself ... But vague individuals, such as "some human," signify the common nature with a determinate mode of existence found in singulars, namely by the distinct subsistence of something. (ST I.30.4)

Thomas discusses the concept of "vague individuals" at more length in his commentary on Aristotle's *Peri Hermeneias*. A "vague individual" signifies the nature *as* determinately existing, without determinately naming the existent itself. As stated in the discussion of question 13, a proper name for Thomas signifies both a determinate nature and a determinate individual.[77] The difference between a vague individual and a determinate one is captured, for Aquinas, by the difference between "Some man is a rational animal" and "Socrates is a rational animal." Likewise, "person" is insufficient for singular reference, which requires both the determinate nature *and* the determinate individual found only in proper names.[78] Moreover, "person" is unique as a vague individual name: whereas most vague individual names signify the nature, "person" signifies the mode of existence, or the individualization, without saying *what* it is that is being individualized (ST I.30.4).

Let us consider what we have found thus far. Natural reason allows us to reason from effect to cause; it thus makes knowledge of God's activity toward the world possible, though only in a "general and confused" manner. We could not know God's essence, or who God is, from natural reason alone. By signifying divine activity, the proofs operated as a "vague individual" name in the ordinary sense, signifying a nature as subsistent (for example, "some first efficient cause") without saying who the individual is. The proofs tell us "someone" is coming, vaguely identifying that it is an individual of a certain nature. Likewise, we find that in naming God as three persons, one adopts an individuated mode of signification, but without specifying an activity or nature. Thus, there is vagueness in terms of both the persons and the nature.

For Thomas, naming God as Father, Son, and Holy Spirit unifies and orders these two vague and errant aspects of our discourse. In naming God as triune, one names God as *this* determinate individual: these names are proper to the persons, and as proper they incommunicably denote the singularity of the individuals. But one also names a determinate nature insofar as one names *the activity of relation*: the Father is the Father in *begetting* the Son, the Son is the Son as *begotten*, and their common spiration is the Holy Spirit. Perfecting our signification of natures and individuals, one is able to refer to or properly name God through faith. In signifying both an individual and a nature, the naming of the Trinity thus parallels the naming

---

77 For example, in the preface to his commentary on the Gospel of John, Thomas distinguishes this Gospel from the Synoptics as the Gospel that tells of divine contemplation. He goes on to say that it is appropriate that John authors gospel, since the name "Iohannus" signifies grace, which is requisite for contemplation of the final end that is above our nature. See *Super Evangelium S. Iohannis* (Rome: Marietti, 1951), p. 3 (para. 11).

78 St. Thomas Aquinas, *Aristotle: Peri Hermeneias*, trans. J.T. Oesterle (Milwaukee: Marquette University Press, 1962), p. 83.

of God by the Tetragrammaton discussed in question 13. Much as the Tetragrammaton incorporates the determinate nature signified by "God" and the determinate individuality of *"qui est,"* Thomas' doctrine of the Trinity incorporates the determinate nature of the relations and the determinate individuality signified by "person."

Thomas explicates the relations within the Trinity by way of the five notions—the abstract ideas by which we understand the distinctions between the persons. For Thomas, there are both abstract and concrete names with respect to the divine essence; there must also, then, be abstract and concrete names for the persons. The notions, in signifying the activities of relation, are the abstract terms. They do not, of themselves, signify the individuals acting, but rather what they do. These notions, as he says, cannot be known by natural reason; rather, they are the ideas by which we explain what is believed through sacred doctrine (ST I.32.1).

In question 32, Thomas explains that there are five notions that constitute the relations between the persons, and thus their identities. He defines them as follows:

> I answer that, a notion is the proper idea whereby we know a divine Person. Now the divine persons are multiplied by reason of their origin: and origin includes the idea of someone from whom another comes, and of someone that comes from another, and by these two modes a person can be known. Therefore the Person of the Father cannot be known by the fact that He is from another; but by the fact that He is from no one; and thus the notion that belongs to Him is called "innascibility." As the source of another, He can be known in two ways, because as the Son is from Him, the Father is known by the notion of "paternity"; and as the Holy Ghost is from Him, He is known by the notion of "common spiration." The Son can be known as begotten by another, and thus He is known by "filiation"; and also by another person proceeding from Him, the Holy Ghost, and thus He is known in the same way as the Father is known, by "common spiration." The Holy Ghost can be known by the fact that He is from another, or from others; thus He is known by "procession"; but not by the fact that another is from Him, as no divine person proceeds from Him.
>
> Therefore, there are Five notions in God: "innascibility," "paternity," "filiation," "common spiration" and "procession." Of these only four are relations, for "innascibility" is not a relation, except by reduction, as will appear later [ST I.33.4 ad 3]. Four only are properties. For "common spiration" is not a property; because it belongs to two persons. Three are personal notions—i.e. constituting persons, "paternity," "filiation," and "procession." "Common spiration" and "innascibility" are called notions of Persons, but not personal notions, as we shall explain further on [ST I.40.1 ad a].

The notions let us know the divine persons, and distinguish them, because the relations signified are oppositional; if the Father is known by "paternity," and the Son by "filiation," then they are clearly distinct. These notions constitute the activity by which the persons exist, but the persons themselves are the agents of the action. The notions thereby come to signify God's essence indirectly, as considered in the activity between them.

Thomas argues that the notions are implicit within scripture, as they are "contained" within the concrete names of the persons. One could ask, though, why he deems it necessary to explicate them. Thomas explains that the knowledge of divine persons—and thus, of the notions—was necessary first and foremost for the right idea of creation. "The fact of saying that God made all things by His Word excludes the error of those who say that God produced things by necessity" (ST I.32.1). In other words, knowing the Trinity and the notions through sacred doctrine change our conception of how God relates to the world. At this point, Thomas is actually understating what the five notions do. For, they do help one to think of how God created the world out of love, and in freedom, but they also suggest how God's internal activity relates to God's activity *ad extra*. The notions establish a correlation between the Trinity and God's activity toward the world, such that in light of the notions we understand how *this* God could be the one whose existence we discover via natural reason's demonstrations. In short, the five notions personalize the ideas found in the five ways, establishing the relations between the persons as the interior activity that is the condition for God's causal relation to creation in the five ways. These activities then can be appropriated to the divine persons, even though strictly speaking acts *ad extra* are acts of the divine essence.

This significance of the notions can be demonstrated by examining the parallels between the five ways (ST I.2.3) and the five notions of the Trinity (ST I.32.3). To recap, the five ways for demonstrating God's existence are prime mover, first efficient cause, a being necessary of itself, maximum being, and governance of the world. The five notions are innascibility, paternity, filiation, common spiration, and procession. In both order and content, the notions parallel the five ways, while surpassing them in mode of signification. Consideration of each of these in detail will demonstrate their parallels. There are of course, significant differences; the notions of the Trinity cannot be known by natural reason (ST I.32.1), and represent the *real* relations of the Trinity; the five ways represent only rational relations from God's standpoint. These differences will become clearer through specifying the parallels between the five ways and the five notions.

1. First, the notion of innascibility parallels the first way's proof of a "prime mover." For Aquinas, innascibility is a notion proper to the Father, even though one does not often name the Father by this notion. The Father is "innascibile" because there is no principle or cause outside of Him from which He comes (ST I.33.1). This notion of being "from no other" (*quod a nullo*) strongly parallels the language of the demonstration of the "prime mover," which is moved by no other. The prime mover must be in act of its own nature in order to reduce the potential of others to act: "Therefore it is necessary to arrive at a first mover, put in motion by no other (*quod a nullo movetur*); and this everyone understands to be God" (ST I.2.3). To name God as Father via innascibility thus allows that God, as from no other, *could* be the prime mover of the world.

2. While the Father may be known by innascibility, one also names the Father by *paternity*. This relation parallels and surpasses the second way's proof that reasons to a first efficient cause. An efficient cause occurs in a series of causes, and an intermediate efficient cause is the effect of a previous one; as discussed earlier, a "first efficient cause" is thus best conceived as the cause of a series of intermediate

causes; without a first efficient cause, one could not think of the intermediate causes (i.e., the causes in a series) as intermediate.[79]

In ST I.46.2 ad 7, Thomas compares the series of efficient causes to a series of begetters; given that the Father *begets* the Son, a parallel between divine paternity and a first efficient cause becomes conceivable. In the Trinity, however, the Father relates to the Son in paternity as Begetter to Begotten while sharing the same essence. In divine paternity, cause and effect are clearly identical, distinguished only by their relation. This identity in procession, indicates for Aquinas that generation is *proper* to God and only analogically appropriate to creatures by participation, even though our mode of signifying generation is proper to creatures (ST I.33.2). Both efficient causality and generation find their primary analogate in the Father's activity, and can thus be appropriated to the Father: "For this preposition from (*ex*) sometimes implies a certain relation of the material cause; which has no place in God; and sometimes it expresses the relation of the efficient cause, which can be applied to God by reason of His active power; hence it is appropriated to the Father in the same way as power" (ST I. 39.8).

Scriptural references undergird Aquinas' reasoning, since it is from scripture (and sacred doctrine) that we are able to name God as Father. Thus, the *sed contra* is Psalm 88:27: "He shall cry out to me: Thou art my Father." Likewise, the reply to objection 4, which orders generation properly to God and derivatively to creatures by distinguishing the *res significata* from the *modus significandi*, relies upon Ephesians 3:14: "I bend my knee to the Father of my Lord Jesus Christ, from whom all paternity in heaven and on earth is named." This reply indicates, again, that divine paternity is the primary analogate for creaturely paternity, even if we know creaturely paternity first; paternity is "first in God and then in creatures (*per prius sit in Deo quam in creaturis*)" (ST I.33.2 ad 4). In light of sacred doctrine, God's paternity is perceived as the primary analogate of the second way of efficient causality.

3. The third way argues for God's existence based on the concept of a being necessary of itself, and this parallels the notion of filiation—the Son's procession from the Father. The argument of the proof is problematic, most notably in the argument from the possibility of things not-being to the possibility of everything not-being, from which only nothing could come.[80] If everything that is were only possible, then there would be no reason that anything had been reduced from potential to actuality; therefore, there must be a being that exists necessarily, and does so of itself: "Therefore we cannot but postulate the existence of some being having of itself its own necessity, and not receiving it from another, but rather causing in others their necessity. This all people speak of as God" (ST I.2.3). As Preller notes, the existence of this being is only "necessary" based upon the existence of an actual, moving, world of possibility and contingency:

---

79 The argument given by Aquinas is close to Aristotle's *Metaphysics* 994a1-19.

80 See Preller, *Divine Science*, pp. 126-31 for his full discussion of the problems with this proof.

That such a being is not the God of Aquinas may be seen from an examination of the status of its "necessity." It is the necessity that must be granted to the immediate cause of an actually existent entity ... Furthermore, its causal efficacy, like that of the first mover and first efficient cause, is not defined as different in kind from that of the intermediate causes.[81]

Only as cause of the contingent world can we deem this being "necessary" according to natural reason.[82] Moreover, while the necessary being's causality is somewhat different from intermediate causes, it does still remain of the same kind, or genus, as worldly causality.

The third notion, however, names a being whose existence is not necessarily tied to the world. As was discussed previously, the name "*qui est*" of Exodus 3:14 names a being who exists of itself. As was noted in the section on the divine names, "*qui est*" is appropriated to the Son, "inasmuch as in God's word to Moses was prefigured the delivery of the human race accomplished by the Son" (ST I.39.8). This name is most appropriate to the filial mode in which God exists of God's own self.[83] As the emanation of the Son from the Father, divine filiation is the activity of a being necessary of itself. It therefore takes up the concept of "necessarily existent being" by naming the Son as a unique being necessarily subsistent of itself. The Son is necessarily existent, not in the sense of being a condition of the world, but rather as proceeding eternally from the Father. Thus, the Son is a being necessarily existent of himself, and one that gives other beings their necessity, since the Son's being as "Word" implies God's intention to create—"for God by knowing Himself knows every creature" (ST I.34.3). Aquinas argues in a similar fashion in ST I.39.8, showing that "All things were made by Him (Jn. 1:3)" should be appropriated to the Son as "the principle from a principle"—closely connecting the Son's role as first begotten (and necessarily existent) with filiation. As begotten but not made, the Son exists apart from the world, yet also causes the existence of the world. Filiation is a mode of necessary being from which the world can proceed, yet in which the freedom of God's creation is nonetheless apparent.

4. The fourth way demonstrates the idea of a "maximum being" that possesses the superlative form of perfections: most true, most noble, and therefore "most existent" (*maxime entia*, following *Metaphysics* II). The proof presents at least two logical

---

81 Ibid., p. 128. I take Preller's comment that the first cause does not differ "in kind" from intermediate causes as indicating that they share the same genus, even if there are important differences between them. I say this, because it seems important to recognize that a "first cause" is not subject to the same limitations as intermediate causality (what we see in the world), while admitting that the idea of a first cause does not adequately capture the uniqueness of divine causality, and in its inadequacy remains much like worldly causality.

82 Ibid., p. 128.

83 Aquinas thus distinguishes between the name as essential and as appropriated to the Son; it is appropriated to the Son on account of the likeness of the Incarnation of the Word to God's giving the Name to Moses in Ex. 3:14. However, because the name signifies the mode of existence of the whole Trinity, it can also be taken as an essential name.

difficulties. The first is the inference from a perfection in each category to the unity of these perfections; the participatory forms of each perfection do not necessarily presuppose that all of the perfections would be united. Moreover, as Preller notes, one can only argue from the existence of certain properties to the "maximum" in a generic sense: since the maximum is a member of the same genus, it would only be the "maximum" of the general class. One cannot argue from the class to a transcendent, non-generic "maximum" in any meaningful sense. Such a "generic" notion of being, truth, and nobility contradicts God's simplicity. As Preller writes, "God would be highest in the general class of existent and good things, just as fire is highest in the general class of hot things. But God, for Aquinas, is not in any general class."[84] The limitation of the proof again comes down to a problem of signification: even if the maximum were far more good and far more true than any other member of the class, one could not thereby infer a singular mode of existence; one ends up limited by the *modus significandi* of things to a "maximum being" whose existence is still not of itself or simple.

On the other hand, the fourth notion of common spiration does possess the singularity lacking in the fourth way. The Father and the Son, as one common principle, spirate the Holy Spirit.[85] Common spiration, as the love that proceeds from the perfect equality between the Father and the Son, is the unity of truth and existence in the divine simplicity. As simple, and as the act shared by the two persons of the same nature, the spiration of their love into the Holy Spirit is the first, maximal outpouring of love and being. Moreover, in that the Spirit is a singular person (*suppositum*, distinguished from the Father and Son by relations), the spirit is a unique, non-generic or classificatory unity of the transcendentals appropriate to God's simplicity and uniqueness. While incorporating the content of the fourth way, common spiration is a goodness that is not attached to the world, and therefore need not be considered as within a genus or species. The Spirit, commonly spirated by the love and unity between Father and Son, signifies *eminently* the divine unity of the transcendentals, in which the goodness, truth, and beauty of worldly things may participate without undercutting its simplicity and uniqueness.

5. The fifth way, the governance of the world, strongly parallels the procession of the Holy Spirit. The governance of the world demonstrates that nonrational things are directed towards their ends. The tendency of these things to fulfill their natures indicates that something is directing their activity, and this is called God (ST I.2.3). The procession of the Spirit is a procession of will, indicating that God is not simply a knowing subject but also one who can act. In that the procession of the Spirit can be properly named "love" (ST I.37.1) or "gift" (ST I.37.2), it is the internal act that proceeds through the Father's knowing Himself in the Son (*filioque*) as the internal condition and ground for God's being towards the world. As Thomas writes in I.45.6: "But to the Holy Ghost, Who has the same power from both, is attributed

---

84 Preller, *Divine Science*, p. 133.

85 They are common as they spirate once, but two spirators as Father and Son are two *supposita* (ST I.36.4).

that by His sway He governs, and quickens what is created by the Father through the Son."[86] Through the activity of the Spirit, *all* creatures—not just those which are not self-directing—are directed toward their final end. The Spirit thus takes up the proof of the governor of the world and deepens its meaning to include both nonrational creatures and rational creatures as well, all of whom are moved by the Spirit's grace both in and above their natures.

In looking at the five ways in light of the five notions, their order and combination take on new significance. As Preller has noted, the five ways often seem opposed to one another. It is difficult to see, for example, how God could be both the God of the third way and the God of the fourth or fifth way, especially when one considers the importance Thomas places on God's simplicity. Moreover, while the second and third ways are not contradictory, it is not clear how they fit together; how ought we to understand that God is a "first efficient cause" and "necessarily existent"?[87] There is, in short, no warrant for reconciling or harmonizing these two ideas.[88] The vagueness of each of the five ways—that "someone" is there—results in a vagueness of the five ways in relation to each other that cannot be reconciled via natural reason.

By assuming the ways into the notions and appropriating these activities to the persons, sacred doctrine transforms the apparent contradictions among the five ways *into the relations that distinguish the persons*. Once we name God as triune, it is conceivable how God could act toward the world in diverse ways, while remaining simple. If the relations, then, are the primary analogates of the five ways, then we can conceive how it is this God who is described by the five ways. As Thomas states in question 13, the names we attribute to God can all consider God from various standpoints, even though the object they all name is eminently simple:

> Therefore, as diverse perfections of creatures respond to one simple principle, the divine perfections are represented in the variety and multiplicity of creatures; as the variety and multiplicity of the concepts of our understanding respond to one who is wholly simple, according to our imperfect mode of understanding concepts. And therefore names attributed to God, although they signify one thing, nevertheless signify it under multiple and diverse reasons, and they are not synonyms. (ST I.13.4)

The five ways, then, are not synonymous; rather, they refer to God's simple nature from a variety of standpoints, emerging from worldly causality, each of which

---

86 See also *Summa Contra Gentiles*: "If, then, drive and motion belong to the Holy Spirit by reason of love, the government and propagation of things is fittingly attributed to the Holy Spirit." St. Thomas Aquinas, *Summa Contra Gentiles*, Book 4, trans. C.J. O'Neil (Notre Dame: University of Notre Dame Press, 1975), p. 120.

87 For a recent argument that the five ways can be united through philosophical reason, see John R. Wilcox, "The Five Ways and the Oneness of God," *The Thomist* 62 (1998), pp. 245-68.

88 My thanks to Peter Ochs and Jamie Ferreira for helping to clarify this issue.

reflects a different relational aspect of God's own triune life, insofar as each can be appropriated to a person (or to two persons, in the case of common spiration). Showing the primary analogate for the multiple types of causality in the world, the five notions incorporate natural reason's understanding of the world into discourse about God while reshaping it through eminent signification. The five notions represent a "diversification"[89] of faith, considering things we know by natural reason in the light of faith.

The parallels between the notions and the ways have several important consequences, first and foremost in terms of how we read the proofs. If anything, the parallels confirm the contingency of the proofs—their failure to refer necessarily due to the impossibility of properly signifying God's simplicity. They can be taken as descriptions, and they fix the reference when one speaks of God. As descriptions, they can only have a contingent relation to who God is; God could be God without any of the five ways being true.[90] This confirms the role of demonstrations by natural reason as "preambles" to the articles of faith. As "preambles," they can make intelligible to a nonbeliever what a believer affirms by faith, thereby either serving an apologetic function or acting as "minimal dogmatics."[91] Far more important than any logical flaws within the proofs, then, are the deficiencies in the proofs' modes of signification, as this precludes the possibility of singular reference. Only in naming God as triune through sacred doctrine does the singular referent of the proofs come into view.

The primary disparity, then, between naming God in faith and by natural reason is in their modes of signification. As Preller writes, "The *id a quo* of 'God' as that term is used in natural theology has such a radically different *modus significandi* from the *id a quo* of 'God' as that term is used in dogmatic theology, that the two could not be explicated in terms of the same conceptual framework or logical space."[92] The difference between the five ways and notions, in terms of their ability to signify God's individuality, confirms Preller's reading. This should not, however, mislead one into thinking that the language of natural reason plays no role in sacred doctrine. Insofar as the five notions of the Trinity parallel the five ways of question 2 in content while surpassing the proofs in their mode of signification, they redescribe that which we know by natural reason. In the five notions, we find the theological reason internal to sacred doctrine for Thomas' argument that God's existence can

---

[89] "*Cognitio Dei* is *diversified* in the presence of an Aristotelian demonstration." The *addition* of a proposition from natural reason expands the world as it is considered in the light of faith. Rogers, *Thomas Aquinas and Karl Barth*, p. 180.

[90] The five ways thus function as "*manuductions*" in Michel Corbin's sense, leading us into the interpretation of the world of faith but thereby being relativized and rendered contingent in their very application. See *Le Chemin*, p. 743.

[91] See Eugene F. Rogers, Jr., "How the Virtues of an Interpreter Presuppose and Perfect Hermeneutics: The Case of Thomas Aquinas," *Journal of Religion* 76 (1996), pp. 70-73.

[92] Preller, *Divine Science*, p. 144.

be demonstrated in five ways.[93] The rationale for the five ways, then, while related to causality, is properly understood in relation to *divine* causality.[94] No longer does one demonstrate that "that which we call God" must exist because the world is here. Rather, *because* one can name God as Father, Son, and Holy Spirit, and refer to intellect and will as internal to the Triune Life, one can state in belief how *this* God has created the world.

As the five notions appropriate the five ways to the divine persons, conceiving of the divine relations as the source of God's relation to the world, they permit us to have a *discursive* conception of who God is. We use the language of the five ways to explicate who God is, while transforming its signification in light of scripture. Such a discursive conception is important precisely because it allows us to have an object appropriate to our discursive intelligence, one to which we can assent and to which we can direct our actions as an end. The language of the five ways provides the material discourse for speech about God, while the mode of signification found in the notions ensures that we speak of God as one unknown. Emptying description of its content and denotation of its materiality, the language of faith brings the simplicity and self-subsistence of God into our view. Through such remotion, we are able to apprehend God in a mode appropriate to our intellect, even if this apprehension remains deficient with respect to the being we seek to understand.

In the notional naming of the Trinity, Thomas combines a determinate signification and a determinate nature, integrating both concrete and abstract names into our language about God. The notions, then, are an *eminent* mode of discourse in the Dionysian sense. Earlier in this chapter, it was suggested that the proofs were more properly read as apophatic statements than as predicative statements about God. In light of the notions, the significance of this reading can be more clearly explicated. The five ways, as a negative theology, abstract God's causality from worldly causality. The eminent sense, which draws upon both the concrete and abstract modes of signification, includes this negative moment within it, thereby affirming the primacy of God's causality, and the participation of worldly causality therein. Much as Dionysius' eminent sense is the ordering of affirmative and negative statements, Thomas' doctrine of the Trinity orders our knowledge of the world, both abstract and concrete, to properly speak about God.

---

93 The close parallels between the order of the notions and the proofs makes this a more tenable reading than that proposed by Lawrence Dewan, who reads the first four ways as related to the *prima pars* of the Summa, with the fifth way (governance of the world) constituting a starting point for the second and third parts of the *Summa*. See Lawrence Dewan, "The Number and Order of St. Thomas's Five Ways," *The Downside Review* 92 (January 1974), pp. 1-18.

94 In *Thomas Aquinas and Karl Barth*, Rogers develops parallels between three ways of speaking about God and the three persons of the Trinity. The parallels are the *via negativa* to the Father, the *via causalitatis* to the Son, and the *via eminentiae* to the Spirit. While Rogers is correct, these *viae* do not correspond exactly to the five ways; they are the modes of signification, rather than *what* we actually say.

This is a significant point, because it shows how even when he appears to be a natural theologian, Thomas may be more deeply Dionysian than readers have previously thought. In an essay on Dionysius, Michel Corbin argues that while Thomas recognizes the importance of the *triplex via* in Dionysius' work, he does not properly employ it in his own:

> To better discover the play of this movement of thought, we will note that Thomas Aquinas has never developed his reprise of the *triplex via* in the direction of a redoubled negation, of a comprehension in which transcendence (*hyper*) is as immediately heard and posed in the discourse of humanity as its negation ... The eminence becomes then simple eminence expressable by the superlatives, and negation occupies the last place.[95]

On Corbin's view, Thomas' reading of Dionysius abstracts from Christology, collapsing the *triplex via* into natural theology:

> He [Thomas, in reading Dionysius apart from Christology] can speak anew of the creation in making it an abstraction from the event of Jesus Christ, in omitting that which had been eschatological for the Fathers of the Church ... What will one obtain in this term if not the identification of the triple way with the "natural theology" as a preamble to faith?[96]

Thomas' incorporation of the five ways into his doctrine of the Trinity—one might say, their assumption by divine discourse—renders Corbin's reading problematic. I would argue, contra Corbin, that Thomas *does* practice the triple way of Dionysius, and that his "super-eminent" discourse is the doctrine of the Trinity. The doctrine of the Trinity, incorporating both our affirmative and negative statements about the world, as well as our concrete and abstract modes of signification, is not a "simple" eminence; it moves through the negation and *apophasis* of the five ways, into the subsistent signification of the persons, and on to a signification surpassing metaphysical theology. Thomas does not reduce Dionysius to a discourse on an Aristotelian prime mover; he makes the Aristotelian prime mover, and its accompanying scientific knowledge of the world, a moment in our eminent discourse about God.[97] Corbin's reading—surprising in light of his other defenses of Thomas' method—shows how deeply engrained the view of Thomas as a natural theologian is, and how much we still have to learn about how to read Thomas.

---

95 Corbin, "Négation et Transcendance," pp. 58-9.
96 Ibid., p. 66. While it will not be discussed here, the parallels between Thomas' doctrine of the Trinity and his Christology, in terms of their use and ordering of signification, would help to show that Thomas does employ the triplex via in relation to Christology.
97 See O'Rourke for discussion of how Thomas' reflections on being reshape the Aristotelian prime mover, in terms of dynamism and generosity.

VI. Conclusion: Trinity and Charity

In signifying God both personally and substantially, the Trinity names God as determinately and properly as the Tetragrammaton. The Trinity, then, becomes a way of speaking eminently, a transformation of natural reason through the Dionysian ordering of predication. Deficient with respect to our understanding and signification, even while appropriate to the thing signified, the Trinity eminently permits denomination without description—even turning description into denomination, as with the transformation of the five ways. It thereby leads our language beyond our understanding, but this also allows us to direct our actions to an end in a new way—as Thomas writes in ST I.1.1, as is necessary for salvation.

The use of nonintellectual language to describe this mode of signification—"allows us to direct our activity towards an end," "signify God as one unknown," "empties our intellectual capacities of any content"—is not accidental. This mode of signification represents the "material moves" of faith.[98] To signify in this way is a movement of the will, which impels (or inspires) the intellect to assent to this object (ST II-II.2.1). To connect naming God with the work of the will makes the most sense when we remember that sacred doctrine deals not only with God's effects in the world, but primarily with God's effects of grace. In grace, God's name is given to humanity through scripture, and through this written effect our will moves the intellect to assent. Like liturgy and the sacraments, scripture is a visible, material effect through which God moves the will. It is a movement of the will because the will is where God moves humans by grace to fulfill and act above our natural capacities.[99] Through sacred doctrine's effects of grace, the intellect turns to an object that it could not know in and of its own capacities (or, through creative grace).

This epistemic loss is all to our gain as creatures. It allows us to *act*, as creatures, towards our proper end of participation in divine life through the theological virtues—faith, hope and charity. The naming of God in sacred doctrine, then, opens the possibility of charity, and directing our love toward God in a new way. While this connection between the theoretical and the practical may often be overlooked, in no small part because of the compartmentalization of ethics and theology, they are clearly very closely linked for Thomas. Moral activity, as "the way of the rational creature into God" (*prae*. I-II) is a part of Thomas' ordering of the *cosmos* to God. Through faith, participation in God's knowing creatures more intimately than we know ourselves leads to participation in charity and distinguishes it from Aristotelian friendship. If this is the case, then faith's perfection of natural reason, precisely through the transformative inversion of signification, transforms practical reason as well. The transformation of friendship into charity by faith then becomes

---

98 See Preller, *Divine Science*, pp. 266-71.

99 See Rogers, *Thomas Aquinas and Karl Barth*, p. 193: "Thomas thinks of the will as another locus of divine activity. Better: 'the will' is the name for the place where God primarily addresses, engages, and involves human beings ... *For that very reason* God's activity in that place, God's taking that field, salvation's occurrence and working out just there can only be the work of grace alone."

the logical outgrowth of sacred doctrine's consideration of all things as *revelabilia*. Thus, as sacred doctrine transforms natural reason's ability to name God, the pragmatic dimension of sacred doctrine can now be examined, as charity reshapes justice, friendship, and virtue.

Chapter 4

Charity, Friendship and Justice in the *Summa Theologiae*

I. Introduction

This chapter explores St. Thomas Aquinas' conception of friendship as the pragmatic dimension of naming God. As discussed in the last chapter, sacred doctrine redirects our language from the world to God. This eminent mode of signification opens a new form of singular reference unavailable to natural reason. Since sacred doctrine is, in Thomas' words, both theoretical and practical, this reshapes the pragmatics of naming God—the way of life opened through this mode of relation. Thomas articulates this in his discussion of charity.

A first step into linking the semantic and pragmatic dimensions of naming God is Thomas' account of the theological virtues. Faith is the first theological virtue in the order of generation, and thus, a material cause of charity. Charity—*friendship* with God—is the goal that faith seeks, and thus the final cause with regard to theological virtue (ST I-II.62.4). Shaped by the theological virtues, religious language intends a different reference, and a different practice. Faith finds its completion in charity: as faith directs our language from creatures to God, so too charity directs our love from creatures to God.

If, as the previous chapter demonstrated, sacred doctrine reorients language through the Dionysian *triplex via*, then the question becomes whether or not charity reorients the moral life in a similar fashion. This sounds strange, since Thomas' ethics are frequently read as the development of an Aristotelian moral philosophy. However, it is worth noting that in his discussion of love, Thomas refers to Dionysius as frequently as Aristotle, in saying that love produces union (ST I-II.28.1) and ecstasy (ST I-II.28.3). These are not merely passing references; rather, they serve to explicate human love in its participation in divine love, as *God* suffers ecstasy. As will be discussed further below, charity both affirms the particulars of Aristotelian ethics and denies their limits, gesturing toward a transcendent love. It is by moving through the various dimensions of Aristotelian ethics that Thomas articulates a Dionysian ethic in imitation of divine love, as the "motion of the rational creature to beatitude" (ST I.2, *proemium*)—which reciprocates God's action towards us, thereby constituting friendship.

As was discussed in the previous chapter, a Dionysian approach involves attending to both the abstract, universal aspects of life and the concrete, particular features of creation, affirming them all in their respective places in creation as multiple, diverse reflections of the one divinity. Reading Thomas' ethics from a Dionysian perspective thus serves to highlight several important features. First, it helps to show how the apparently hierarchical order of charity can likewise be read as an affirmation of materiality, embodiment, and love of one's neighbors. Charity, as love of God, is only complete when it unfolds into love for creation, as represented by the soul, neighbor, and body. Second, the ecstatic dimension of divine love highlights how friendship with God unfolds into a self-diffusive concern for justice and the activity of virtue. As part of this ecstasy, Thomas reshapes the obligations and responsibilities of the moral life, extending them beyond the Aristotelian *polis* in the love of enemies. Third, much as Dionysian mystical theology is only complete in attention to particulars, involving both divine names and symbolic theology, it is in the practical life that Thomas finds the completion of our speculative desire for God. Fourth, and finally, the Dionysian framework of Thomas' ethics can help a reader to attend to the interplay between scripture and philosophy therein.

Before diving into Thomas' work, it may help to summarize the contemporary importance of these features of Thomas' moral philosophy. First, charity's connection of friendship with justice raises important questions for contemporary understandings of friendship with God. Often, when authors invoke the rhetoric of friendship with God in contemporary settings, the relationship is described in personal terms that privatize or spiritualize the relationship, divorcing it from other dimensions of life. It is not surprising, in this light, that friendship often is ignored in discussions of ethics. However, Thomas' understanding of the connection between charity and justice—and his scriptural warrant for this link—may help to historicize our conceptions of friendship, and to interrogate modern assumptions regarding friendship's place in moral philosophy and theology. For if Thomas is right, then friendship with God is not a private relationship, but rather a love that opens onto a life of virtue, justice, and concern for the world; only *through* this motion into the world does beatitude become possible. Ecstatic concern for others is, as we shall see, an imitation of the Incarnation and divine descent.

Second, for Thomas, the practical intellect and virtues are especially fitting vehicles for our motion toward beatitude. This fittingness can be explicated by briefly contrasting God's knowledge and ours. God knows individuals and events singularly, by knowing the eternal law through the Son. We, on the other hand, only know universals in the intellect; we do not know singulars. Through the passions and habits of the virtues, our practical wisdom pays attention to the particular and contingent features of events and situations. Practical wisdom is more capable of attending to singulars—and thus "knowing" things as God knows them—than our speculative intellect. This shapes the order of charity, as the exercise of practical wisdom is directed toward future speculative participation in charity; our journey as "wayfarers" toward the beatific vision meanders through our practice of this friendship.

Third, through practical wisdom, we come to a deeper understanding of the science of God; from love comes a new form of knowledge. The light of faith and sacred doctrine reshape practical wisdom through the theological virtue of charity, the form of all the virtues (ST II-II.23.8). As the form, charity is not simply a "supernatural" habit that tops off the natural virtues like a maraschino cherry; more like a transfusion, it filters through them and reshapes their actions from within. The order of charity includes our distinctively human features and the relationships that individuate us within society. Our creaturely rationality, political nature, and embodiment particularize the general character of God's activity, reshaping it for *human* participation in the divine life. The order of charity does not only mean that the body, neighbor, and soul are understood in light of God; it also means that we only really understand *scientia Dei* through these aspects of life. Our understanding of the higher levels of the hierarchy is reshaped in light of the lower, and only then does our participation in *scientia Dei* come to fruition. Only at the lowest level of the hierarchy do we know God most fully, as it is by the works of the body that we come to a perfect enjoyment and knowledge of God (ST II-II.25.5).

This Dionysian element of charity help to show how Thomas' ethics fit into the broader theological framework of the *Summa*. Thomas' soteriology contextualizes his concern for the practical life. The ethics are central to the *Summa*, precisely because God's salvation of humanity through the Incarnation intends to bring us to friendship, through participation in the good life of God. Following the order of charity demonstrates how each aspect of ethical reflection refers in its own way to God's governance of the world and love for humanity. This can help to illustrate how Thomas' understanding of God's providence and predestination, grace and free will, and habits and passions all shape his view of friendship with God, and how his expansive theological doctrines are at work in the slightest internal movements of the soul.

In explicating the order of charity, this chapter will focus primarily on the treatise on charity from the *secunda secundae* of the *Summa Theologiae*. To help clarify how charity is both friendship and true human happiness, and to better grasp the particularities of Thomas' thought, reference will also be made to his scriptural commentaries, his commentaries on Aristotle, and the disputed questions on charity. Explicating this order and clarifying the human mode of participation in friendship with God will articulate the pragmatic dimension of Thomas' account of naming God.

II. Friendship with God: The Primacy of God's Love

As mentioned in the last chapter, Anna Williams has noted that Thomas takes the language of friendship as describing sanctification in ways that go beyond his theological predecessors. However, given his extensive philosophical training and deep Aristotelianism, it is still surprising that Thomas describes charity as friendship. Friendship, in Aristotle, involves strict equality, reciprocity, and acts that benefit one another, and all three features are in conflict with the transcendence of a unique, self-sufficient God who creates and moves all things. The reciprocity or mutual giving constitutive of friendship would seem to be impossible. As Paul Wadell writes, the claim that humans can be friends with God seems nothing short of blasphemous,[1] and Aristotle thought such friendship impossible.[2]

Nonetheless, Thomas begins the *Summa*'s treatise on charity by affirming that charity *is* a friendship between God and humans. He bases this affirmation on Jesus' statement to the disciples: "I will not now call you servants ... but My friends" (John 15:15).[3] Because of this friendship of Jesus for the disciples, Thomas affirms that friendship between God and humans *is* possible, even if this appears to contradict Aristotelian principles. As he explains, there is a "communication" between God and humanity that establishes a basis for mutual well-wishing and reciprocity. Beginning within these parameters, friendship with God serves as a node in which central theological principles harmonize and merge, as Thomas draws upon God's election and providence, grace, free will, and merit, and Christology to unpack this relationship.

Thomas' commentary on the passage from John, to which we shall return in more detail, is particularly instructive in showing how these issues fit together. While the scriptural passage indicates an equality of the disciples with Jesus, this equality is not an independently established fact. Rather, the equality between Jesus and the disciples is made possible by God's activity: "I *have called* you friends, because I have disclosed to you everything that I heard from my Father." Christ's activity initiates and enables the friendship. This activity is "disclosed" in a twofold sense; it is spoken to and exemplified for the disciples by Jesus. Thomas thus uses Aristotle to demonstrate the genus and species of the love of charity, but Aristotelian science does not thereby determine its individual form.[4] Charity, as friendship, begins unilaterally with God's elective call.

In this text, God's calling of the disciples makes equality possible. This may sound strange, because placing the emphasis on God's activity of calling us would seem to emphasize the inequality between God and creatures. However, through divine communication, humans can participate in the divine life; God chooses and calls (*dilectum*) humans to friendship, establishing the framework within which friendship with God takes shape. God's primary action makes possible a derivative equality between God and humans.

God's creation of friendship connects Thomas' analysis of charity with his discussions of providence, predestination, grace and free will. One of the primary loci in which Thomas treats the issue of human equality with God is condign and congruent merit, in his explication of providence and predestination. Condign merit indicates the extent to which there can be equality between humans and God, whereas congruent merit is only proportional, and thus would not be a sufficient basis for

---

1 Paul Wadell, *Friendship and the Moral Life* (Notre Dame, IN: University of Notre Dame Press, 1989), pp. 120-1.

2 NE, viii.7, p. 204.

3 ST II-II.23.1 *sed contra:* "*Sed contra est quod Io. 15,15 dicitur: Iam non dicam vos servos, sed amicos meos. Sed hoc non dicebatur eis nisi ratione caritatis. Ergo caritas est amicitia.*" See Anthony W. Keaty, "Thomas' Authority for Identifying Charity as Friendship: Aristotle or John 15?" *The Thomist* (1998) 62: 581-601.

4 Keaty, "Thomas' Authority for Identifying Charity as Friendship,", p. 585.

friendship. Within the providential context of human merit before God, grace and free will bring condign merit to fruition. A brief discussion of these topics will show how charity is the culmination of these systematic topics in the *Summa*.

Providence is acting towards the future in light of the past and present: God's providence is the ordering of things to their end, and especially toward the end of divine goodness (ST I.22.1). As Daniel Westberg writes, glossing Thomas' distinction of God's providence from human prudence, "The commanding of things to be ordered towards an end, concerning which he has right reason, is fitting for God."[5] As Westberg goes on to explain, God's providence involves both intellect and will. God's providence is foreknowledge of the "type" of God's effects; the type pre-exists in God's mind, and then is actualized in creation.[6]

For Thomas, providence is especially important because of its connection with divine justice.[7] God is provident in providing for things to be ordered to their ends— God provides created things with the ability to fulfill their diverse natures. In that flowers flower, wolves can act as wolves, and rocks rock, the diversity of God's creation is fulfilled; these can fulfill their natures, because God has justly provided them with what is required for the actualization of their potentials.[8] Providence is, in short, God's distributive justice—God's acting in a virtuous or prudential manner, for the good of all creation.[9]

While God's providence is necessary with regard to universal causality (what God wills will come about), the particular causality with respect to individual creatures may be either necessary or contingent. The contingencies of particular causality allow for human freedom *within* the universal causality of God's providence. God's particular causality, as a specific combination of necessity and contingency, calls for humans to act rationally and freely *through* the exercise of the virtues. God is provident to humans, by allowing humans to exercise *prudence* and thereby fulfill

---

5 Daniel Westberg, *Right Practical Reason: Aristotle, Action, and Prudence in Aquinas* (Oxford: Clarendon Press, 1994), p. 231.

6 More could be said about the meaning of Christ as "exemplar," through whom God knows creation, and the relation of Christ's exemplarity to divine types. For the moment, I leave this as a question. See Lee Yearley, "St. Thomas Aquinas on Providence and Predestination," *Anglican Theological Review* 49 (1967), pp. 409-23; Denis J. Bradley, *Aquinas on the Twofold Human Good: Reason and Human Happiness in Aquinas' Moral Science* (Washington, DC: The Catholic University of America Press, 1997), pp. 128-34; Eleonore Stump, "Providence and the Problem of Evil," in *Christian Philosophy*, ed. T.P. Flint (Notre Dame, IN: University of Notre Dame Press, 1990), pp. 53-61.

7 Yearley, "St. Thomas Aquinas on Providence and Predestination", pp. 414-15.

8 Where there are defects, Thomas argues, these exist so that the greater diversity and flourishing of the world may be made evident. This is his rationale for natural evil, such as animals eating animals and the general cycle of generation and corruption; see I. 22.2.

9 One of Thomas' most extensive texts on providence is *The Literal Exposition of Job: A Commentary on Providence* (Atlanta: Scholars' Press, 1988).

our rational natures. Our voluntary virtue is thus a sign of God's distributive justice, enabling us to act according to our natures.[10]

Distributive justice, however, gets us nowhere in terms of friendship with God. While God provides for us according to human nature, we still remain quite distant from God. Thomas' commentary on Aristotle's *Ethics* demonstrates his awareness of this distinction:

> The reason for this difference (i.e., between friendship and justice) is that friendship is a kind of union that cannot exist between widely separated persons; but they must approach equality. Hence it pertains to friendship to use an equality already uniformly established, but it pertains to justice to reduce unequal things to an equality. When equality exists the work of justice is done. For that reason equality is the goal of justice and the starting point of friendship.[11]

While justice establishes equality in human relations, a "wide separation" remains between God and creatures. Providence does not establish the conditions for charity; it therefore falls to predestination to reduce this inequality.

Thomas' reflections on predestination are central to the possibility of friendship with God. Thomas' discussion of the relationship between providence and predestination is instructive:

> I answer that it is fitting that God should predestine humans. For all things are subject to his providence, as was shown above [ST I.22.2]. Now it belongs to providence to direct things towards their end, as was also said [ST I.22.1, 2]. The end towards which created things are directed by God is twofold; one which exceeds all proportion and faculty of created nature; and this end is life eternal, that consists in seeing God which is above the nature of every creature, as shown above. The other end, however, is proportionate to created nature, to which end created being can attain according to the power of its nature. Now if a thing cannot attain to something by the power of its nature, it must be directed thereto by another; thus, an arrow directed by the archer towards a mark. Hence, properly speaking, a rational creature, capable of eternal life, is led towards it, directed, as it were, by God. The reason of that direction pre-exists in God; as in Him is the type of the order of all things towards an end, which we proved above to be providence. Now the type in the mind of the doer of something to be done, is a kind of pre-existence in him of the thing to be done. Hence the type of the aforesaid direction of a rational creature towards the end of life eternal is called predestination. For to destine, is to direct or send. Thus it is clear that predestination, as regards its objects, is part of providence. (ST I.23.1)

Both providence and predestination are "types" existing in the divine mind, prior to the creation of any creatures; predestination is the act of governance that proceeds through divine providence to bring humanity to the vision of eternal life. While it

---

10 For an in-depth study of contingency, providence, and the virtues, see John R. Bowlin, *Contingency and Fortune in Aquinas' Ethics* (Cambridge: Cambridge University Press, 1999).

11 St. Thomas Aquinas, *Commentary on Aristotle's Nicomachean Ethics*, trans. C. Litzinger (Notre Dame, IN: Dumb Ox Books, 1993), p. 501.

proceeds through providence, predestination is nonetheless distinct from providence, in ordering us to an end beyond our natural capacity.[12] In flowing from providence, it parallels the cultivation of friendship on the basis of justice; God's providence and justice are preconditions for the more radically equal love of friendship to which God predestines humanity.

While Thomas' definition of predestination describes God's plan for charity, it does not show how humans and God can be equals. He explicates this in terms of the roles of grace and free will in charity. Thomas initially addresses this issue in terms of God's foreknowledge of merit in I.23.5. The implications are profound. If God's foreknowledge of our merit is the cause of our predestination, then our activity would seem to be the cause of predestination; we would acquire grace by works (Pelagianism). Rejecting the solutions of Origen and the Pelagians *tout court*, Thomas considers a third alternative at more length:

> And so others said that merits following the effect of predestination are the reason of predestination; giving us to understand that God gives grace to a person, and preordains that He will give it, because He knows beforehand that he will make good use of that grace, as if a king were to give a horse to a soldier because he knows he will make good use of it.

This view is appealing, because it recognizes that predestination is principally (first) God's activity, yet preserves the independence and causality of human freedom. Thomas, however, sees the cost of this view is high: "But these (i.e., those who hold this view) seem to have drawn a distinction between that which flows from grace, and that which flows from free will, *as if the same thing cannot come from both.*" Thomas understands why someone would want to keep God's activity and our activity distinct. However, the cost of this view is that our exercise of free will limits God's providence and grace to external causality.

Instead, Thomas affirms that grace and free will are the dual causes of the same event, such that grace works *through* free will rather than being limited by it.[13] He compares the relation of grace and free will to primary and secondary causes, in which the primary cause is active through the secondary cause:[14]

> Now there is no distinction between what flows from free will, and what is of predestination; as there is not distinction between what flows from a secondary cause and from a first

---

12 In "The Theological Transformation of Friendship" L. Gregory Jones links the possibility of friendship with God with Thomas' Christology (p. 386). While this is correct, it is christological as the enactment of God's providence and predestination towards us. In this light, it may be more possible to say that friendship with God has a Trinitarian ring to it for Thomas, where Jones sees that it does not (pp. 398-9).

13 This conception of God's activity as radically transcendent precisely in working intimately through creation, and its status as a rule for Christian doctrine and practice, is well formulated by Kathryn Tanner, *God and Creation in Christian Theology: Tyranny or Empowerment?* (London: Blackwell, 1989).

14 Yearley, "Providence and Predestination in St. Thomas Aquinas," pp. 417-18.

cause. For the providence of God produces effects through the operation of secondary causes, as was shown above [ST I.22.3]. Wherefore that which flows from free will is also of predestination. (ST I.22.4)

Since grace informs the will, the will can be the secondary agent for God's predestination.

From the identity of action between grace and free will, Thomas is able to formulate a "reason of predestination" through a distinction between particular and universal effects of predestination. With regard to particular effects of predestination, our actions or merits can be the final or material causes of the effect of predestination, as our worthiness before God can be the end toward which we act. Since final causes serve as first principles in practical matters, merit can be called the "reason" of a particular effect of predestination. Or, if we have acted meritoriously, our action may habitually prepare us for further grace. As the material that grace can further inform, our merit is thus a "reason" for a particular effect of predestination in the sense of a material cause (though, of course, such merit is *already* informed by grace). As Thomas writes, "Thus we might say that God pre-ordained to give glory on account of merit, and that He pre-ordained to give grace to merit glory."

However, with regard to universal or general predestination, it is clear that merit is incapable of being a reason for predestination:

> In another way, the effect of predestination may be considered in general. Thus it is impossible that the whole of the effect of predestination in general should have any cause as coming from us; because whatsoever is in man disposing him towards salvation, is all included under the effect of predestination; even the preparation for grace. For neither does this happen otherwise than by divine help, according to the prophet Jeremias (Lam. 5:21): "convert us, O Lord, to Thee, and we shall be converted." Yet predestination has in this way, in regard to its effect, *the goodness of God for its reason*; towards which the whole effect of predestination is directed as to an end; and from which it proceeds, as from its first moving principle. (ST I.23.5, my emphasis)

Since all of our actions are acts of secondary causality, in principle our actions cannot account for the whole series of effects. *Divine* goodness is the reason for the whole act of predestination. The identification of free will and grace permits us to say that our actions are the "reasons" for particular effects of predestination, since grace works causally through free will. However, in that free will is the site for the operation of grace, the *whole* of the operation should be attributed to God.

This intimate coworking of grace and free will in predestination suggests how God's unilateral and generous love can nonetheless lead into a reciprocal union with humanity. The rule concerning divine and human agency that Thomas establishes here comes to fruition in his explanation of charity as a supernatural habit, which enables properly *human* acts (ST II-II.23.2, discussed below). Because God's goodness—not human goodness—is the primary reason for predestination, God makes us who we are supposed to be, so that we can participate in the divine life. As Joseph Wawrykow writes: "There is no dignity or merit in the person that would 'cause' God to choose that person for eternal life. Indeed, that there comes to be a special dignity or worth in the one predestined by God is itself due to God's decision to manifest the divine goodness through the election of this person to salvation."[15]

As Wawrykow has argued, Thomas' views on predestination enables his reformulation of condign and congruent merit in the *Summa*. Condign merit indicates the possibility of having the same *character* as God, and thus being worthy of friendship.[16] Strictly speaking, the action of the Holy Spirit in grace is condignly meritorious, as the Spirit is divine. Insofar as the Holy Spirit moves the will, the will also participates in God's nature, and thus can merit condignly. As our merit may be the reason for effects of predestination in a secondary and particular way, so too are we able to merit eternal life condignly through free will as a "subsequent cause," a cause ordained by God out of God's mercy (ST I-II.113.3 ad 2).[17] In the mature teaching of the *Summa*, Thomas distinguishes the work of the Spirit and of the will only for speculative purposes, such that the condign merit of the Spirit can be said to be our own. "What belongs naturally to the Spirit comes into the purview of those possessed and directed by the Spirit. Similarly, grace as habitual endows the individual with new being. It transforms the person and makes him, in the words of II Peter, a sharer in the divine nature."[18] By working through the will, grace enables the voluntary human love of God's goodness, on the basis of God's love for God's goodness.

Question 114 of the *prima secundae* clarifies the sense in which the conjunction of our action and God's grace establishes the equality necessary for charity. The causality of free will merits *congruently*: "for it would seem congruous that, if one does what one can, God should reward her according to the excellence of her power" (ST I-II.114.3). However, in that the grace of the Holy Spirit is *also* operative in the same activity, the action is condignly equal: "And the worth of the work depends on the dignity of grace, whereby a person, being made a partaker of the Divine Nature, is adopted as a son of God, to whom the inheritance is due by right of adoption, according to Romans 8:17: 'If sons, heirs also'" (ST I-II.114.3). In that the Holy Spirit acts through the will in a way that is absolutely equal to God, our action can be said to be equal to God's activity. Charity as friendship with God therefore

---

15 Joseph Wawrykow, *God's Grace and Human Action: "Merit" in the Theology of Thomas Aquinas* (Notre Dame, IN: University of Notre Dame Press, 1995), p. 157.

16 Given our state of sin, there is a dual reason for our need for grace—first, to be cleansed of sin, and then to be elevated. See ibid., p. 192.

17 Wawrykow (ibid., p. 80) makes his argument in the course of reading the development of the concept of merit in Thomas' work "In the *Summa*, there is the most intimate connection between the *ordinatio* involved in merit and grace: As the equivalent of predestination, the ordination is the cause of grace, and because God ordains someone to achieve eternal life (through this person's merits), God's grace consequently moves the individual to the acts which bring him to God." As Wawrykow notes (p. 73), in Thomas' early writings, condign merit is linked with distributive justice, and thus with *proportionate* equality. In the *Scriptum*, Thomas denies that one can merit condignly first grace.

18 Ibid., p. 195.

becomes possible, because God is being friends with God through our activity.[19] According to our nature, the actions are just; according to divine activity, they raise us to friendship with God. Because God's Trinitarian love works through us, Thomas conceives of grace as the beginning of our growth into friendship with God.[20]

By articulating how human virtue participates in divine love and actualizes God's predestination, Thomas establishes a theological framework for his discussion of charity as friendship with God. Thomas' thought, here, is as much scriptural as systematic. Predestination and charity are explicitly linked in Thomas' commentary on the scriptural warrant for ST II-II.23.1: "I do not call you servants ... but friends" (John 15:15). As we saw above, this call is an election to friendship, God's voluntary elevation of humanity.[21] In its interweaving of central theological topics, Thomas' commentary on these verses is breathtakingly rich. As James Weisheipl writes, "Among all of Thomas' writings on Scripture none surpass the *lectura* on John's Gospel. It is sublime in its theological profundity, particularly in its discussion of the last discourse of Jesus (Jn. 14-17)."[22] Thomas' scriptural commentary illustrates how predestination, merit, and the co-operation of grace and free will inform how charity synthesizes the Summa's disparate systematic discussions of predestination, grace, and virtue.

There are three central points Thomas makes in the commentary on John 15. First, the beginning of friendship is God's gracious election or love of us. Second, a mark of friendship is the revealing of secrets, as this unites the souls of the lovers. Third, John 15 makes an important distinction between servants and friends, particularly regarding the role of rational and voluntary operations in the fulfillment of precepts and commands. By clarifying these three points, we will better understand the *communicatio* (sharing) that God undertakes with humanity as the basis for friendship, and how the divine initiative for friendship creates the space and capacity for human response. The passage from John 15 is as follows:

---

19 Paul Wadell connects charity with grace, but does not put it in the context of God's predestination. See Wadell, *Friendship and the Moral Life*, pp. 120-41. The importance of this connection, apart from the coherence of the *Summa* itself, lies partly in its prominence in Thomas' scriptural interpretation of friendship, as discussed below.

20 As Wawrykow notes, ST I-II 114.6 discusses a proportionate friendship between humans and God on the basis of our agency. However, given Thomas' comments on participation in the divine life, it would seem that a friendship that is equal with God is more properly the focus of Thomas' discussions of predestination and charity. Proportional friendship, like distributive justice, is a precondition for this more radical friendship. See Wawrykow, *God's Grace and Human Action*, pp. 216-19.

21 As Thomas describes it in the *Summa*, dilection or choice is a feature of the rational love of friendship, insofar as it allows one to love another for his or her sake. See ST I-II.26.3.

22 James A. Weisheipl, F.P., *Friar Thomas D'Aquino: His Life, Thought, and Work* (New York: Doubleday, 1974), p. 246.

This is how my Father is glorified: you are to bear fruit in plenty and so be my disciples. As the Father has loved me, so I have loved you. Dwell in my love. If you heed my commands, you will dwell in my love, as I have heeded my Father's commands and dwell in his love. I have spoken thus to you, so that my joy may be in you, and your joy complete. This is my commandment: love one another, as I have loved you. There is no greater love than this, that someone should lay down his life for his friends. You are my friends, if you do what I command you. No longer do I call you servants, for a servant does not know what his master is about. I have called you friends, because I have disclosed to you everything that I heard from the Father. You did not choose me: I chose you.[23]

In the *Lectura Super Johannem*, Thomas reads John 15 as deeply shaped by God's election and predestination of the disciples. Election, the primacy of God's love in choosing us, forms the context and the means by which friendship with God becomes possible. In Jesus' speech to the disciples, the Father's love for the Son is clearly primary. Thomas makes it clear that the love of Father and Son involves an equality of nature, whereas the love for the disciples is an adoptive love that proceeds by likeness. The activity of the Trinity, in its strict equality, raises the unequal activity of the disciples to dwell in the Father's love.[24] Human participation is only possible on the basis of this communication of the triune love to us by the Son. This signifies that all of our works—and our dwelling in God's love—are possible by grace.[25] Likewise, in that "You did not choose me: I chose you," God's election of us serves as the clear beginning of our ability to choose rightly and be deemed friends of God.[26] Since we tend to think of ourselves as the cause of friendship,[27] Thomas interprets Jesus as saying this to order the love of the disciples and make it plainly clear that God's love causes this friendship.[28] As in ST I.23.5, God's goodness is the cause of predestination, and here again it makes space for secondary activity on the part of the disciples.

Predestination takes the shape of friendship because Jesus discloses to the disciples "everything that I have heard from the Father." Thomas indicates that disclosure is a true sign of friendship, for a friend "reveals to his friend the secrets of his heart."[29] This emphasis on secrecy marks a turning in Thomas' theory of friendship; secrecy is particularly important to the Stoics, and through them to monastic conceptions of friendship, as it is linked with cultivating interior virtue, in ways that are not as

---

23 John 15: 9-16 (NRSV).
24 St. Thomas Aquinas, *Super Evangelium S. Ioannis Lectura* (Turin: Marietti, 1952), p. 377. Chapter 15, lecture 2: "sed notandum, quod ly sicut quandoque denotat aequalitatem naturae, quandoque autem similitudinem actionis." Further citations will be by chapter and lecture number in parentheses. Thomas takes the opportunity to reject the Arian view that the love for the Son is the same as the love for the disciples, and thus that the Son is less than the Father.
25 Aquinas, *Lectura Super Iohannem*, 15 (2).
26 Ibid., 15 (3).
27 Keaty, "Thomas' Authority for Identifying Charity as Friendship," p. 600.
28 Aquinas, *Lectura Super Iohannem*, 15 (3).
29 Ibid.

central to Aristotle.[30] God has shared with us what God wishes, as sacred doctrine is the revelation to us of the end toward which the world was created. Bearing these secrets makes us, as Thomas cites St. Gregory, "guardians of the soul," and we hold them close to our hearts by obeying and keeping God's commands.[31] While Thomas here shows interest in the internal character of friendship, this interior dimension will also be complemented by an exterior focus on the relationships between the disciples, as guided by John 15.

Thomas notes a difficulty here: the communication between the Father and the Son would seem to be unavailable to us as humans, since unlike the Son we cannot know God's essence: yet, "if all is made known to them, it follows that the disciples know (*sciebant*) the same as the Son."[32] Thomas' response demonstrates the distinctive way we participate in this friendship; while we clearly cannot know things in the same way as God does, we can know the same things in a different way. God's commands are disclosed to us in a manner fitting our intellect, and not in the same way as the Father or Son.

Secrets are disclosed to us as a "foretaste" (*praelibatio*) of the participation in the divine life that is to come.[33] This "foretaste" is appropriate to our intellectual and perceptual faculties. Thomas distinguishes two ways in which one can teach or know a science. One knows a science perfectly when one knows both the principles of the science and its singular conclusions. This is *scientia Dei*, as had by God, the Son, and the blessed. A second way to know or teach a science is to communicate the first principles without explicitly drawing out the conclusions.[34] While imperfect, this can still be considered knowledge, in that the conclusions are "virtually" contained in the principles, and may become known from them. The "imperfect" knowledge is appropriate to our rational capacity, as we are able to know things under universal forms rather than as singulars.[35] It is also appropriate to our status as "wayfarers" on a journey to beatitude.[36]

In living out fidelity to these secrets, by attending to particulars through practical wisdom and the infusion of grace in theological virtue, our participation in *scientia Dei* and our friendship with God deepen. Through the acts of charity, we come to a *practical* knowledge of singular conclusions from the principles of faith. We keep the precepts of God close to our hearts by loving each other; as Thomas says, we

---

30 For example, see Seneca, "On the Tranquility of the Soul," trans. M. Hadas, in *The Stoic Philosophy of Seneca* (New York: W.W. Norton, 1958) and Aelred of Rievaulx, *Spiritual Friendship*, trans. M. Laker (Kalamazoo: Cistercian Publications, 1977).

31 Aquinas, *Lectura Super Iohannem*, 15 (3).

32 Ibid.

33 Ibid.

34 Ibid.

35 See, for example, ST I.85.2 ad 2.

36 Aquinas attributes *both* sorts of knowledge to Jesus, in that in the hypostatic union he participates in the divine life *both* as the Son and also according to human nature—a "beholder" and a wayfarer. St. Thomas Aquinas, *De Caritate*, trans. L. Kendzierski (Milwaukee; Marquette University Press, 1960), p. 83.

remember God's love in loving the neighbor.[37] The disclosure of secrets, then, is not only in accord with our psychological faculties, but also with our existence as political or communal animals; we "keep" these secrets by disclosing this love to one another. As Thomas says, "As God is the object of faith, so is God the object of charity" (ST II-II.23). The theological virtues of faith, hope and charity thus deify us and lead to our participation in the divine life.[38]

The disclosure of secrets is an important mark of God's friendship with humanity, as it establishes a mutual communication. Still, it would not be enough for friendship for there to be a one-way communication from God to persons. While that would be love, it would not allow for the love of friendship, since humans could not reciprocate God's love by wishing God well for God's sake. The crucial, missing element would be the rational operation of human beings. The disclosure of secrets therefore allows for a new level of reciprocity. By communicating with us in the disclosure of secrets, making us "guardians of the soul," God allows for rational fellowship and true friendship, as we participate in "conversation" with God and the angels in our "spiritual life in respect of the human mind" (ST I.23.1 ad 1).[39]

This rationality is central to Thomas' interpretation of Jesus' call of friendship to the disciples. By saying "I no longer call you servants ... but friends," Jesus marks the inclusion of our rational capacities within the love between humans and God. Like Aristotle, Thomas sees servitude (or slavery) as precluding the possibility of friendship.[40] Servants, for Thomas, do not share in the reasoning of the master that directs them to their end. In that God has disclosed the secret of divine life through Jesus, thereby engaging our rational capacity, we can move ourselves to do the will of God (again, we see the interplay of grace and free will discussed earlier).[41] God's revelation makes possible our reciprocation, as God wills that we should be saved in a manner that makes us worthy and capable of friendship with God. The shift from servitude to friendship, then, is a change in the love between us. God's action makes evident our proper end of friendship. Insofar as sacred doctrine makes it possible for us to freely and rationally love God and obey God's precepts, we are no longer servants, but friends.

This shift from servitude to the friendship of charity reshapes the human pursuit of the good. On Thomas' view, while we find our true happiness in obedience to God's precepts, this obedience is better described as friendship. Because we have some knowledge of what God seeks, and we voluntarily share in God's pursuit of the

---

37 Aquinas, *Lectura Super Iohannem*, 15 (3).
38 See Jean Porter, "De Ordine Caritatis: Charity, Friendship, and Justice in Thomas Aquinas' *Summa Theologiae*," *The Thomist* 53 (1989), p. 204.
39 Joseph Bobik lists a number of "*communicationes*" of God and humanity, but leaves out the *conversatio* of the mind, which is common to all who participate in charity. See Bobik, "Aquinas on Friendship with God," *New Scholasticism* 61 (1986), pp. 269-71.
40 NE, viii.11; *Commentary on Aristotle's Nicomachean Ethics*, p. 518.
41 Aquinas, *Lectura Super Iohannem*, 15(3).

good, we can fulfill God's precepts for God's own sake, rather than simply out of self-interest or utility.[42] The distinction between friends and servants thus allows Thomas to place importance on the *interior*, voluntary quality of action as an expression of one's character. Servants who do not participate rationally in their lord's deliberations may also fulfill the precepts, but such an external fulfillment of one's duty is more likely to arise out of fear of punishment than out of any genuine interest in seeing the action come to fruition.[43] When rationally engaged, however, servants are able to appreciate for themselves the end toward which the lord is directing the action. Out of appreciation of the lord's goodness, they may wish the project well not only for their sake, but for the sake of the lord as well, and such rationally engaged obedience is more properly considered friendship than servitude.[44]

In that charity requires a participation of our rational nature, we can see the importance of sacred doctrine and its reorientation of language. Since sacred doctrine reorders our discourse and our mind from things to God, without the mode of signification by which we consider things as they are ordered to God, our intellects could not intend things for God's own sake. It is theoretically possible that we could be moved by God to act in accord with God's will in other ways, but insofar as God wills not only that we do God's will, but also that we do it freely and as friends, our rational participation is required, and sacred doctrine enables this mode of participation.

If reason must be engaged for friendship to be possible, then this is a necessary condition for determining what Thomas means by *communicatio*. As Joseph Bobik has suggested, God's *communicatio* to humans includes the sacraments,[45] yet it seems to me that it must include a great deal more as well. God's *communicatio*, for Thomas, is a sharing with us, but first and foremost must be a sharing with our rational nature. This aspect of *communicatio* is often neglected in recent appropriations of Thomas' thought. To generalize for a moment, much of the recent retrieval of Thomas' work for Christian ethics has rightly put the emphasis on *what* is communicated to us by God's revelation through sacred doctrine. Included under this heading would be an emphasis on the virtues, the importance of community, and a recognition of the validity of passions as expressions of moral judgment. *How* God communicates these aspects of the moral life to us has received far less emphasis in recent Thomistic ethics. Contemporary virtue theory, for example, often risks placing almost all of the emphasis on the role of moral virtue in moral philosophy. The role of theory is often neglected, if not out and out criticized. For Thomas, given that humanity's *telos* is friendship with God, we cannot separate the practical life from the theoretical or intellectual life of the soul.[46] Conversely, recent appropriations of Thomas' account

---

42 Ibid.
43 Ibid.
44 Keaty, "Thomas' Authority for Identifying Charity as Friendship," p. 600.
45 Bobik, "Aquinas on Friendship with God," pp. 269-71.
46 A reading of Thomas' work along these lines is A.N. Williams, "Mystical Theology Redux: The Pattern of Aquinas' *Summa Theologiae*," in *Spirituality and Social Embodiment*,

of contemplation, such as Levering's *Scripture and Metaphysics*, should attend more closely to how contemplation flows from praxis.

A truly Thomistic ethic, then, would require the integration of theory and praxis. The recent shift toward virtue and practice may, in fairness, be a response to an excessive intellectualism in modernity, including within Thomism. However, until we seek to integrate the practical and intellectual lives, we may not know what it really means to be an intellectual in the Thomistic sense. To move toward this goal, it is necessary to examine how Thomas integrates contemplation and practice in the order of charity, as the love of God renews one's love for one's neighbor, and the world.

III. Friendship With the Soul: Love and Knowledge

When one thinks of charity, its two precepts come to mind: love of God and love of neighbor. It may be surprising, then, that Thomas places love of one's soul between love of God and love of neighbor, and that love of the soul takes precedence over love of neighbor. This priority of the soul plays an integral part in Thomas' hierarchical ordering of charity. As Jean Porter has noted, it gives precedence to love of oneself over love of the neighbor;[47] one is not permitted to do anything that would jeopardize the possibility of the soul's eternal happiness with God. From the moment love of the soul is privileged, charity cannot be described simply as an equal regard for all creatures—or even for all humans.

However, this emphasis on the unequal regard of charity risks overlooking a crucial feature of this order: the order of charity enables specifically human friendship with God. The soul, as that which makes us uniquely human over against other creatures, is what is most our own. Love of the soul mediates between love of God and love of neighbor. Because the soul is the seat of our humanity, love of the *human* neighbor becomes part of charity as well. Even as it appears to privilege the self over others, love of the soul binds us to them. Through love of the soul, love of God begins its journey into the world.

Two aspects of the soul's place in charity must be examined. First, as that aspect of us which is most loved in charity, how does the soul allow us to be friends with God? Second, why does Thomas give the soul priority in the order of charity? Answering these questions will enrich the idea of friendship with God by showing how charity is God's friendship for humans *as* human. Moreover, in that our neighbors also participate in the life of glory that awaits us via the rational capacities of their souls,

---

ed. J.G. Jones and J.J. Buckley (Oxford: Blackwell, 1997), pp. 53-72. While I am in strong agreement with Williams, particularly on the unitive aspects of contemplation as the relation between God and humanity, the work of this chapter tries to extend this line of thought by exploring *how* this unity is a friendship—in terms of equality, reciprocity, virtue, and adhenece to the other's good.

47 ST II-II.26.4; Porter, "De Ordine Caritatis," pp. 199-200.

love of the soul unfolds into charity's love of the neighbor, as will be discussed in the next section of this chapter.

For Thomas, how humans move and act can only be fully understood in comparison with the movements and actions of other living things. Articulating the features of moral action, and the capacity of the soul, as what is right for humans, thus has the form of a "moral ecology."[48] All motion, or action, is motion towards an end (ST I-II.1.3). We share with other living things the capacity to act towards an end. Humans, however, are distinctive in that we move not only by sensible appetites and feeling, but also have a rational capacity for movement. Where a tree or dog is immediately moved toward its end, either by desire for nourishment or its senses, properly human movement towards an end proceeds via practical reason. As Thomas writes:

> Now, besides these three powers, the vegetative, the sensitive, and the appetitive, some animals also have the capacity to move from one place to another. Some, too, i.e., human beings and any other kind of beings, if such exist, resembling or even perhaps excelling mankind, have, in addition to these four capacities, the power of understanding or intellect. The beings "more excellent" are the immaterial substances and the heavenly bodies, the latter, however, only if they are alive. Among living corruptible beings the human race alone is endowed with intellect.[49]

In moving ourselves rationally, we do not solely deliberate about the means to an end; we can reflect upon and choose the ends toward which we act as well.[50]

For example, if my neighbor is hosting a barbecue, and leaves a steaming plate of hamburgers on the back porch when she goes to welcome the guests, both a dog in the neighborhood and I can smell them—they smell delicious, and we both want to eat one (or two). Yet while I apprehend them as *a* good, I can reflectively say to myself, "Those burgers are not yours, so you shouldn't eat them," or, "Those burgers have more fat than I should be eating." The taste of a burger is not the only good I apprehend. I can act toward the end of community and respect for other persons and their property, or act for my health, rather than acting toward the end of immediate culinary satisfaction. As a rational being, I can choose not only the means to the end, but also the end toward which I will act. I can decide which end should serve as the first principle of my action ("For the sake of harmonious community, I will not eat my neighbor's burgers") through practical reason.

For the dog, however, the wafting burger-odor presents itself immediately as an end toward which to run. Its sensitive appetite moves the dog. While the dog may deliberate about the best way to get to the burgers, going over or under the fence,

---

48 I borrow this term from John Bowlin.

49 St. Thomas Aquinas, *Commentary on Aristotle's De Anima*, trans. K. Foster and S. Humphries (Notre Dame, IN: Dumb Ox Books, 1994), p. 93 (Book 2, lecture v).

50 Daniel Mark Nelson, *The Priority of Prudence: Virtue and Natural Law in Thomas Aquinas and the Implications for Modern Ethics* (University Park, PA: Pennsylvania State University Press, 1991), pp. 48-50.

it does not choose the end toward which it acts. It *acts*, and so much the worse for the burgers. In that we can deliberate not only about means, but about the ends toward which we act as well, we have a practical wisdom distinct from other living creatures. As Daniel Westberg writes:

> Yet as self-movers such animals [i.e., nonrational] are limited in the ends they have. Although they receive the principle of movement, the form, through sensation, they do not set for themselves the purpose of their action or movement; this is given to them by nature, and they are moved by instinct to do something through the form apprehended by sensation.[51]

Since the dog is moved immediately toward its end by its nature, eating as a means of self-preservation is necessarily its final end and thereby the first principle of its activity. For humans, reason intervenes, acting as a "second nature" that frees us from the necessity of sensitive appetites. The rational capacity of the soul thus makes us distinctively human: "For a person is lord of his actions by reason and will: as free will is said to be a faculty of will and reason" (ST I-II.1.1).[52] Where the intellectual capacity of the will is inactive, we act as other animals do.

Since the end toward which something acts becomes a first principle of its activity, this end becomes a mark which distinguishes a species. Humanity is therefore in a strange position. Since we can choose the end toward which we will act, it is difficult to see what shared end would define our species. Some people choose to be sports fans, others patrons of the arts, and still others patrons of the local bar. What could we all have in common as a final end?

For Thomas, our final end is to actualize the rational capacity by which we choose particular ends. Insofar as we can act on the rational capacity that is most our own (among material creatures), we flourish in a distinctively human way. This flourishing of our practical and theoretical rationality is *beatitude*. Because our flourishing is connected with intellective activity itself, our perfect beatitude cannot be found in created things (ST I-II.2.8); it is, rather, in relating to things through the work of reason. Rather, our perfect beatitude is found in the beatific vision of God after death, where we exercise reason contemplatively and without interruption.[53] The work of reason is distinctive form of flourishing, and it makes possible a happiness unavailable to other creatures with whom we share the world.

In identifying our beatitude with contemplation, Thomas seems quite close to Aristotle's account of *eudaimonia*. Yet there are important differences. While Aristotle certainly thinks that we can achieve some contemplation, he does not think that we can approach the happiness of the gods. Through grace, however, Thomas thinks this is possible for us, and likewise friendship with God. As Thomas writes

---

51 Westberg, *Right Practical Reason*, p. 49.

52 See Ralph McInerny, "Ethics," in N. Kretzmann and E. Stump (eds), *The Cambridge Companion to Aquinas* (Cambridge: Cambridge University Press, 1993), p. 197.

53 And, moreover, in contemplating God one contemplates the universal good rather than a particular one, which is proper to the notion of an ultimate end.

in the questions on charity, "According as anything shares with us in the society of rational natures, so it is lovable out of charity. Therefore rational nature is the object of charity."[54] The rational capacity of the human soul, then, allows us to participate in charity, makes conceivable our adoption by God, and permits friendship with God to be the final end of humanity.[55] Beatitude, in this sense, surpasses the contemplative happiness available in Aristotelian friendship, through the graciously transformed relation of charity.

This creates an even stranger puzzle: if beatitude, as humanity's final end, is the vision of the divine essence, then it would seem that we cannot act toward our final end in a properly human manner. In the last section, we saw that Thomas interprets Jesus' calling the disciples to friendship as engaging their rational natures. And yet, if we seek to love the God whom we do not know naturally, then how can we voluntarily appropriate this knowledge? How to act toward an end above our nature, while preserving it?

The solution to this problem rests in the possibility of supernatural habits. Only if something is superadded to our nature can we become aware of our final end, and thus act toward the final end in properly human manner. This "addition" takes a twofold form: extrinsically, it is sacred doctrine, which is revealed so that we can order our actions in light of our final end (ST I.1.1). Intrinsically, the graceful work of the Spirit moves the free will in writing the "new law" on our hearts. The new law is written on our hearts in the form of the theological virtues—faith, hope and charity. The supernatural habit of charity perfects human nature taking the form of *voluntary* human action, and redirecting it toward God.

To clarify Thomas' account, a brief discussion of habits is necessary. The virtues, as habits, are the ways in which the human soul becomes a self-moving agent. Thomas borrows Aristotle's definition of a habit as "a disposition whereby that which is disposed is disposed well or ill, and this, either in regard to itself or in regard to another."[56] Since a habit shapes the way we consider something in the world, it determines how we will act towards it; quoting Ibn-Sina, Thomas writes "habit is that whereby we act when we will" (ST I-II.49.3). Because human virtue moves us to act toward a particular good end, virtues are habits that dispose us to the good (ST I-II.55.1). The theological virtues, then, are principles whereby humans "may be directed to supernatural happiness" (ST I-II.62.1). As directed toward God, and to direct *us* toward God, the theological virtues differ from moral and intellectual virtues (ST I-II.62.2) in content; however, as "exemplate" human virtues, while

---

54 Aquinas, *De Caritate*, p. 61, article vii.

55 To touch briefly on an issue that is too wide-ranging to address here, while our rational capacity would permit us to be friends with God, it does not effect this communion. Rather, our participation in charity would be effected through the exercise of the virtues.

This view of charity is consistent with several recent interpretations of natural law and the virtues in Thomas: Bowlin, *Contingency and Fortune in Aquinas' Ethics*; Daniel Mark Nelson, *The Priority of Prudence*; Eugene F. Rogers, Jr., *Sexuality and the Christian Body: Their Way Into the Triune God* (London: Blackwell, 1999).

56 Aristotle, *Metaphysics* v.25, quoted in ST I-II.49.1.

disposing us to divinization, they nonetheless work within us in the same habitual manner as natural virtue.

Since charity is to be friendship, and this requires voluntary action in the form of habits, Thomas' discussion of the question of whether or not charity is created in the soul (ST II-II.23.2) becomes especially important. He discusses three potential objections to his view, which are significant because he breaks with received opinion on this topic. First, since charity properly speaking is God's love of God's self, charity cannot be something created. Second, God quickens the soul by charity as the soul quickens the body. Thus, by analogy, since the body is *immediately* quickened by the soul, so too God immediately quickens the soul in an uncreated way. The third objection states that what is created cannot lead us to the perfection of the divine life, so that if charity is our participation in the divine life, it cannot be created. Together, the objections make a strong case that charity should not be considered something created in the soul. As Thomas reports, Peter Lombard held this view.[57]

Against these received opinions, Thomas argues that the habit of charity is created. His response condenses and orders the various features of voluntary action, habits, and grace and free will discussed above, microcosmically incorporating the issues of predestination and merit laid out in the preceding sections of this chapter. The soul cannot direct itself to a love that is greater than what we can know or love. If the Holy Spirit moves the soul immediately, then the Spirit is the efficient cause of the act of charity, and our merit would be impossible:

> But if we consider the matter aright, this would be, on the contrary, detrimental to charity. For when the Holy Spirit moves the human mind the movement of charity does not proceed from this motion in such a way that the human mind be merely moved, without being the principle of this movement, as when a body is moved by some extrinsic motive power. For this is contrary to the nature of a voluntary act, whose principle needs to be in itself, as stated above (ST I-II.6.1): so that it would follow that to love is not a voluntary act, which involves a contradiction, since love, of its very nature, implies an act of the will. (ST II-II.23.2)

Thomas' comments in *De Caritate* are likewise illuminating:

> Therefore, if the soul does not effect an act of charity through some proper form, but only because it is moved by an extrinsic agent, i.e., by the Holy Spirit, then it will follow that it is considered only as an instrument for this act. There would not be, then, in humanity the power to act or not to act, and one would not be able to gain merit. For only those things are meritorious which are in us in a certain manner [i.e., voluntary].[58]

---

57 ST II-II.23.2. See Keaty's discussion, "Thomas' Authority for Identifying Charity as Friendship," pp. 595-8.

58 Aquinas, *De Caritate*, p. 22.

Therefore, the Spirit cannot dwell immediately in the soul, since this would undercut the whole process of making us worthy of friendship with God.

Thomas therefore argues that the Spirit dwells in the soul through the creation of a supernatural habit: "Therefore it is most necessary that, for us to perform the act of charity, there should be in us some habitual form superadded to the natural power, inclining that power to the act of charity, and causing it to act with pleasure" (ST II-II.23.2). The Spirit creates the supernatural habit of charity in the soul. By dwelling in us through a habit, rather than moving us extrinsically, the Spirit allows the human will to be the efficient cause of the action, so that acts of charity "proceed from an intrinsic principle."[59] Even as the acts of charity surpass our natures, they complete them as voluntary acts of love. The infinite love of the Spirit works via the finite form of habitual human action. By creating this habit, the Spirit enables action toward our final end through our will. The will is the subject of charity (ST II-II.24.1). The intellective will apprehends love of God as good because the Spirit has habituated the soul to see love of God as good. The Spirit, named "love," creates in us a love of God; as intellectually engaged in this activity, we become worthy through grace of friendship with God.

It is important to note, moreover, that Thomas privileges charity as the greatest of the theological virtues because it relates to God through love rather than knowledge. In so doing, he displaces Aristotle's privilege of the intellectual virtues over the practical virtues.[60] For material things studied by Aristotelian science, Thomas agrees with Aristotle that knowledge is the most complete relation. However, insofar as love tends to God as God is, rather than God as conceived in our intellect, love tends to a greater good than natural knowledge of God (ST II-II.23.6), or the knowledge of God that we have in faith. Charity, then, leads to a closer union to God, and a deeper participation in *scientia Dei*. Thus, while beatitude is contemplation, it is more properly the contemplation internal to friendship—a contemplation *through* love rather than privileged over it. Charity's existence as a habit within the soul highlights Thomas' emphasis on the voluntary aspect of charity, both with and against Aristotle. The question still remains, however, how other aspects of human life, especially community and embodiment, are brought into the order of charity, extending friendship with God into the world.

IV. Love of Neighbor: Virtue and Beatitude

We have seen how charity, as the final end of humanity, directs human action to its proper goal and fulfillment. However, while charity as love of God engages our rational capability for participation in the divine life, our discussion to this point says little about human action in the world. In that our proper end is not found in this world, need we concern ourselves with action at all? Could we not simply forgo attachment to the world, and live a contemplative life directed solely towards God?

---

59 Ibid., p. 21.
60 See NE book x.

If this were the case in Thomas' account of charity, it would be both surprising and very troubling. First, it would be surprising, since Thomas is deeply committed to the Augustinian view of charity as love of God *and* love of neighbor.[61] Thomas' commentary on John indicates his clear perception that the fruit of God's predestining love is our mutual love for one another. It would also be very troubling, since, if love of the neighbor were not included in charity, then charity, as Fergus Kerr writes, "perhaps begins to remind us of that vision of an invulnerable and impersonal love such as Socrates describes in the *Symposium*."[62] Such a view of charity would deny the world any place in blessedness—an almost Gnostic love of God. It would not take our personal attachments and relations seriously, becoming a love that denied rather than redeemed the social and corporeal aspects of our humanity.

Once again, the language of friendship provides Thomas with a way to explicate a world-oriented account of charity. Friendship has two crucial components. First, one loves a friend as who the friend is, for the friend's own sake (ST II-II.25.2). Secondly, one loves the good of the friend; that is, one loves that which the friend finds to be good, for the sake of the friend. In friendship with God, God loves us, by bringing us to our fullest happiness (the fulfillment of the life of the soul), but also loves what we find to be good, by bringing us to this end through the activity of this life. In response to God's initial act of friendship, we love God *and* that which God finds to be good—creation. And, since a neighbor is able to love God, we love the neighbor out of charity as well. In truth, we have already seen this order at work: in charity, we love our soul because it is loved by God for its ability to participate in the divine life. A reshaped love of neighbor follows a similar path.

While the initial step into the world is straightforward, it raises significant questions. Does one love the good that is loved by God for its own sake, or as a means to the end of loving God? In loving the neighbor on account of God (*propter Deum*), is one "loving" the neighbor in an instrumental fashion? Friendship with God may not be real friendship for the neighbor.[63] It is at least conceivable that in charity, one would have a love of friendship for God, but a concupiscible love for other humans. In order not to treat others as means rather than ends, love of God must entail love of others for *their* own sake (*propter proximi*). Thomas, however, says that God alone is loved for God's sake in charity, thus raising intriguing and difficult questions about charity's perfection of the moral life.

Thomas begins to resolve this difficulty through the likeness between love of soul and love of neighbor. In the neighbor, we recognize another person with the rational capacity for participation in divine life, ordered to the same final end as oneself. The

---

61 See Keaty, "Thomas' Authority for Identifying Charity as Friendship," pp. 590-4.

62 Fergus Kerr, "Charity as Friendship," in *Language, Meaning, and God* (London: Chapman, 1987), p. 18. Kerr reads Socrates as deflecting interest away from the particular, individual friendships that we engage in in the world, treating them as transient moments on the passage to the highest good with no intrinsic value of their own.

63 Don Adams, "Loving God and One's Neighbor: Thomistic Charity," *Faith and Philosophy* 11 (1997), pp. 207-10.

neighbor, like the self, has an intellective capacity in the soul; thus, one can love the neighbor for her ability to participate in charity. Once aware of our likeness to God, and the neighbor's likeness to us, we can love the neighbor as ourselves. In this sense, the neighbor is "another self"; the placing of the love of soul above love of neighbor in the order of charity is therefore not necessarily an egoistic hierarchy. Rather, by love of the soul we become aware of how to love *someone* as ordered to God, and thus to love another. The self is, for Thomas, the first neighbor; by learning to love the soul in charity, we also learn how to love other neighbors.

Because we love the neighbor as ordered to the same participation in the divine life as our own, Thomas' comments on the love of the soul are instructive for how charity loves the neighbor as a friend. As with the soul, the neighbor is loved on account of her final end. Thus, to love the neighbor *propter Deum*—on account of God—is in fact to love the neighbor as who the neighbor most intimately is. This point is crucial, because loving the neighbor "on account of God" could be taken in an instrumental fashion, but this is clearly not how Thomas sees it.[64]

When one considers Thomas' discussion of how one loves the neighbor in charity, it becomes clear that friendship with God is a friendship for the neighbor as well. Yet charity differs from worldly friendship, as it no longer intends the good or the character of other humans, but rather the goodness and character *of God*. God, who is loved essentially in charity, is both the formal object and a "material" object of charity; God is the one loved, and the one in light of whom one loves others. Insofar as in charity one loves the neighbor "in that he may be in God," the habit of charity directed toward love of God may have the neighbor as its material object as well (ST II-II.25.1). As Jean Porter has shown, charity may share the same material object with Aristotelian friendship, as both love the neighbor; it differs, however, in having a distinctive formal object.[65] Charity is the shared journey to friendship with God, through engagement with neighbors and the world.

Thomas' discussion of love of neighbor enriches and clarifies charity's connection with predestination. Charity only includes creatures able to participate in divine fellowship; irrational creatures cannot be loved out of charity (ST II-II.25.3). The limits of charity thus parallel the limits of God's predestination. In charity, one can love irrational creatures insofar as their existence and well-being can contribute to one's own (or others') participation in charity. In other words, one should act justly towards them as a furtherance of God's providence, but one does not love them charitably.[66]

---

64 Ibid., pp. 213-16.

65 Jean Porter, "Salvific Love and Charity: A Comparison of the Thought of Karl Rahner and Thomas Aquinas," in E.N. Santurri and W. Werpehowski (eds), *The Love Commandments* (Washington, DC: Georgetown University Press, 1992), pp. 250-1.

66 And thus, while the animal-rights questions would seem to be precluded by their exclusion from charity, it is at least possible that the ordering of one's actions toward all

In light of this parallel, we can take up once again Thomas' discussion of humanity as "particular causes" of predestination. In loving the neighbor in charity, one loves the good loved by one's divine friend. Thus, loving the neighbor in charity makes us the secondary cause of God's predestination *of neighbors* to the divine life. In charity, Thomas' mental gymnastics on grace and free will come to a remarkable fruition. While God is the final end of charity and the primary cause of grace, the secondary causality of our virtue becomes the site through which the neighbor is brought into the divine life (and, likewise, in reciprocal fashion). Our love for neighbors *propter Deum* is not outside God's providence: *through* our friendship, God's love for humans is enacted. As Thomas writes, one human cannot be the final end of another in charity, but one can act "ministerially" to help bring about God's love for another (ST II-II.25.1 ad 3). Such secondary, particular causality, in light of God's election, is consistent with Thomas' interpretation of John 15, in that God's election and love leads to mutual love among the disciples and thereby their mission to the world. Friendship with one another both seeks and enacts friendship with God.

To highlight charity's place in God's predestination sounds shocking. Yet given the connections between grace, free will, and charity, it is appropriate. Human action particularizes divine love; as Thomas writes, in charity one has an obligation to love more those to whom one is closer. This greater love has two sources: on the one hand, one has an obligation to love some more dearly, namely parents; but one also has natural affection for some neighbors more than others (ST II-II.26.6). Charity's grace does not contradict the natural love of humanity, which attends more closely and strongly to some people than to others. It is to these individuals—family, friends, members of one's own community—that one most often and most fully acts as an agent of God's predestination and love, bringing them into the life of charity in a more complete, personal way.

However, one could ask in Kierkegaardian fashion if Thomas is to some degree misunderstanding the nature of the term "neighbor." For, if grace works through nature, and the Spirit moves us to charity through human friendship, then there is the risk that one would identify human love and charity. For Kierkegaard, and many modern theological ethicists, this would effectively deny the universality of *agape*, rendering it preferential and even exclusive. This risks reducing the divine good to a particular human community, and even to the good of *some* humans at the expense of others. Where Kierkegaard would emphasize the tension between divine command

---

God's creatures in terms of justice may be an outgrowth of charity. If one acts toward all things insofar as they further participation in the divine life, this may require more justice and stewardship than we currently employ. Such justice arguably could have considerable bearing on questions of treatment of animals. I am grateful to Mark Ryan for pressing me to reflect on the relation of nonrational beings to charity.

and human passionate preference,[67] Thomas argues that passion and command work together.

Thomas recognizes this risk very clearly, and thus emphasizes that love of enemies perfects charity, opening charity beyond our exclusionary preferences. Once again, Thomas' scriptural commentaries help to clarify how charity reshapes the moral life and extends it beyond the parochial limits of the Aristotelian community. The John commentary makes it very clear that charity's command to love one's enemies transforms one's habits and virtues, directing the particular goods of one's actions toward the universal end of charity for all of humanity. It is only in light of this command, and its reshaping of the passions and virtues, that Thomas sees the greater love for some neighbors as directed toward the common good that God seeks for all of creation. Consider, then, the Sermon on the Mount's articulation of this command:

> You have heard that they were told, "Love your neighbor and hate your enemy." But what I tell you is this: Love your enemies and pray for your persecutors; *only so can you be children of your heavenly Father*, who causes the sun to rise on good and bad alike, and sends the rain on the innocent and the wicked. *If you love only those who love you*, what reward can you expect? Even the tax-collectors do as much as that. (Mt. 5:43-46, my emphasis)

While apparently impossible in worldly terms, love of enemies is the *sine qua non* for being an adopted child of God, through conforming one's character to God's. Charity, as friendship with God via love of God's Son, thus requires love of enemies (ST II-II.25.8). Thomas interprets this Gospel passage through a tripartite distinction that respects the reality and concreteness of human nature as a political and communal animal.

The first way to love one's enemy is to love an enemy as such. Loving one's enemy as one's enemy, however, would imply loving that which one found hateful or evil. For Thomas, since we always act toward apparent goods, love of an enemy as such is impossible. Since love of enemies as such would involve love of that which is evil, Thomas, following 1 Corinthians 13:4, deems this sort of love "perverse." For such love of enemies, Joab upbraids David: David loved his son over all of Israel, even though Absalom rebelled against him (2 Sam. 19:6). Charity, then, cannot love the enemy as such in this way.

The second way in which one can love an enemy is according to the enemy's nature (*quantum ad naturam*). For Thomas, the meaning of this is twofold: first, loving the enemy as a rational creature, but also thereby loving the enemy as a potential participant in the divine life. Enemies are not "contrary to us, as human and capable of happiness" (ST II-II.25.8 ad 2). Given this capacity, the enemy should be included within our neighbor-love. This is not to love the enemy as such, but rather to love the enemy as ordered to God, with God as the enemy's final end. "For since

---

67 See Søren Kierkegaard, *Works of Love*, trans. H.V. Hong and E.H. Hong (Princeton: Princeton University Press, 1995).

one loves the neighbor, out of charity, for God's sake, the more one loves God, the more does one put enmities aside and show love towards the neighbor: thus if we loved a certain man very much, we would love his children though they were unfriendly towards us" (ST II-II.25.8 ad 1). As God brings rain on everyone, so too in charity one should be open to loving the enemy.

The third way one can love the enemy is individually, with a "special movement of love towards our enemies (*in speciali moveatur motu dilectionis ad inimicum*)" (ST II-II.25.8). This cannot be required, because according to Thomas such a special movement towards all rational creatures (i.e., all included in neighbor-love) is impossible. However, even if this individual love is not required, one's character must be so shaped that one *could* act in this way toward a particular enemy if the situation arose—say, if an enemy needed food or drink, or a wounded enemy was captured. "That one should actually do so, and love one's enemy for God's sake, without it being necessary for one to do so, belongs to the *perfection* of charity."

Thus, while the first way of loving the enemy is deemed perverse, both the second and third ways pertain to charity. These two ways of loving the enemy help to clarify how love of an enemy is both a *precept* and a *perfection* of charity. One must love the enemy, as a precept, as part of the ordering of one's soul: "Now it is absolutely necessary, for the fulfillment of the precept, that we should inwardly love our enemies in general, but not individually, except as regards the mind being prepared to do so, as explained above" (ST II-II.25.9). This preparation of the soul (*praeparationem ainimi*) is a *habitual preparation*. Charity, as an ordering of the soul in friendship with God, is not simply concerned with external acts, but first and foremost with a reshaping of character. As a habit (ST II-II.24.12) infused by the Spirit, and created in the soul, charity does not forget our other attachments and loves, but it does require that we consider those in a new light. This precept prepares us for the perfection of charity in which we actively love those opposed to us.

In that charity as a habit orders our mind and soul, we can see how it is the form of the virtues (ST II-II.23.8) and a virtue (23.5). As the form of the virtues, charity reshapes how we look at the world, and reshapes and redirects the other virtues.[68] Where the virtues would otherwise be shaped solely by our human perceptions of friendship, enmity, likeness and difference, in light of charity we are habituated to consider all fellow rational beings as potential participants in the divine life. As Thomas writes in *De Caritate*, "We are bound by the affection and the carrying out of the works of charity, by which we love all our neighbors and pray for them, not to exclude even those who are not joined to us by any special bond, as for instance those who live in Ethiopia."[69] The possession of charity as a habit is central to considering neighbors and things in the world as ordered to God.

As a virtue, charity guides our action in the world. In charity's love of enemies, it exemplifies two central features of virtue. First, in seeking to overcome the hostility between enemies, charity is a virtue in that it seeks a good that cannot be achieved

---

68 Porter, "Salvific Love and Charity," pp. 252, 259.
69 Aquinas, *De Caritate*, p. 70, article viii.

without difficulty. The functionality of charity is part of its goodness, since as humans this good cannot be conceived without its accompanying difficulty. Second, and equally importantly, charity is *externally* directed. One cannot be charitable in the best sense simply by focusing on interior action. The perfection of charity, as Thomas states, is connected with showing signs of love to one's enemies. Such love, directed to the enemy, is a perfection in that it seeks to overcome evil by good. This external focus, as well as the emphasis on functionality, manifests the Aristotelian dimension of Thomas' ethics even in his appropriation of Augustinian charity. Broadly speaking, one could say the following: the primacy of the perfection of charity over its habituation exemplifies Thomas' decision in favor of the externality and functionality of Aristotelian ethics over a Stoic conception of virtue as an interior activity.[70]

That charity has an Aristotelian shape, even while articulated scripturally, raises questions about the relation between Aristotle and sacred doctrine at the most detailed level of the *Summa*. In his tripartite distinction of how one ought to love enemies, is Thomas writing as an Aristotelian philosopher, or as a scriptural theologian? Resources within Thomas' writings could support both interpretations. First, Thomas' tripartite distinction of love of enemies (as such, habitually, and perfectly) exemplifies Aristotle's understanding of potential and actuality in the soul's agency. As Thomas elucidates in his commentary on *De Anima*, a proper understanding of the potential and actuality of the soul involves three steps rather than two, and this can be explained in light of the preceding discussion of charity.

First, the soul can be in potential with regard to an activity if it is completely devoid of a habit. If the soul does not possess the habit, there is no way in which it can act towards its end or goal. In such "primary potency," the soul can only become active if an exterior agent moves it, ordinarily by teaching.[71] Such primary potency can be seen in Thomas' discussion of love of enemies in two ways. First, if one loved an enemy as such, acting against God's good and against one's own good, the soul would be in primary potency with regard to virtue. This unformed potential requires action from without if it is to become charitable; the habit must be placed in the agent by another in order for its actuality to become possible; for a theological virtue such as charity, as we have seen, this is brought about by the Spirit.

The second type of potential is the possession of a habit that is not currently actualized. One only makes the transition from unformed potential to habitual potential when the habit needed for agency is within oneself, but not yet completely

---

70 My remarks on virtue here are largely indebted to John Bowlin's reading of virtue in Thomas. See *Contingency and Fortune in Aquinas' Ethics*, pp. 138-67. Bowlin notes an interesting tension in Thomas' work, particularly around the virtues as possessed by Adam, since in paradise they seem to lose their functionality. What is equally interesting, if not more so, is that God would seem to have a *functional* set of virtues, in that God's justice and love are directed to the overcoming of evil. This is a point that is merely raised here to point the way to further study.

71 Aquinas, *Commentary on Aristotles's De Anima*, II.xi, p. 116.

actualized.⁷² The possession of charity habitually orders one to God, and habituates one in love of enemies, preparing the soul. When one has a habit, one possesses its form in an imperfect sense, since one does not act according to its principles. The habit, however, by reshaping one's passions and how one relates to both friends and enemies, sets the stage for acts of charity.

When one acts externally, the habit is perfected.⁷³ Acting toward others lets one see, visibly, the specific consequences held within the habit in one's soul. In loving the enemy individually (*in singuarli*) (25.9), one actualizes the form of charity within the world. By so acting, one possesses the habit perfectly. In this tripartite distinction of the activity of charity, then, Thomas follows Aristotle closely on the agency of the soul.

He is not, however, following Aristotle blindly. Thomas' account of love of enemies is guided throughout by his reading of the Gospel of John. As we saw earlier, Jesus communicates to the disciples "all he has learned" from the Father, in the mode of a foretaste (*praelibatio*). This is an "imperfect" knowledge, because only the first principles are communicated. By living in light of its principles and actualizing this habit in their lives, the disciples attain the "perfect" knowledge of a wayfarer. Through love of neighbor, habitually placed in one by sacred doctrine and the Spirit, and perfected in love of the enemy, one keeps in mind (*commemorat*) God's love for us.⁷⁴ When one loves an enemy, as one who is ordered to God, one draws out the singularity of God's love for this one creature, participating as fully as one can in the *scientia Dei*.

Given John's focus on disciples' love for one another, and generally hostile rhetoric towards outsiders, one could scripturally question why Thomas privileges love of enemies as the perfection of charity. The short answer is that for Thomas, love of enemies is a perfection of charity, because *this is the nature of divine love*. He foregrounds Jesus' statement "no greater love hath man than this, that he lay his life down for his friends." This statement, prefiguring Jesus' crucifixion, seems to indicate that love of friends rather than enemies is the perfection of love, in terms of its plain sense.⁷⁵ As Thomas notes, however, humans were *not* friends of God as such when Jesus died. If anything, on account of sin we are God's enemies. Thomas takes Jesus' statement, then, as saying that the greatest love is to die so that others *may* be friends, even though they are currently enemies. "To which is said, that Christ did not lay down his life for us as enemies, that of course we would remain enemies, but that he would make us friends; for while they were not yet friends as lovers, nevertheless they were friends as loved."⁷⁶ God's love, then, is such as to make friendship where there had been hostility, overcoming evil with good (Rom. 12:21, quoted in II-II.25.9). The crucifixion and resurrection here become the perfection of

---

72 Ibid., p. 116.
73 Ibid., p. 117.
74 Aquinas, *Lectura Super Iohannem*, 15 (3), pp. 409-16.
75 Ibid., 15 (2), pp. 232-5.
76 Ibid., 15 (2), pp. 243-7.

charity, as a divine act of love of enemies, to bring about friendship. Our "perfection of charity" participates therein, as an imitation of Christ. This is a subtle, yet crucial move; Thomas effectively reads the John passage figuratively, in light of Matthew 5:44 and other passages, so as to open the language of friendship beyond a closed circle of disciples.

Similarly, by loving an enemy as ordered to God, one makes goodness and peace out of evil and hostility; one thus participates as fully as humanly possible in God's love for the world. Love of the enemy is a perfection of charity according to our natures, just as God's love for humanity was perfect charity on God's part *ad extra*. In loving the enemy, creating good out of evil, one intends the good as God intends it.[77] As Thomas notes, where such a shared intention is found, one can say that there is equality, thereby making friendship possible. We have perfect charity in the form appropriate to our "wayfaring" status by actualizing love of enemies.

Love of enemies shapes charity, as it leads to peacemaking and wisdom. Peacemaking, like love of enemies, makes one a child of God. Thomas argues that peace is a proper effect of charity (ST II-II.29.3), and in ST II.45.6 he links wisdom with peace as well. He attributes wisdom to peacemakers because there is only "obedience to reason" within their hearts, setting conflicting wills in order and directing them to a common end. The making of peace is a participation in "the likeness of the only-begotten and natural son of God ... Who is Wisdom Begotten. Hence by participating in the gift of wisdom, humanity attains to being a child of God" (ST II-II.45.6). Peacemaking, then, is our participation in God's charity, an *imitatio Christi* by which we merit the adoptive status of God's children. This gives wisdom, as peacemakers are infused with a knowledge of God's will for humanity, as embodied in the Son.

Thomas' account of charity thus has both scriptural and Aristotelian sources, and this raises important questions for interpretation of the influence of his sources.[78] Given the historical proximity of the works discussed here—the scriptural commentaries, Aristotelian commentaries, and the *Summa* all being written in the same period[79]—it is difficult to accord priority to philosophical or scriptural sources. Nonetheless, our engagement with these various works of Thomas shows that in the *Summa*, Aristotle's thought operates in the service of sacred doctrine, and not vice versa. Christology occupies the pre-eminent place in his thinking about love of enemies. Thomas makes use of Aristotle's understanding of the soul to explain the potency and actuality of the habitual precepts and singular perfections of charity. To be sure, Aristotle could not have imagined such a habit—let alone that it is a habit for

---

77 As Thomas writes in ST I.19.9, God wills evil accidentally, in properly and intentionally willing the good; that is, evil is only an object of the will as that which is to be overcome or healed, rather than something willed of itself.

78 Bradley, in *Aquinas on the Twofold Human Good*, argues at length that one should not read Thomistic ethics apart from its theological context, and challenges a number of recent philosophical attempts to do so.

79 Weisheipl, *Friar Thomas D'Aquino*, pp. 241–92.

the good. In charity, the soul works in the same way as it does for natural habits and actions; however, the end toward which the soul operates is scripturally informed. The Aristotelian approach to friendship and the activity of the soul serves a heuristic purpose, helping to explicate the morality and psychology Thomas finds implicit within scripture. This confirms, on a concrete level, Alasdair MacIntyre's summary of Thomas' approach:

> In the best accounts of the virtues to be given so far, inadequacies are remedied by using the Bible and Augustine to transcend the limitations ... of Aristotle ... and by using Aristotle as well as Augustine to articulate some of the detail of the moral life in a way that goes beyond anything furnished by Augustine.[80]

Of course, the perfection of charity is not the whole story. God wants humans to be friends with God, but *as* humans. Within our embodied and corrupted lives, perfect charity is often unattainable. As previously noted, one cannot make the movement of singular love requisite for perfect charity toward all individuals. The order of charity is not simply God at the pinnacle, with the soul, neighbor, and body as derivative participants. To paraphrase *Animal Farm*, some neighbors are more equal than others.[81] But charity also takes into account our communal and political natures, as is evident from Thomas' discussion of just warfare.

In light of the above connection between perfect charity and peacemaking, Thomas' claim that war can be justified is particularly striking. It is in the context of the treatise on charity that he makes this argument, and our ability to wage war justly is clearly meant to be understood *within* the precept, "love your enemies." It seems fair to ask, how can one love one's enemies and wage war on them at the same time? This question is reinforced by Thomas' placement of warfare, in a section treating the "vices opposed to charity" (*vitiis opponuntur caritatis*, introd. II-II.34), and especially those vices which are opposed to peace. Given the importance of peace as the perfection of charity, as seen above, one would hardly expect to find any of these actions being justified. Nonetheless, Thomas affirms that a just war is possible. So, in the light of charity, war—what is it good for?

The specifics of Thomas' account of a just war are well documented and have been the source of extensive scholarly debate and research.[82] Specifically, three criteria must be met for the war to be just: the authority who wages the war must be a sovereign, the war must be waged for a just cause (i.e., those attacked must

---

80 Alasdair MacIntyre, "Aquinas and the Rationality of Tradition," in *Three Rival Versions of Moral Inquiry: Encyclopedia, Genealogy, and Tradition* (Notre Dame, IN: University of Notre Dame Press, 1990), p. 141.

81 See Porter, "De Ordine Caritatis," p. 205.

82 Recently, see Darrell Cole, "Thomas Aquinas on Virtuous Warfare," *Journal of Religious Ethics* 27 (1999), pp. 57-80. My focus here will be the justice of going to war (*jus ad bellum*), not just conduct within warfare (*jus in bello*). See also James Turner Johnson, "Aquinas and Luther on War and Peace: Sovereign Authority and the Use of Armed Force," *Journal of Religious Ethics* 31 (2003), pp. 3-20.

have acted unjustly, so that the war is for restitution), and thirdly the belligerents must have a "rightful intention" (*intentio recta*) that intends either the furtherance of goodness or the avoidance of evil as its end.[83] A war that is deficient in any of these three features cannot be considered a just war (ST II-II.40.1).

It is important to note that war, considered in itself, can be just but not charitable. War, as contrary (opposed) to peace, cannot be peaceful in itself. A just war is one that aims at peace, seeking justice for the end of charity. In seeking to further good, and to overcome evil, war may make a just peace possible. Such a just peace, according to Thomas, is intended by God as our final end: "Those who wage war justly aim at peace, and so they are not opposed to peace, except to the evil peace, which Our Lord 'came not to send upon the earth' (Mt. 10:39)" (ST II-II.40.1 ad 3). An unjust peace, on Thomas' view, would create a conflict between the peace toward which we are predestined and God's providential justice that orders all things. Only through the idea of a peace based on justice—and which thus may require war on occasion—can God's predestination fulfill rather than dissolve God's law and providence.

In this light, it is especially interesting to consider Thomas' reflections on the role of prelates and priests in warfare. On Thomas' account, it is unlawful for prelates and priests to fight for two reasons (ST II-II.40.2). First, the bustle and antagonism of warfare are detrimental to contemplation. The second reason, however, interests Thomas far more. Clerics, on Thomas' view, are directed toward the ministry of the altar, "on which the Passion of Christ is represented sacramentally." Insofar as one is participating in the sacraments, one should not fight in a war, since the shedding of blood is not fitting for one participating therein. However, priests may minister to those who are engaged in battle, so as to "afford spiritual help to those who fight justly." Thus, for Thomas, priests may endorse (but not engage in) warfare where the war is just, insofar as it may be a precondition for the peaceful love that is the perfection of charity (ST II-II.40.2).[84]

What is striking about Thomas' just war theory, when read in light of the treatise on charity, is that it shows just how important justice and virtue are as preconditions for the friendship of charity. Given that peacemaking is a participation in the divine life, Thomas' willingness to defer peace where required for the sake of justice is deeply striking. A love of God that radically ignored or denied the value of justice to others—an *egoisme à Dieu*, if you will—would fail to be a friendship of character in the truest sense. Thomas is thus very close to Aristotle on the relation between friendship and justice, even in discussing friendship with God. As God's character refuses to separate justice and the peace of friendship, so too does charity. One need not, in my opinion, walk away from Thomas' text convinced that pacifism is an untenable position. Particularly given the strictures on warmaking by those who take

---

[83] As Cole notes, this is not a Cartesian-style intention, but rather one that is manifest in what is actually done. Cole, "Thomas Aquinas on Virtuous Warfare," p. 72.

[84] That priests were the only ones who received the sacraments, and that they were not to participate in warfare, raises interesting questions as to who can participate in warfare in light of the extension of sacraments to all members of the Church.

the sacraments, as well as the difficulty of intending a just war, there would seem to be resources within Thomas' account for a pacifism built on the virtue of charity, provided that justice is taken into account. However, what both pacifists and just war theorists alike should take from this treatise is a deep respect for its recognition of the importance of holding justice *and* the peacemaking of love of enemies together.

To conclude, charity extends love to neighbors, performing the ordering of humanity to God that is revealed in sacred doctrine. As communicated by God to us through scripture, and as first communicated to the disciples, divine love works to call us to friendship. As the naming of God in sacred doctrine orders our language to God, so too love of neighbor orders our relations to others toward God as well. Our mode of participation, like the mode of signification of religious language, remains imperfect; our limitations and faults make perfect charity impossible in this life, yet this transforms and redirects the shape of community. Nonetheless, in that charity may be a habit that orders and directs just actions in the world, we can come to a limited perfection of "wayfaring" charity that lets us see through a glass darkly the beatific friendship of charity.

V. Love of the Body: Rejoicing in the Passions

Given his philosophical training, it is perhaps not surprising that Thomas frequently describes human beatitude in intellectualist terms. Beatitude is contemplation, participation in God's reflection on God's self; charity is a spiritual communication between God, angels, and humanity. Given this intellectualist or spiritualizing language, one would expect the outward, worldly life of the body to take a secondary role. In keeping with this approach, Thomas describes charitable love of the body as an "overflow" from one's love of the soul, but the body *per se* does not share in charity (ST II-II.25.5).

Even so, while the body's role in charity appears to be secondary, it nonetheless takes on great importance. As Thomas writes, it is through the body that one comes to a perfect knowledge or enjoyment of God in this life. The body is not just a central part of human life, but an essential aspect of divine charity. In an essay on John 6, Michel Corbin notes that for Thomas, Jesus' Incarnation is the outgrowth— or "overflow"—of the love of the Trinity, the self-diffusion of divine goodness extending love to creation and humanity. The divine love of charity operates through condescension, lowering itself to take on material form, precisely so that creation can be raised into spiritual fellowship. This is not, as Corbin notes, a change in God, but rather a change in creatures. The eminence of divine love is found in its self-abasement, which signifies the sureminence of divine love in the Dionysian sense.[85] Thus, when human charity overflows into the love of the body, this is an affirmation,

---

85 Michel Corbin, "Le Pain de la Vie: La lecture de Jean VI par S. Thomas d' Aquin," *Recherches des Sciences Religieuses* 65 (1977), pp. 107-38. Corbin also highlights the eucharistic and sacramental dimension of Thomas' understanding of the Incarnation.

anticipation, and imitation of divine goodness—an act of faith, hope, and love, reciprocating Christ's generous gift and bringing creation into divine fellowship.

In addition to the Incarnation, the body is also important in charity for its functional and external activity, extending charity into the world and establishing relations between people. The love of the body is connected with its ability to be an "instrument of justice" (Rom. 6:13, quoted in II-II.25.5). Love of the body, then, furthers this chapter's reflections on the relation between charity and justice. This section will focus on the *passionate* nature of embodiment. Passions, the emotions and feelings by which we interact with the world in a bodily way, are central to Thomas' account of human action and agency. Shaping what we do as well as why and how we do it, passions play a central role in human intentionality, and must be taken into account.

Passions are our bodily responses to events around us. When ordered by virtue, they tell us what is right and wrong with our world.[86] On an Aristotelian view, that we feel a greater attachment to parents than to strangers is not a selfish interest; it may rather be a passionate signal that we *owe* more to our parents than to others. By helping us to discern what we owe to different others, the passions play a central role in our acting justly in the world. Insofar as charity orders the passions and appropriates their activity toward a new end, it thereby enacts the relation between love of God and justice in the world.

A number of recent scholars on Aquinas have focused on the importance of the passions in Thomas' account of love and friendship.[87] More often than not, their focus has been to emphasize the role that our emotional and embodied selves play in moral deliberation, challenging intellectualist and deontological reductions of the value of emotional attachments. While their work will guide this reading, the focus here will be somewhat different, exploring the role of passionate embodiment in the order of charity. To this end, this section focuses on fear, a passion that remains in charity. The reshaping of fear in charity will help us to understand two important features of Thomas' work: first, how charity takes embodiment seriously, and second, given the body's connection with justice, how the new Law of charity fulfills rather than dissolves the old Law and its concern for justice.

A recognition of the reality of fear is central to Thomas' moral psychology. Properly distinguished by the temporality and quality of its object, fear regards a future evil which may befall us, one that from our present vantage point appears "irresistible" (*cui resisti non potest*, I-II.41.2). Fear's complex character locates it within the irascible passions. Thomas distinguishes the irascible passions from the concupiscible passions by two important features. First, irascible passions are

---

86 Diana Fritz Cates, *Choosing to Feel: Friendship and Compassion in Aristotle and Thomas Aquinas* (Notre Dame, IN: University of Notre Dame Press, 1997), pp. 21-3.

87 Cates, *Choosing to Feel*; Wadell, *Friendship and the Moral Life*, and *The Primacy of Love: An Introduction to the Ethics of Thomas Aquinas* (New York: Paulist Press, 1992); G. Simon Harak, *Virtuous Passions: The Formation of Christian Character* (New York: Paulist Press, 1993).

complex and intellective, regarding future goods and evils that are difficult to attain or avoid. Second, the irascible passions move one to action in a way the simple, concupiscible passions do not.[88]

The difference between concupiscible and irascible passions can be seen by distinguishing sadness and fear in two parallel instances. For example, if I am playing soccer, and my opponent cleats me from behind, my reaction will be one of pain. This immediate suffering is a concupiscible passion; an evil (i.e., pain and bruising) has befallen me, but there is nothing I can do about it, since I immediately feel it. However, if I am running toward the ball, and see that my opponent is about to kick it, I may gauge by our respective positions that the ball is going to strike me squarely in the face. I'm about to take one for the team, and it looks for all purposes unavoidable. This is a future yet irresistible evil, and my reaction is the irascible passion of fear.

Because the evil has not yet happened, fear can move me to act in a way that the concupiscible passion cannot. Thomas describes the movement of fear as "contraction." While the biological explanation is specious (i.e., bodily fluids flowing to the center of the body), he nonetheless seems correct about the psychological response, as one cringes in fear. I may hunch over and turn away, to try to take the impact on my back or avoid the ball if possible. I may "contract" to avoid the soccer ball because I like having my front teeth; insofar as I do, fear leads me to act. I may also take counsel from others to help me overcome the evil I face (in this case, "Duck!"). The danger foreseen is the efficient cause of the fear, and it is foreseen as a danger because of a good that I seek or wish to maintain. The good that one loves is thus the material cause of fear (ST I-II.43.1). Fear moves one to act to protect the good that one loves.

The fear proper to charity is fear of God. Discussed in the context of the theological virtue of hope in the *secunda secundae*, Thomas' analysis of fear of God draws heavily on his general understanding of fear. Thomas recognizes the strangeness of saying that one fears God, since God is one's final end and perfect beatitude, yet the fear of God is central to his scriptural tradition.[89] Thomas therefore makes a distinction between two ways of fearing God—the fear of a servant (*timor servilis*) and the fear of a child (*timor filialis*). While filial fear and servile fear initially seem opposed, Thomas' analysis brings them into an order in which *both* remain in charity. The ordering of the passions demonstrates how the change in John 15 from "servants" to "friends" affects us in bodily terms.

Servile fear is a fear that seeks to avoid punishment (ST II-II.19.2). Servile fear is not interested in the commands of a lord for their own sake; rather, a servant seeks to avoid the pain and suffering a lord can inflict in punishment. The servant fears

---

[88] Wadell, *The Primacy of Love*, pp. 98-101; Harak, *Virtuous Passions*, p. 94.

[89] In the sed contra to ST II-II.19.1 (*Utrum Deus possit timeri*), Thomas cites Jeremiah 10:7 ("Who would not fear you, King of the nations, for fear is a fitting tribute for you?"), and Malachi 1:6 ("If I am a master, where is the fear due to me? So says the Lord of Hosts to you, priests who despise my name.").

punishment out of self-love, wishing to avoid distress. This manifests the disordered aspects of servile fear, which takes bodily preservation as its primary good. Its sense of self-love is restricted to the nonrational self and excludes the work of reason. Servile fear is thus an "inordinate" fear, restricting not only the movements of the body but the movements of the soul as well (ST I-II.44.4).[90] Likewise, servile fear fulfills God's commands begrudgingly and only as commanded, remaining estranged from God. Because this fear is opposed to reason, it is also opposed to freedom, and thus considered in itself an evil (ST II-II.19.4). However, it is the servile aspect of fear, not fear itself, that is the evil. This understanding of the passion clearly parallels the discussion of servants found in Thomas' commentary on John.

The fear of a child (*timor filialis*) differs from the fear of a servant in the object of its fear. The child fears guilt (*timor culpae*) because guilt brings *separation* from the parent. The good that the child seeks to uphold is the relationship with the parent. To avoid separation, then, one seeks to reside in the will of the one whom one loves: the fear of a child draws her closer to the object of her love. Moreover, to avoid separation, one seeks to do what the parent desires. Seeking counsel and engaging one's rational capacity, the fear of a child is thus a properly-ordered fear (ST I-II.44.2). In filial fear of God, one seeks counsel in the Law, and strives to fulfill the commands so as to avoid the evil of separation from God's will.

As Thomas points out, however, filial fear does not simply negate servile fear, but rather integrates and reorders it. Filial fear retains self-love (*amor sui*) from servile fear, but redefines it (ST II-II.19.6). Whereas servile self-love consisted in avoidance of pain, self-love in the filial sense is love of one's relationship to God, and of one's ability to exercise reason. Filial fear arises when the intellective conversation of reason (and thereby the possibility of friendship with God) is threatened. Self-love remains, but it is love of the self in relation to God; the fear of punishment is lost. Filial fear drives one to act or seek counsel so as to retain the possibility of one's final end or beatitude in the life of the soul.

Filial fear, as the ordering of servile fear to a more human conception of self-love, could be called "good" servile fear. This reordering of fear parallels the connection between being a "friend of God" and a "good servant" noted earlier in Thomas' commentary on John 15. The analysis of fear, however, adds to our earlier discussion by showing how the passions and bodily aspects of humanity are integrated into charity. Only when the passions are properly shaped by the virtues, so that the body and the mind are brought into harmony, is participation in the divine life possible. Thomas clearly and emphatically states that fear remains in the life of charity, and *in patria* as well (ST II-II.19.11), in that continued filial fear is connected with an increase in charity (ST II-II.19.10).

Fear does not lead to wisdom only in the intellective sense, but rather to reverence of God and obedience to God's precepts, shaping one's practical deliberation and

---

90 Inordinate fear, as opposed to moderate fear, affects not only the body but also the soul (ST I-II.44.4).

activity.[91] In that the body, as an "instrument of justice," becomes an instrument for the fulfillment of these precepts, one comes to love it properly.

Fear remains within charity, and helps impel us to obey God's law; this is useful in terms of understanding how one can prefer some neighbors over others. For Thomas, the hierarchy of relations with neighbors is based on the law; in charity, one should love more those whom it would be more of a sin *not* to love under the law. As Thomas writes:

> One's obligation to love a person is proportionate to the gravity of the sin one commits in acting against that love. Now it is a more grievous sin to act against the love of certain neighbors, than against the love of others ... Therefore we ought to love some neighbors more than others. (ST II-II.26.6)

This love, Thomas continues, not only regards exterior actions, but the interior affections as well. In charity, one's affections toward certain neighbors, friends, or family members are taken seriously.[92] Thomas expects that one would love a friend more passionately than an enemy, even if one loves both of them in charity. Similarly, one should love one's parents more as regards what one owes to them, while one's love for a spouse is more intense in feeling on account of the closeness of the union (ST II-II.26.11).[93] The fear of separation, from both God and certain neighbors, leads to a more intense demonstration of love towards them.

Fear's continuance within charity thus creates space for the other passions by moving one to uphold the law—the counsels that keep one close to God. The specific precepts of the law regarding duties to parents, spouse, and community order and validate the passions that attach us to those around us. In charity, however, these passions (and the fulfillment of the law) are ordered by charity's habitual precept to love *all* who can participate in the divine life. Charity, as a virtue, means one no longer loves parents or natural kin as such; but rather, that in light of one's love of God, one habitually orders the affections and passions that bind one to a specific community.

Still, Thomas recognizes, more than many Christian theologians, the risks involved in attachment to family, natural origin, and community. These attachments and our passionate commitments are as likely to be obstacles to love of God as conduits thereto. The passions, one could say, do not directly *refer* us to God. Indeed, in many of his examples of whom one should hate on account of love of God Thomas names family and friends, precisely because the passions can misdirect one's attention. Commenting on Luke 14:26 ("If anyone come to me and hate not his father and mother, wife and children, brothers and sisters, even his own life, he cannot be a disciple of mine"), Thomas writes:

---

91 ST II-II.19.7.
92 Aquinas, *De Caritate*, p. 77.
93 Ibid., p. 80.

We are commanded to hate, in our kindred, not their kinship, but only the fact of their being an obstacle between us and God. In this respect they are not akin but hostile to us, according to Micah 7:6: "A man's enemies are they of his own household".[94]

The risk of these passions, on Thomas' view, is that excessive attachment to one's family will lead one to injustice. Nonetheless, without an appropriation of the passions and an ordering of them within charity, one could not love God humanly. Charity demands, then, both love of enemies, and enmity toward those we love; the affections that join us more closely to some neighbors must be both affirmed and denied for the full fruition of friendship with God.

Charity thus includes love of the body as an "overflow" of the love of the soul. Love of the soul leads to a just love of one's embodied life in family and community as well. Practically speaking, then, the love of charity overflows into the body as a concern for justice. Properly ordered by charity, the passions allow us to pay more adequate attention to the particulars that determine a rich conception of distributive justice. As Diana Cates writes, "Construed in light of his theory of the passions, Thomas' reflections on the deliberative process also suggest that ordinate passions make possible a more complete knowledge of particulars (represented by the minor premise)."[95] While charity habitually orders us to equal regard for all persons as potential participants in the divine life, the passions help us to act more strongly toward those around us. One could borrow the following from a bumper sticker: charity teaches us to think globally, and the passions move us to act locally. Such local action, moreover, allows for a richer conception of distributive justice, as it integrates the multilayered and complex relationships of society *within* the love of charity.

The love of charity, through its incorporation of the body, manifests a concern not only for self and neighbor with regards to supernatural happiness, but also according to our nature, taking seriously what is required for distributive justice. As Westberg writes:

> Having the right end, namely the attainment of God through love, does not guarantee good actions, because as Thomas so frequently states, right action is a matter of proper ends *and* right choice of means. Having the right ultimate end is necessary for complete virtue but not sufficient: one continues to need prudence to judge not only particular action, but the secondary ends which now become means to the ultimate end.[96]

---

94 ST II-II.26.7 ad 1. Likewise, in his discussion of love of enemies as such (which, as we have seen, is a sin), Thomas' example is David's love of Absalom, since Absalom has rebelled against him and the rest of the people of Israel, and yet as his son David still loves him more than all of Israel.

95 Cates, *Choosing to Feel*, p. 23. While in this passage Cates is discussing acquired (i.e., natural) moral virtue, *Choosing to Feel* argues for the centrality of the passions to charity and supernatural virtue as well, and I am in agreement with her on this point.

96 Westberg, *Right Practical Reason*, p. 255, my emphasis.

Directing oneself to God—seeking to remain close to God's heart—*requires* the exercise of the virtues of prudence and justice, both as habits and as actions, and this only occurs through the passions. Friendship with God, then, not only accomplishes God's predestination of humans to participation in the divine life, but likewise moves one to an affective concern for justice in the world as well. Without the passions, as shaped by a fear of separation from God, charity's engagement with the world would remain incomplete.

Conclusion: Charity as Eminent Friendship

In exploring Thomas' discussion of friendship with God through the order of charity, several central points have emerged. First, while Thomas' ethics draw upon Aristotle, his discussion of charity is intimately connected with the systematic theology of the *Summa*; in charity, we see the workings of grace and free will, the importance of the Incarnation, and the practical outworking of his views on predestination. Second, as these systematic concerns run through the discussion of charity, a new form of friendship emerges that subverts Aristotelian friendship from within his terminology. Third, in attending to each level of the order of charity, we have seen how charity, while a spiritual fellowship, also integrates other dimensions of human life—psychology, sociality, and embodiment. Explicating these points, and considering the relation between the pragmatics of charity and the semantics of naming God, will provide a concluding summary of Thomas' thought and lay the groundwork for a transition to and comparison with the poststructuralist thought of Derrida.

First, it is clear that in his discussion of the moral life in the *secunda pars* of the *Summa*, Thomas' concerns are primarily theological. His discussions of the role of grace in the formation of habits, and especially in the supernatural habits of faith, hope, and charity, demonstrate a profound integration between the practical life and scriptural interpretation. In Thomas' interpretation of the Gospel of John, systematics and ethics are at one. Given the chronological proximity of the commentary and the *Summa*, as well as the consonance between their views, it is reasonable to argue that the *secunda pars* is as much about God's activity toward us, and how we should reciprocate such love, as a study in the intentionality and structure of human moral action. The perfection of human action in charity and friendship with God is, at the same time, the perfection of God's plan for humanity within creation. Charity demonstrates the coherence of Thomas' thought in a way that is not only overarching and systematic, but intimately at work throughout the particulars of human life as well.

Second, Thomas' discussion of charity imagines a new, transcendent possibility of friendship that differs from Aristotle in terms of orientation, activity, and politics (in the sense of determining the shape and limits of community). In seeking to love God for God's sake, charity is a fellowship that Aristotle could not imagine, and through the activity of the Spirit, an equality between God and humanity emerges that overcomes the great distance which rendered such friendship impossible. It also, significantly, extends the idea of equality to all participants in charity, much further than the equality of complete Aristotelian friendship. In its activity—keeping secrets of God close to one's heart, and remembering the love that Christ showed in his life, crucifixion, and resurrection—the activity of this friendship differs from Aristotelian friendship as well. In charity, it is a friendship based upon character and goodness, but the character and goodness that constitute the relationship are divine.

Finally, the politics of charity differ from Aristotelian friendship, which only extends between those of the same rational nature—those who share the same language, and are of the same city, and most likely of the same age and gender. As love of enemies is both a precept and perfection of charity, it opens the community of faith beyond self-enclosed limits. The possibility of charity and its habitual ordering of our actions change the shape of friendship. While charity directs us to love of those for whom we have affection, such as family and friends with whom we share a common upbringing, familial tie, or natural origin, it at least makes conceivable the idea of a friendship based upon something radically different. Only by ordering these relationships in light of the love of enemies does one come to love friends and family as neighbors, and thus grow into friendship with God. This is, at the least, a displacement of Aristotelian essentialism as a basis for friendship, even if it does not dispense with the Aristotelian model entirely. Charity thus goes beyond Aristotelian friendship, both "vertically" and "horizontally," raising one toward a transcendent friendship with God, but also opening new possibilities of friendship within humanity as well.

Third, while charity is a transformation of friendship, it nevertheless respects the integrity of human activity. Charity may direct us to a new end, but as the form of the virtues, it integrates and affirms human nature. This happens at each level of the order of charity. In order for charity to be voluntary, and thus truly a reciprocal relationship, it requires creation of a supernatural habit. In order for charity to be social and political, it cultivates love of neighbor, and affirms one's obligations to parents and community as integral aspects of the common good. In order for charity to be affective and embodied, it integrates the passions, which move one toward love of God and neighbor. In each way, charity becomes friendship in the deepest sense, as God's love affirms and blesses the embodied, finite character of human activity, allowing us to reciprocate God's action as who we are. Here, the Thomistic principle that grace perfects nature rather than destroying it bears its most remarkable fruits.

In light of these points, the relationship between naming God and friendship for Thomas can be clarified. In looking at these issues together, two points of confluence become clear, and they point toward reading the discourse on charity in a Dionysian direction. The first is that charity, on the part of God, is an *eminent* love or friendship. That is, it is a friendship that we can only represent or imitate at a distance, in the diverse actions of charity as a habit and as a relationship to God and the world. Much as naming God involves both concrete and abstract modes of signification, so too charity involves both concrete actions and abstract precepts. There must be a general, or universal, love of all neighbors, but this cannot annihilate the particularity of one's attachments to family, friends, and community; one will love some neighbors more than others. Simultaneously, one must "hate" those for whom one has affection, precisely so as to negate the limited, even exclusionary character of a love based on human affection. In the perfection of charity, in which one loves an enemy as an individual, one most closely imitates divine love, but one does so by concretely loving this one enemy, but also by thereby showing that one's charity does extend universally, to potentially include any neighbor. Thus, we see a Dionysian pragmatics at work, as both the concrete and abstract aspects of the human moral life are both affirmed and denied, so as to lead toward an eminent love that imitates the divine *caritas* that transcends representation.

Second, Dionysian metaphysics conceives of creation as the self-diffusion of divine goodness, its ecstatic unfolding out of love. This begins as descent, from spiritual goodness into its imitation in material forms, but then through the material returns to itself in an ascent. Naming God, in both *The Divine Names* and *The Mystical Theology*, reflects this pattern. In charity, a similar descent/ascent pattern can be discerned, since one begins in the order of charity with the spiritual love of God, which unfolds into concern for one's neighbors' spiritual goods, and finally to love of the body. In the love of the body, moreover, one practices justice as the unfolding of divine good in the world. This "descent," however, also brings about an ascent, as one is thereby raised into greater spiritual fellowship with God, wisdom, and enjoys God as perfectly as a wayfarer can in this life. The order of charity is, in a sense, a hierarchy: spiritual goods are privileged, and some neighbors are granted greater proximity. But as with Dionysius, the point of such hierarchy seems to be to show the radically kenotic nature of love, its unfolding across such boundaries and barriers.

If charity follows the descent/ascent pattern of the Dionysian good, it also thereby acts as an *imitatio Christi*. It imitates Christ's Incarnation, and thereby establishes the likeness and union requisite for human friendship with God. To be sure, the union and friendship are not as strong as the union and love in the Incarnation itself, but they participate in charity to the extent that God deigns to count us as friends. In these ways, Thomas' account of charity integrates an Aristotelian ethics into a Dionysian theology, directing the workings of human action toward an eminent, transcendent end that we know in faith, christologically.

Looking at naming God and friendship, then, as the semantic and pragmatic dimensions of singularity, serves a valuable purpose in interpreting Thomas' work. In looking at Thomas' account of naming God, it became clear that sacred doctrine enabled new modes of reference and activity, but this may still have seemed somewhat inchoate. However, looking at charity along with Thomas' account of theological language illuminates how sacred doctrine's naming of God enables a way of life, not just an abstract set of principles. In charity, the life of sacred doctrine unfolds in a series of relations that exceed and transform the limits of Aristotelian friendship.

Thus, to this point, we have explored two accounts of naming and friendship. The essentialist approach to both cognitive and ethical relations found in Aristotle has been displaced by the Thomistic emphasis on the relation to God that is more intimate than we can know—both in terms of our language and our friendships.

Thus, in both Aristotelian and Thomistic thought, naming and friendship converge, as semantic and pragmatic correlates. A third convergence of naming and friendship, as found in the work of Jacques Derrida, will point us toward further questions regarding Thomas, the Dionysian tradition, and whether they break with Aristotelian essentialism and its exclusivity. The ethics of deconstruction, then, will enable a further reflection and evaluation in the conclusion on the significance of Thomas' work, in thinking the naming of and friendship with God.

Chapter 5

Naming the Impossibility of Friendship: On Jacques Derrida

> These people here will go away saying that we are friends of one another—for I count myself in with you—but what a friend is we have not yet been able to find out.
>
> —Plato, *Lysis*

To this point, we have explored the convergence of names and friendship in traditional Christian theology and philosophy as studies of singularity. In the work of both Thomas and Aristotle, naming, as a way of singularly identifying, has been closely related to both friendship and necessary knowledge. For Thomas, this is especially true for relation to God: without the eminent discourse by which one names God and "knows" God in faith, one could not love God for God's own sake in charity. The identity of naming, through eminent discourse, guides and stabilizes the path of friendship.

Over against these approaches, the work of Jacques Derrida questions the assumptions of the linkages between friendship, singularity, and knowledge in the activity of naming. In thinking of friendship as exceeding what can be named, Derrida's work dislocates the philosophical conceptions of naming and friendship, rethinking both practices through the subversion of metaphysics. If the singular object of either a cognitive or ethical relation cannot appear as such, then one's intention of that object is unsettled from its inception. The impossibility of presence, perhaps the most widely-known idea from Derrida's work, requires that one think of relation as exceeding cognition, such that the other's singularity exceeds the thematic or designative grasp of the subject. If the relation to the other exceeds representation, then this reshapes conceptions of both friendship and the naming of God.

The trajectory of Derrida's work parallels the concerns of this study; his early work, in its focus on writing and textuality, examined the logic of proper names. More recent work has built upon these reflections in terms of naming God and the relationship between deconstruction and negative theology. In the last few years, friendship has become a central topic in Derrida's articulation of the ethical and political import of deconstruction, particularly in his reworkings of the concepts of responsibility and decision. Of particular interest here will be his arguments that relation exceeds cognition both linguistically and ethically, in the openness of prayer as an address beyond predication and in the openness of friendship beyond brotherhood and natural origin. This leads to what I would term a *counter-convergence* of naming God and friendship: a convergence of ideas of friendship and naming that goes beyond the cognitive, essentialist emphasis that predominates in Aristotle and is at work within Thomism as well.

This chapter explores the significance of the deconstruction of conceptions of proper names and friendship for theological reflection, and it therefore proceeds in several steps. First, it will analyze Derrida's deconstruction of the connection between proper names and identity, and how this reshapes our understanding of singularity. The second section then builds upon this discussion by developing Derrida's thought on the issue of naming God in light of the work of Martin Heidegger and Emmanuel Levinas, with particular attention to the topics of prayer and praise. The third section of the chapter then considers Derrida's work on friendship, exploring Derrida's conception of friendship in dialogue with his friend and colleague Maurice Blanchot. The parallels between Blanchot and Derrida help to clarify the ways in which Derrida's work on friendship challenges the limits of Aristotelian friendship. This establishes a basis for the chapter's concluding synthesis, which brings together Derrida's discussions of naming God and friendship in terms of *testimony* as a relation to the other that refuses cognitive determination.

The latter part of the chapter thus serves both critical and constructive purposes. In demonstrating the impossibility of naming properly or being friends with another as such, deconstruction gives rise to a noncanonical, alternative version of love and friendship. Our primary concern in considering these issues is to see if they provide a viable alternative to Aristotelian singularity, perhaps avoiding its essentialist implications, particularly in terms of a reduction of friendship to fraternal likeness and natural origin.

The progression of this chapter moves toward this essay's concluding comparison and analysis. In his engagement with negative or apophatic theology in "How Not to Speak: Denials" and *Sauf le Nom*, Derrida re-reads both Augustine's work and that of Pseudo-Dionysius—central sources for Thomas' understanding of divine names. Rereading these sources with Derrida sets up an engagement between Thomas and Derrida, and brings the relationship between deconstruction and theology into greater relief and clarity, in terms of their understandings of language and their conceptions of responsibility, friendship, gift, and singularity as well. In rethinking the politics of friendship in light of the command to love one's enemies, Derrida tacitly enters into conversation with Thomas' own politics, as this command is a central precept of charity. The respective convergences between naming God and friendship in each author's work will enable a conversation and rethinking of their respective politics and views on community and friendship.

A preliminary definition of deconstruction would be that deconstruction exhibits the ruination at the heart of any conceptual unity. Kevin Hart provides a concise definition that highlights two central features of deconstruction: "its ability to show that what seems to be a monistic whole is always already doubled, and its tendency to double itself."[1] Deconstruction takes such doubling as both positive and negative:

---

1 Kevin Hart, *The Trespass of the Sign: Deconstruction, Theology, and Philosophy* (Cambridge: Cambridge University Press, 1989), p. 117.

if a concept is ruined at its heart, then it is impossible. And yet, simultaneously, this "ruin" also lets the concept be itself. The ruin that deconstruction speaks to is the condition of possibility for a concept, even while being its condition of impossibility.

To exemplify this constitutive "doubling" or ruin, let us consider an example of friendship. Aristotle undertakes what could be termed a phenomenology of friendship in book ix of the *Ethics*, when he inquires as to the essence of friendship. The content of this passage is well-known, but let us pay attention to how Aristotle's argument presents the essence of friendship:

> Friendly relations with one's neighbors, and the marks by which friendships are defined, seem to have proceeded from a man's relations to himself. For (1) we define a friend as one who wishes and does what is good, or seems so, for the sake of his friend, or (2) as one who wishes his friend to exist and live, for his sake; which mothers do to their children, and friends do who have come into conflict. And (3) others define him as one who lives with and (4) has the same tastes as another, or (5) one who grieves and rejoices with his friend; and this too is found in mothers most of all. It is by some one of these characteristics that friendship too is defined.
> Now each of these is true of the good man's relation to himself. (NE ix.4)

In defining the qualities that constitute friendship, it happens that these qualities are most present—apparent, and knowable—in self-love. Since self-love has all of the qualities of friendship, it is the *best* example of friendship that one could have. Self-love's privilege in Aristotle is unquestioned. Yet self-love is still only an *example* of friendship—it is not the essence of friendship itself. For if one could be friends simply with oneself, then in the best friendship there would be *no* friends.

Aristotle was clearly aware of this problem: "Whether there is or is not friendship between a man and himself is a question we may dismiss for the present; there would seem to be friendship *insofar as he is two or more*."[2] The meaning of this statement is twofold: first, there is friendship if there is more than one person; but second, one loves *oneself* properly—as does a person of good character—in friendship with another. One loves oneself well by loving others, in justice and friendship. Only one's openness to the other in justice and virtue distinguishes the self-love of the good from the worst egoism.[3] Self-love, to be self-love, requires friendship with another. Friendship must be with more than one, doubling itself to make self-love; self-love must be deferred, and not fully present in order to appear. Here, even while acknowledging the stated privilege of self-love in Aristotelian friendship, one can recognize that its difference from itself, in its openness to the other, constitutes its very possibility and origin.

While self-love's exemplarity founds the order of complete, fraternal friendship that Aristotle held so dear, its constitution in this passage opens a series of questions regarding both its priority and its politics. Self-love, from which all Aristotelian

---

2   NE, ix.4, p. 228.
3   Ibid., ix.8.

friendship proceeds, is not the first friendship to come onto the scene. The first friend that we encounter in this passage is a mother. Maternity is associated with the two active qualities of friendship, which are *more* of the essence of friendship than being-loved. The figure of the mother is called up within this discussion to manifest certain qualities of friendship. Yet, strangely enough, once friendship is conceived within the parameters of self-love—where both loving and being-loved occur simultaneously, as *present*, so that friendship is between those who are the same and reciprocal—maternal friendship recedes from view. Non-oppositional difference never appears as such; only a trace is found in the mother's figuration of difference as that which can be neutralized, and this trace is always already effaced in its presentation. In this case, the mother is called up to figure the properties of friendship, and then suppressed; in the process, sexual difference is excluded from friendship proper.[4]

Derrida often reads the effacement of sexual difference as representative of the effacement of singularity, via the privileging of relations that are presentable and therefore knowable. It is only a short step from love of self to love of "another self," as Aristotle describes friendship, precisely in the love of the brother.[5] Once the neutralization of difference is effected, *philia* is thought within the realm of the same. The point here, however, is that a double gesture constitutes the identity of this friendship: on the one hand, the repetition and differentiation of loving in friendship, and thus its difference from itself, but also its effacement of non-oppositional difference in neutralizing sexual difference. Both gestures contribute to the exemplary privilege of a certain conception of friendship.

This discussion of friendship in Aristotle raises two important questions about the conception of friendship within philosophy. First, as self-love requires openness to the other, otherness would seem to be at the heart of philosophy's self-constitution. The openness of good character to the other in justice and virtue illustrates that a restricted alterity is conceivable within philosophical friendship. But second, the limits to this openness are seen in the exclusion of the mother from friendship; the self constituted in this openness always risks effacing its nonsimple origin. It risks thinking the other simply as another self, foreclosing difference and doing violence to the other. As Derrida writes, "Invention of the other—is it the absolute initiative for which the other is responsible and accountable? Or is it rather the other that I imagine

---

4 With regard to friendship between husband and wife, Derrida reads Aristotle as stating that a friendship of the highest sort is only possible insofar as both husband and wife have virtue—and thus, to the extent that the wife is virile, so that friendship even in this case would seem to remain fraternal. See Jacques Derrida, *Politics of Friendship*, trans. G. Collins (New York: Verso, 1994), p. 168.

5 As quoted before: "Parents, then, love their children as themselves ... and brothers love each other as being born of the same parents; for their identity with them makes them identical with each other (which is the reason why people talk of 'the same blood,' 'the same stock,' and so on). They are, therefore, in a sense the same thing, though in separate individuals" (NE, viii.12, p. 213).

as a retention of my psyche, my soul, my mirror image?"[6] The proximity of these two gestures—openness to and assimilation of alterity—in Aristotle's discussion of self-love is remarkable. This proximity of hospitality and xenophobia, apparently arising in tandem, will be our explicit concern later in this chapter, and it gives a preliminary sense of the stakes involved in questioning the philosophical conception of friendship. To approach this question in light of Derrida's corpus, our focus will first turn to deconstruction's displacement of the philosophical understanding of names and singularity.

I. Names and the Im(possible) Possibility of Singularity

As discussed in chapter 2, Kripke's work exemplifies two central philosophical doctrines challenged by deconstruction: first, the idea of necessary identity, and second, scientific knowledge as the *telos* of language and relation. As Kripke argues, proper names as rigid designators have a necessary identity unchanged in all possible worlds. As an identity that is true in all possible worlds, rigid designation is an immediate, unmediated identity. This identity of proper names, for Kripke, is central to the possibility of *scientific* discovery. Analogously, self-identity is equally central to the establishment of scientific necessity in the transcendental projects of Kant and Husserl. Thus, from its first challenges to necessary identity, Derridean deconstruction has interrogated this philosophical conception of proper names. By showing the impossibility of thinking identity without difference, deconstruction calls such singular reference and its ensuing necessity into question. Derrida's approach to proper names challenges Kripke's theory of reference, and exhibits how deconstruction rethinks singularity in light of the impossibility of presence.

Derrida's early work can be described as a Socratic questioning of necessary identity—identity of consciousness, the *cogito*, or a transcendental signified. As Derrida discusses in *Speech and Phenomena*, Husserl's phenomenology privileges speech over writing because of speech's apparent self-presence to the speaker; in this self-presence, speech manifests the identity required for a purely scientific thinking better than writing does. Husserl then demonstrates that this self-presence is at work even more purely within thought, which requires no external expression whatsoever. By showing that the "spacing" associated with writing and difference is internal to both thought and speech (most basically, in that these must be excluded for speech and thought to be conceived), Derrida undoes their apparently necessary identity, and their privilege over writing. In order to be itself, the transcendental ego must differ from itself, spatially and temporally, exhibiting the movement that Derrida terms *différance*.[7]

---

6 Jacques Derrida, "How Not to Speak," quoted in Richard Kearney, "Derrida's Ethical Re-turn," in G. Madison (ed.), *Working Through Derrida* (Evanston: Northwestern University Press, 1993), p. 29.

7 See, in particular, Jacques Derrida, *Speech and Phenomena and Other Essays on Husserl's Theory of Signs*, trans. D. Allison (Evanston: Northwestern University Press, 1973), pp. 85-7.

Where *Speech and Phenomena* calls into question the necessary identity of consciousness, *Of Grammatology* overturns the necessary identity of proper names, and the privileged place they occupy within metaphysics. *Of Grammatology* is perhaps best known for Derrida's critique of Saussure's theory of the sign, but the notion of the proper name is central to the contradictions and aporias that arise therein. For Saussure, a sign is composed of two parts: the signified (i.e., the referent) and its signifier (that which indicates the referent). Derrida shows two important tenets of Saussure's theory to be incompatible with each other, and here again we are dealing with the privileging of speech over writing due to its presence of intention and certainty of meaning. The first tenet is that signifiers are arbitrarily related to their signified; given the variety of ways in which languages describe the world and divide it into namable entities, one cannot simply see a word as representative of an object. Rather, a word acquires its meaning through its place within a system of signs and in its differences from other signifiers; it is through these differences within language that a signifier is linked with its signified and set in place.

Saussure's second, contradictory tenet is that sound has a "natural bond" with meaning; phonic signifiers are intrinsically and necessarily related to the meaning which they signify. Based on this natural or essential connection, Saussure can treat writing as exterior to the proper essence of language. This thesis is central for relegating the arbitrariness of the sign (the relation between signifier and signified) to a secondary role. If the arbitrariness of the signifier remained primary, meaning would only be produced through the differences between signs and would have *no* necessity; linguists could not hope to discover anything in a scientific fashion. Because of this "natural bond," Saussure can claim that the meaning of a graphic signifier is actually determined by the meaning of the phonic sign that it represents— a meaning that, as proper and essential to the linguistic system, gives the *necessity* requisite for linguistics to become a science of language. The phonic sign connects with one meaning; it signifies singularly, much like a proper name, as we shall see. However, Saussure must then turn around and exclude the phonic sign because it is in fact a material element spoken within time and space; only by such exclusion can the *langue/parole* opposition of his work take shape.[8] This is the first indication that there is "archi-writing" at work within speech. Rather than writing being dependent upon speech for its meaning, speech is rather a form of writing.[9]

Derrida's concern is not to privilege writing as such over speech, but rather to demonstrate that the self-presence and identity of the privileged concept is constituted through its differential elements. Writing must be made derivative, exterior (spatially differentiated), and subsequent (temporally differentiated), in order for speech to maintain its natural bond to meaning. Inverting Saussure's argument, Derrida argues that this movement of *différance* constitutes the meanings of speech and writing. As Derrida writes in "Différance":

---

8 Jacques Derrida, *Of Grammatology*, trans. G. Spivak (Baltimore: Johns Hopkins University Press, 1976), pp. 27-73.
9 Derrida, *Of Grammatology*, pp. 44-68.

What is written as *différance*, then, will be the playing movement that "produces"—by means of something that is not simply an activity—these differences, these effects of difference. This does not mean that the *différance* that produces differences is somehow before them, in a simple and unmodified—in-different—present. *Différance* is the non-full, non-simple, structured and differentiating origin of differences. Thus, the name "origin" no longer suits it.[10]

This unmotivated movement of the trace can only be thought in its effacement; the trace, irreducible to its effects, makes possible the opposition of speech and writing while simultaneously exceeding and undoing this opposition. *Différance* appears only as a trace, in the production of differences:

> The trace, where the relationship with the other is marked, articulates its possibility in the entire field of the entity, which metaphysics has defined as the being-present starting from the occulted movement of the trace ... When the other announces itself as such, it presents itself in the dissimulation of itself [i.e., the trace].[11]

The sign's constitution by differences, such that it never presents what it signifies as such, enables a relation to alterity, since one no longer claims to grasp the other, or what is signified, in the act of signifying.

In Kripke's philosophy, rigid designation provides the necessity that Saussure's naturally bonded signifier seeks. The rigid designation of proper names is another one of Derrida's targets in *Of Grammatology*, since singular reference appears to exceed the sorts of signification that Derrida describes. The rigidly designative reference of proper names is at the heart of Kripke's conception of how language relates us to things and persons.[12] While Derrida does not address Kripke's theory directly, his reading of Levi-Strauss on proper names can be brought into conversation with Kripke's argument.[13]

---

10 Jacques Derrida, "Différance," in *Margins of Philosophy*, trans. A. Bass (Chicago: University of Chicago Press, 1982), p. 11.

11 Derrida, *Of Grammatology*, p. 47.

12 See Kripke, *Naming and Necessity*, p. 127.

13 The differences between Derridean and Kripkean approaches to proper names are addressed by Christopher Norris in *The Deconstructive Turn: Essays in the Rhetoric of Philosophy* (New York: Meuthen, 1983) and Michael Spikes in two articles in *Soundings* and *Christianity and Literature*. Spikes's defense of Kripke is weakened by his failure to address the substance of Derrida's argument regarding names rather than just language in general. Moreover, his interpretation of Kripke fails to note the importance of the noncircularity condition (that I cannot simply use a name as I want to use it, but as *others* use it in order for it to refer) to Kripke's argument; this introduces a differential element into Kripke's account that is perhaps overlooked by both Norris and Spikes. For Spikes' views, see "Self-Present Meaning and the One-Many Paradox: A Kripkean Critique of Derrida," *Christianity and Literature* 37 (1988), pp. 13-28, and "Present Absence versus Absent Presence: Kripke Contra Derrida," *Soundings* 75 (1992), pp. 333-55.

Derrida's texts define proper names in a manner similar to Kripke. Derrida broaches the subject in discussing Levi-Strauss's anthropological analysis of the Nambikwara, and his analysis of their prohibition of speaking proper names:

> Before we consider this [the prohibition within Nambikwara culture of pronunciation of proper names], let us note that this prohibition is necessarily derivative with regard to the constitutive erasure of the proper name in what I have called arche-writing, within, that is the play of difference. It is because the proper names are already no longer proper names, because their production is their obliteration, because the erasure and the imposition of the letter are originary, because they do not supervene upon a proper inscription; it is because the proper name has never been, *as the unique appellation reserved for the presence of a unique being*, anything but the original myth of a transparent legibility present under the obliteration; it is because the proper name was never possible except through its functioning within a classification and therefore within a system of differences, within a writing retaining the traces of difference, that the interdict was possible, could come into play, and when the time came, as we shall see, could be transgressed; transgressed, that is to say restored to the obliteration and the non-self-sameness [*non-propriété*] at the origin.[14]

I quote this paragraph in its entirety because it articulates the crucial features of the Derridean approach to the problem of proper names. First, that a proper name is a "unique appellation reserved for the presence of a unique being" indicates that proper names epitomize singular reference, and a proper name, if it existed, would rigidly designate *one* entity. Derrida's argument, summarized here, is that what appear as proper names or singular appellations within language are *not* proper names. If language is constituted through the differences of signifiers, then what appears as a proper name is already no longer unique, but rather is inscribed in a differential system of signification.

As Derrida writes soon after, "When within consciousness, the name is *called proper*, it is already classified and is obliterated in being named. It is already no more than a so-called proper name."[15] Thus, proper names do not appear as such within language; already differing from themselves in their meaning, the singular reference of naming is impossible within a system of classification. As Geoff Bennington writes, "Naming does violence to the supposed unicity it is supposed to respect, it gives existence and withdraws it at the same time."[16] Singular reference is deferred through the signifier, even though the signifier is also the condition for such singular reference, as without the attempt to refer there would be no singular appellation at all.

---

14 Derrida, *Of Grammatology*, p. 109.

15 Ibid., my emphasis. Also p. 112: "To name, to give names that it will on occasion be forbidden to pronounce, such is the originary violence of language which consists in inscribing within a difference, in classifying, in suspending the vocative absolute."

16 Geoff Bennington, "Derridabase," in *Jacques Derrida*, trans. G. Bennington (Chicago: University of Chicago Press, 1993), p. 106.

The question that faces us, then, is whether Kripke's account of "rigid designation" present a picture of reference in which names have an identity independent of difference. Certain features of Kripke's "picture" would seem to indicate that this is the case. In that proper names are purely ostensive, and depart from the descriptive sense which requires a knowledge of the "totality" of the language, then if a name designates something in all possible worlds, its identity would seem to be prior to any differentiation or classification. Moreover, as initial baptism is a logical condition for the coherence of the theory of reference, his view does seem to posit an unmediated identity as the basis for reference.

However, this picture oversimplifies Kripke's account, and leaves out several important qualifications to his work. First, a name can only refer if its reference is noncircular. I cannot simply use a name as I wish to use a name; I must intend to use the name as others within a community either will use it or have used it.[17] Thus, there must already be some delay, difference, or possibility of repetition within the name in order for it to refer. Even "rigid" designation requires difference in order to maintain the stability of the reference, such that the meaning is never fully present. The causal chain of speakers in the community is as constitutive of a name's rigid designation as the notion of baptism itself. If I name my aardvark "Napoleon," then I am not using "Napoleon" in a way that can refer within my community. The name's reference must extend through time, to refer at all.

The real value of "initial baptism" to Kripke's picture of reference becomes evident when one considers how the noncircular condition treats identity as an effect of repetition and difference. By contrast, "initial baptism" allows us to think of the generation of a name's reference apart from any other names, abstracting the "causal" chain from other words used by the same community. This has two effects: it abstracts from a name's place within language, and from cases where a name may have more than one bearer, imagining an original connection between the name and its referent. This second abstraction, in John McDowell's terms, leads to an abstraction of the "chain of reference" from the world.[18] Further, when one considers that one properly names in relation to a world, one recognizes that the first abstraction from language *does* have a significant impact on the theory. Anyone named "Junior" or "the third" is well aware that his name is already classificatory even in being "proper." If reference is always already in relation to the world, then it is already improper, dissimulating the singularity of a proper name so it never appears as such.

These reflections do little to disturb the *workings* of Kripke's account of proper names, or the function they serve in language. However, by problematizing the idea of initial baptism, Derrida's work unsettles the necessary identity of reference, and its scientificity. Derrida's account of proper names places their uniquely appellative, singular address *beyond* language; singular address presents itself only as a trace in

---

17 Kripke, *Naming and Necessity*, pp. 68-72.
18 See John McDowell, "On the Sense and Reference of a Proper Name," in *Meaning, Knowledge, and Reality* (Cambridge, MA: Harvard University Press, 1998), pp. 171-98.

the words that we call "proper names." Singularity, on Derrida's view, exceeds the classificatory schema by which we know what things are, and remains unknowable. Relation to the other *qua* other goes *beyond* the name, since the name remains improper. But relation only goes beyond the name *through* the name, since the dissimulation of singular appellation in a system of classification works to guard the other's alterity. In light of these general reflections on proper names, it is now possible to consider how deconstruction reshapes the specific problematic of naming God.

II. Derrida on Naming God: Between Heidegger and Levinas

A. Levinas on Naming God

Insofar as deconstruction problematizes traditional understandings of the workings of language and discourse in general, religious discourse and the naming of God can be subjected to its scrutiny as well. The privileging of "writing"—the thought of the trace and *différance* as the nonsimple origin of discourse—troubles the naming of God, as all other names. Derrida's early work is emphatic in stating that the trace is not a theological gesture; in particular, the movement of *différance* should not be equated with a negative or apophatic theology even as both share a critical stance towards predication. The trace, for Derrida, exceeds the discourse of negative theology.[19]

Yet as we have already seen, the play of *différance* within naming is not simply a refusal of predication. Naming or singular reference cannot appear as such; but this does not mean that there is *no* signifying of singularity. The deferral of singularity and the differing of names both work to preserve and guard singularity, preventing its reduction to what can be known. While *différance* renders impossible a direct, present naming of God, this impossibility opens a different relation to God, possibly more respectful of God's alterity. In opening this possibility of thinking of naming God without knowing if God is thus named, Derrida's work is very close to the work of Emmanuel Levinas. At the same time, he bears in mind the Heideggerian critique of ontotheology, maintaining a distance from Levinas's exact position. This section will first examine Levinas's views on the naming of God, as well as some of the problems Derrida sees in Levinas's approach. In light of these considerations, one can then clarify how Derrida negotiates the impasse between Levinas and Martin Heidegger regarding revelation, predication, and the naming of God.

In both his phenomenology and his Talmudic interpretation, Levinas's work has contributed to the recent focus on God's name in recent continental thought in important ways. In the Tetragrammaton, God's name disrupts and reorients everyday practices of naming and thematization. According to Levinas's phenomenology of need and enjoyment, human naming is ordinarily undertaken within the ontological

---

19 See Jacques Derrida, "Différance," in *Margins of Philosophy*, p. 6.

realm of enjoyment and with an eye to one's own needs.[20] As Levinas describes it, in our general, thematic practices of naming and signification, my referring to a thing is undertaken solely with the intention of making it a thing in and for myself; the singularity of a name's referent is thought within the scope of my subjectivity.[21] For Levinas, this reduction of the other to cognition—to what is thematizable and representable within language—forecloses the possibility of ethics and responsibility. Insofar as my relation to the other, as cognitive, is demonstrable through discourse, it is a relation that anyone can have to any other, rather than a relation of unsubstitutable responsibility. Enjoyment reduces my infinite responsibility respect for the singular other to a finite, generalized, ontological responsibility.

The priority of ontology thus effaces singularity—the other's first, but my singularity in responsibility *for* the other as well. For Levinas, this effacement is evident in the privileging of the question, "what?" over the question, "who?" within Heideggerian philosophy. Against Heidegger, Levinas seeks to think relation as beyond thematic questions, which limit relation to what is knowable:

> In fact the question 'who is it' is not a question and is not satisfied by a knowing ... The face is not a modality of quiddity, an answer to a question, but the correlative of what is prior to every question. What is prior to every question is not in its turn a question nor a knowledge possessed a priori, but is Desire. The *who* correlative of Desire, the *who* to whom the question is put is, in metaphysics, a "notion" as fundamental and as universal as quiddity and being and the existent and the categories.[22]

While our ordinary uses of language, in their emphasis on knowledge and substance, reduce our relations to things in the world to *what* things can be for me, the face opens a singular relation of desire:

> To be sure, most of the time the *who* is a *what*. We ask "Who is Mr. X?" and we answer: "He is the President of the State Council," or "He is Mr. so-and-so." The answer presents itself as a quiddity: it refers to a system of relations. To the question *who?* answers the non-qualifiable presence of an existent who *presents himself* without reference to anything, and yet distinguishes himself from every other existent. The question *who?* envisages a face.[23]

The privilege of the question "what?" conceals the *address* implicit in any question, the address that envisages the other by speaking *to* them and anticipating a response. It thereby denies the transcendence of desire, its ability to move beyond Being in the ethical relation of *height*. Thematic questioning therefore effaces responsibility for and to the other. "To affirm the priority of Being over existents is already to decide the essence of philosophy; it is to *subordinate* the relation with someone, who is

---

20 Levinas, *Totality and Infinity*, pp. 109-21.
21 Emmanuel Levinas, "Substitution," in *Basic Philosophical Writings*, ed. A. Peperzak, R. Bernasconi, and S. Critchley (Bloomington: Indiana University Press, 1997), pp. 82-7.
22 Levinas, *Totality and Infinity*, p. 177.
23 Ibid., p. 177.

an existent, (the ethical relation) to a relation with the Being of existents, which, impersonal, permits the apprehension, the domination of existents (a relationship of knowing), subordinates justice to freedom."[24]

By contrast, in privileging the question "who?"—a question that calls for a name in response—Levinas conceives an infinite, irreducible responsibility that exposes one to singularity in the movement beyond being:

> The face I welcome makes me pass from phenomenon to being in another sense: in discourse I expose myself to the questioning of the Other, and this urgency of the response—acuteness of the present—engenders me for responsibility; as responsible I am brought to my final reality.[25]

The questioning of the Other calls for a response rather than a thematic answer; humanity is called beyond being to the transcendence of ethics. Before the face, naming and language are redirected toward responsibility and sociality, and it is at this point that naming God becomes central to Levinas.

For Levinas, the Name of God locates the discovery of the ethically responsible subject in the Jewish tradition. Levinas takes the Talmudic interpretation of God's name as signifying an opening to the infinite. For example, when God gives the Name to Moses in Exodus, or speaks at the tower of Babel, God's name withdraws in its presentation. "The square letters [of the Name] are a precarious dwelling from which the revealed Name is already withdrawn; erasable letters at the mercy of the man who copies out."[26] Effacing God's presence while manifesting it, God's name opens the *desire* in which the ethical relation commences. "[But] the proper name, close to what is named, is not connected logically with it; consequently, despite this proximity, it is an empty shell like a permanent revocation of what it evokes, a disembodiment of what is embodied through it." God's withdrawal, in the trace, refuses return to the subject in a finite, cognitively appropriable manner, signifying a relation to transcendence that cannot be appropriated. In its self-evacuation, the name, as the trace of God, can only be grasped in responsibility: "The transcendence of God is his actual effacement, but this obligates us to men."[27] The Name's withdrawal envisages the subject as responsible for others.

---

24 Ibid., p. 45, my emphasis. This famous and vigorous rejection of Heidegger's thought by Levinas is subsequently deconstructed by Derrida in "Violence and Metaphysics," which defends Heideggerian ontology not on its own terms but rather as a mode of guarding alterity— as the possibility of the ethical relation itself. Jacques Derrida, "Violence and Metaphysics: An Essay on the Thought of Emmanuel Levinas," in *Writing and Difference* trans. A. Bass (Chicago: University of Chicago Press, 1978), p. 146.

25 Levinas, *Totality and Infinity*, p. 178.

26 Emmanuel Levinas, "The Name of God According to a Few Talmudic Texts," in *Beyond the Verse*, trans. G. Mole (Bloomington: Indiana University Press, 1997), p. 121. Next quotation, p. 122.

27 Ibid., p. 125.

Insofar as recuperation becomes impossible, the subject is called outside itself to a possibility that exceeds thematization: responsibility to the singular other, to God and before God, to holiness (*sainteté*) or what Levinas calls in his philosophical writings "ethics as first philosophy." This responsibility is one's ownmost possibility, because it comes in the event in which the other appears.[28] In the possibility of substituting oneself for the other, the singularity of responsibility becomes manifest—no one can take my place in this act of substitution, involving singular existents. The concealment of God's faith overturns the order of truth, turning us toward a neighbor and away from the pursuit of knowledge. Moreover, through this moment of proximity or distancing intimacy, Israel's responsibility is founded in response to the giving of the Law that follows. Thus, for Levinas, naming God speaks to the truth of human nature, moving us beyond being and cognition to the singular responsibility for another in the trace of God.

B. The Face and the Name: The Undecidability of Revelation

The preceding section drew upon both Levinas's Talmudic interpretation and his phenomenology to explicate the significance of naming God. While both point to a responsibility beyond being, the parallel between the Name and the face illustrates a tension that is central to Derrida's critical appropriation of Levinas's work. In many ways, both figures do the same work for Levinas, one within phenomenology and the other within Talmudic interpretation. Yet the parallel leads to the following problem: one's being hostage to the other, responsible beyond all indebtedness, is supposed to be a uniquely temporal event that "an-archically" upsets the order of presence in its radical singularity. However, at the same time, the phenomenological exteriority of the face as a feature of our temporal existence points toward a general anthropological possibility *rather* than a revelatory event. Thus, there is a problem in terms of how one reconciles the unique event of revelation in the naming of God and the expression of responsibility in the face as a general, phenomenological possibility. In many ways, this parallelism leaves Levinas open to a Heideggerian critique, in which one could only think the possibility of revelation (and infinite responsibility) on the basis of its revealability, and thus in terms of the very ontology that Levinas hoped to escape.[29]

---

28 Levinas's conception of responsibility is a refusal of Socratic maieutics; this rejection involves a recognition that the other appears in time, *as* time. On Levinas and maieutics, see *Totality and Infinity*, p. 204, and Jacques Derrida, *Adieu: à Emmanuel Levinas* (Paris: Galilée, 1997), p. 42.

29 An example of this criticism would be Gianni Vattimo's criticism of absolute alterity (as conceived by Levinas) as in fact a reduction and ignorance of real, concrete differences that are found within the hermeneutical field of inquiry, and open the possibility of interpretation and judgment. "It is hard to see in Levinas any attention to the 'signs of the times'; all that time, the existential temporality characteristic of man, points towards is the eternity of God, revealed as a radical alterity that calls for the assumption of a responsibility which can only be regarded as historically qualified by accident (the neighbor is to be sure always a concrete,

A brief analysis of the face and the Name can help to demonstrate the parallel between them, the tension that ensues within Levinas's work, and Derrida's response to this problematic. Their parallel can be summarized as follows: both the face and the Name, as *traces* of alterity, guard against the appearance of alterity *as such*. As Levinas writes in *Totality and Infinity*, the face is the appearance of the Other within the same, the irruption of alterity within phenomenology. The face gives itself to consciousness as that which cannot be thematized. "The face is present in its refusal to be contained. In this sense it cannot be comprehended, that is encompassed. It is neither seen nor touched—for in visual or tactile sensation the identity of the I envelops the alterity of the object, which becomes precisely a content."[30] The face, along with its first linguistic expression "thou shalt not kill," is therefore not alterity as such. Rather, through the appearance of alterity in the face, subjectivity is reoriented towards the new possibility of responsibility. The face, then, insofar as it is not the other itself, *guards* the singularity of the other, protecting it from the recuperative activity of subjectivity that would reduce it to a thematic content, and makes responsibility possible.

The similarities of the face to Levinas's discussion of the Name, as described in the previous section, are apparent. Much like the Name, the visage operates as a "precarious dwelling" in which the infinity of the face evacuates itself in its revelation. The singular other never appears by itself. The closest one gets is the face-to-face, in which the face already doubles itself in order to be itself. Both the Name and the face (visage) are deferrals of absolute singularity, but these deferrals also make singularity possible. The Name and the face testify to the other. The singularity of the face is available as *promised* rather than given in the present.

Given the parallel between these phenomena, we can return to the problem noted above. On the one hand, God's Name would seem to be the foundation of responsibility, opening the possibility of singular relation without totalization. On the other hand, a similar irruption of asymmetrical responsibility occurs through the visage of the human other. Particularly as it arises in Levinas's early and more phenomenological works, responsibility appears to be a general possibility within the phenomenal field, apart from any scriptural tradition or historical event of election. If Levinas's phenomenology in *Totality and Infinity* is truly a transcendental phenomenology, then the irruption of the face and the anarchical priority of responsibility are not determined by any empirical, textual, or historical event. This would seem to be consistent with what Derrida has recently termed Levinas's thought of a *"revelation de la Thora d'avant Sinaï."*[31]

---

individual, but that's the point: *always*)". Gianni Vattimo, "The Trace of the Trace," in G. Viattimo and J. Derrida (eds), *Religion* (Stanford: Stanford University Press, 1998), p. 91.

30 Levinas, *Totality and Infinity*, p. 194.

31 Derrida, *Adieu*, p. 204. In addition to Derrida's recent work on Levinas, an important essay on the two thinkers is Robert Bernasconi's "The Trace of Levinas in Derrida," in D. Wood and R. Bernasconi (eds), *Derrida and Différance* (Evanston: Northwestern University Press, 1988), pp. 13-30.

Levinas's thought seems to be caught in the aporia between the following statements: 1) Responsibility arises from a singular event of revelation; 2) responsibility is the deepest feature of human subjectivity, and thus a transcendental condition for the possibility of any event. Levinas clearly sides with the importance of the event of responsibility, downplaying the subjective side of the aporia. Religion, as a re-binding,[32] is where we discover the responsibility that is most human, and its structures temporalize and singularize the participants in responsibility before God. The irruption of the idea of the infinite from within subjectivity temporalizes subjectivity into responsibility, leading the generalizable structure of consciousness beyond itself into its singular temporal existence.[33] The Name discloses an event whose ethical meaning is logically prior to the structure that chronologically precedes it.

Given his valuation of the event over the structure of religion, Levinas places himself in sharp opposition to Heidegger's understanding of the relationship between theology and ontology. For Heidegger, theology is a "science of faith" that is a *regional*, ontic science, that acquires its possibility within *Dasein*'s field of ontological possibility: "[Hence] we can say that precisely because all basic theological concepts, considered in their full regional context, include a content that is indeed existentielly powerless, i.e., ontically sublated, they are *ontologically* determined by a content that is pre-Christian and that *can thus be grasped rationally*."[34] On Heidegger's view, one must think of revealability (*Offenbarkeit*), the condition of possibility, as prior to the event of revelation (*Offenbarung*) itself. Without such a structure (or ground), the event of revelation is inconceivable. Only based upon the Being of beings can one think of something, in particular, as being. Its Being, its showing-forth, must be prior to that which is shown forth. As Derrida will point out, this emphasis on ontological determination shows that, in spite of his disavowal of scientific knowledge, Heidegger remains committed to cognition as the fundamental ground of existence.

Given their respective positions, the contrast between Levinas and Heidegger can now be clarified. Heidegger's formulation of "ontotheology" manifests this structural emphasis when one considers that the primary error of ontotheology—one could say, its exemplary metaphysical gesture—rests in its confusion of the ontic and ontological; in treating God as Being and as a being, theology forgets its ontic character and thinks *Being* poorly, effacing the ontological difference from which its possibility first arose. Levinas, on the other hand, would suggest that even as the idea of God appears within the ontological field, theology nonetheless points to a responsibility and subjectivity that exceeds and *precedes* ontology. The contrast,

---

32 For Levinas's interpretation of the meaning of religion, see Emmanuel Levinas, *Dieu, la mort, et le temps* (Paris: Grasset, 1993).

33 See, for example, Emmanuel Levinas, "God and Philosophy," in *Basic Philosophical Writings*, pp. 129-48.

34 Martin Heidegger, "Phenomenology and Theology," in *Pathmarks*, ed. W. McNeill (Cambridge: Cambridge University Press, 1998), p. 51 (my emphasis).

then, can be summarized in a simple question asked by Levinas: "ontotheology, is it to think Being poorly or to think God poorly?"³⁵

Derrida begins from this opposition between Heidegger and Levinas on the relation between ontology and theology; over against their approaches, he questions how each author privileges one discourse over the other. On Derrida's view, the antinomy between structure and event, as represented by the thought of Heidegger and Levinas, is undecidable. Derrida's view is expressed in the following question and others similar to it:

> In fact, "in truth", it would be only the event of revelation that would open—like a breaking-in, making it possible after the event—the field of the possible in which it appeared to spring forth, and for that matter actually did so ...
>
> Is there an alternative here? Must one choose between these two orders [structure and event, revealability and revelation]? And is this necessary first of all in the case of the so called "revealed" religions, which are also religions of the social bond according to *loving* (love, friendship, *fraternity*, charity, and so forth)? Must one choose between the priority of revelation (*Offenbarung*) and that of revealability (*Offenbarkeit*), the priority of manifestation and that of manifestability, of theology and theiology, of the science of God and the science of the divine, of the divinity of God?³⁶

The thought of these together in their undecidability gives rise to a different, *messianic* thought of religion. The event of revelation, insofar as it gives itself into a generalizable structure (which may then *appear* to be the condition for its possibility), points beyond itself; but, at the same time, the structure as structure presupposes the possibility of a singular event. Iterability and singularity must be thought together, as conditions for one another's possibility, even while undoing one another. For the naming of God to be what Levinas (and Derrida) want it to be, it must *dissimulate* itself in the general structure of language and naming; conversely, for revealability to be the structural possibility of revelation, the unique event of revelation must be thinkable, in its uniqueness.

While Heidegger decides for the ontological difference as constitutive of *Dasein*, and Levinas decides for the event of revelation as proper to human subjectivity, both treat one difference as proper or originary. The problem, on Derrida's view, is that in thinking of one activity as proper, and thus privileging a certain type of difference, other differences are thereby treated as derivative.³⁷ By thinking "derivative" differences only on the basis of the proper, one fails to let them show themselves in their true singularity. Derrida, by contrast, attempts to think through the differing of

---

35 Levinas, *Dieu, la mort, et le temps*, p. 144.
36 Derrida, *Politics of Friendship*, p. 20.
37 See Jacques Derrida, "*Geschlecht*: Difference sexuelle, difference ontologique," in *Psyché: Inventions de l'autre* (Paris: Galilée, 1987), and "At this Moment in This Work Here I Am," in R. Bernasconi and S. Critchley (eds) *Re-reading Levinas* (Bloomington: Indiana University Press, 1991). These works show how the privileging of either ontological or theological difference involves a neutralization of sexual difference, on the parts of both Heidegger and Levinas.

these differences from one another. Derrida's thought of *différance* as a "nonsimple" origin that only "is" in its effects—that is, in *other* differences, not appearing as such—is thus an attempt to dislocate the rule of the proper, and to allow differences to manifest themselves. Only in thinking of these differences, for Derrida, does one truly think through the singularity of the event. Phenomenologically, Derrida's thought could be summarized as follows: differences are only thinkable *as differences* when the propriety of the "as such" is displaced. He thus seeks to reconceive naming God and friendship in ways that minimize the neutralization of difference.

C. Derrida on Naming God

Derrida's reflections on God's name, then, can be interpreted within his broader reflections on the possibility of the event appearing as such to consciousness. A double movement is at work in his conception of its singularity. On the one hand, God's name, as indication and writing, is always different from and a deferral of God's presence to consciousness. On the other hand, only through the name is such a manifestation of God's presence conceivable, and only so does it enter into the realm of possibility. God's name relates us to God and distances us from God. God's name, then, is both the condition for the impossibility *and* the condition for the possibility of relation to God.

Derrida has addressed the issue of God's name through several texts, most notably "How Not to Speak: Denials," and *Sauf le nom*.[38] Both of these texts approach the problem of naming God beginning from the apparent affinity between deconstruction and negative theology, as a discourse that denies the ability of language to speak properly of its referent. By focusing on texts often understood to comprise "negative theology"—specifically, by Meister Eckhart, Angelus Silesius and Pseudo-Dionysius—Derrida distinguishes deconstruction from negative theology.[39] He describes the significance of God's name as follows: "This is what God's name always names, before or beyond other names: the trace of the singular event that will have rendered speech possible even before it turns itself back toward—in order to respond to—this first or last reference."[40] As the trace of singularity, God's name opens the possibility of speech—both as address, and in calling for a response. Without the name there would be no speech, and there would be no relation to the singular event. Such an absolute silence, for Derrida, would be inseparable from

---

38 In addition, one should also note the discussion of God's name in Jacques Derrida, "Des Tours de Babel," recently republished in *Acts of Religion*, ed. G. Anijar (New York: Routledge, 2002).

39 As Derrida himself notes, along with a number of commentators, Derrida's comments on negative theology are shaped around Christian texts, and thus remain haunted by both Jewish and Muslim thinking that remains unaddressed. See Kearney, "Derrida's Ethical Re-turn," p. 43. I am grateful to Robert Gibbs for pointing out this qualification of his reading.

40 Jacques Derrida, "How Not to Speak: Denials," trans. K. Frieden, in H. Coward and T. Foshay (eds), *Derrida and Negative Theology* (Albany: State University of New York Press, 1992), p. 98.

death. God's name signifies the need for speech or discourse in order to create a space where singular relation becomes possible. It signifies this, in part, by always already being a trace: this first speech, only gesturing toward what it names, thereby calls forth *further* speech. "The event remains in and on the mouth ... on the edge of the lips passed over by words that carry themselves toward God ... They name God, speak of him ... a reference to just what the name supposes to name beyond itself, the nameable beyond the name, the unnameable nameable."[41] On Derrida's view, language finds its *possibility* of reference precisely in the words that pass beyond themselves, even in remaining "on the edge of the lips" of the speaker.

Speech, in naming God, is necessary precisely because it is lacking; it is required by the absence of relation, and one's obligation to relate to the other. Without speech there is no singular reference, but speech also fails (i.e., is lacking) in its reference because it is always already too late:

> Order or promise, this injunction (*il faut*) commits (me), in a rigorously asymmetrical manner, even before I have been able to say I, to sign such a provocation in order to reappropriate it for myself and restore the symmetry. That in no way mitigates my responsibility; on the contrary. There would be no responsibility without this prior coming of the trace, or if autonomy were first or absolute.[42]

I am committed to speaking, to naming God, because of the failure to do so, even before being a subject. The necessity of this lack is central to the notion of "denegation" in the title of Derrida's essay.[43] De-negation is speech's sharing or partitioning within itself; naming God must both affirm and deny itself, recognizing its inadequacy as essential to its possibility.[44]

Negative theology exhibits this inevitable lack through its negations of those predicates that deny God's transcendence by speaking on the level of creation. In its claim that God is "unnameable," negative theology asserts the inadequacy of our acts of predication and speech. At the same time, language is required in order to relate one to the absolutely other. However, negative theology likewise seeks to limit this ambivalence. Derrida reads apophatic theology as "hyperessential" in that it seeks to determine the referent of its speech even while manifestly refusing our ability to describe it, particularly in the attribution of praise that determines the addressee. Even as negative theology is addressed *as prayer*, it is addressed to "you

---

41 Jacques Derrida, "Sauf Le Nom (Post-Scriptum)," trans. T. Leavey, in T. Dutoit (ed.), *On the Name* (Stanford: Stanford University Press, 1997), p. 58.

42 Derrida, "How Not to Speak," p. 99.

43 The double sense of *il faut*, as both lack (the origin of desire) and obligation (that which is necessary), can also be read as a challenge to Levinas's opposition of desire and need as infinity and totalizing ontology; caught between the two translations of *il faut*, would one ever be certain that the realm of needs and enjoyment was not the realm of desire and thus responsibility?

44 Derrida, "How Not to Speak," p. 95.

as 'hyperessential and more than divine Trinity,'"[45] retaining a predicative element. Derrida's approach differs from negative theology in arguing that this insufficiency of speech is internal to *all* speech, since speech is lacking from its very origin; the address to the other *qua* other must exceed its determinate address. This leads Derrida to dissociate praise and prayer, over against the hyperessentiality of negative theology that would link them.

In his analysis of prayer, and his dissociation of it from praise, Derrida develops Levinas's idea of speech as address to the other, as an infinite responsibility that avoids thematics. Prayer is central to understanding Derrida's religious reflection, not only in terms of his reflections on theological language, but also for turning these reflections towards responsibility and the possibility of friendship. For Derrida, prayer is first and foremost a structure of address:

> The act of addressing oneself to the other as other must, of course, mean praying, that is, asking, supplicating, searching out. No matter what, for the pure prayer demands only that the other hear it, receive it, be present to it, be the other as such, a gift, call, and even cause of prayer.[46]

Prayer is an undetermined form of address distinguishable from encomium or praise (*hymnein*):

> Praise is not prayer, in this it does not merge with the movement of prayer itself, which does not speak *of*, but *to*. Even if this address is immediately determined by the discourse of encomium and if the prayer addresses itself to God by speaking (to Him) of him, the apostrophe of prayer and the determination of the encomium form a pair, two different structures.[47]

As an address, it cannot be reduced to a predicative "speaking-of" even if prayer occurs in conjunction with the predicative form of encomium or praise. Irreducible to any predication, it is likewise irreducible *to the name* as well.[48] Prayer would even open up beyond the name, addressing the one thematized in the name itself.

---

45 Ibid., p. 110.
46 Ibid.
47 Ibid., p. 111, my emphasis.
48 There is a strong affinity to Rosenzweig here: "The prayer is its own fulfillment. The soul prays in the words of the Psalms: let not my prayer and your love depart from me. It prays to be able to pray—and this is already given to her to do in the assurance of the divine love." For both Rosenzweig and Derrida, prayer would be an activity (if one can call it that) with no purpose outside itself, and without intention on the part of the subject; moreover, for both, it opens onto the thought of the future as a question. See Rosenzweig, *The Star of Redemption*, pp. 184-5.

The reading here, it seems to me, differs from that of John Caputo, who reads the relation of prayer and encomium improperly by making encomium essential to prayer for Derrida. While encomium does determine prayer predicatively, the texts quoted here indicate that it is clearly not an essential feature of prayer itself. Derrida's text is confusing on this point, unless

One could therefore distinguish Derrida's position from that of "negative theology" as practiced by Pseudo-Dionysius and Meister Eckhart as follows: insofar as these authors link encomium with prayer, they hyperessentialize God, thematize the thought of the event, and thereby *limit* the address and responsibility. Insofar as the addressee is nameable, address and responsibility are thematizable and therefore restricted.

> How can one deny that, in this movement of determination (which is no longer the pure address of the prayer to the other), the appointment of the *trinitary* and hyperessential God distinguishes Dionysius' Christian prayer from all other prayer? To reject this doubtless subtle distinction [prayer/praise], inadmissible for Dionysius and perhaps for a Christian in general, is to deny the essential quality of prayer to every invocation that is not Christian.[49]

For Derrida, insofar as the address may performatively exceed its thematization, prayer may exceed the predication through which it appears. If one rejected this distinction, then non-Christian speech could not be prayerful. Moreover, Derrida emphasizes that in prayer, one's addressee is never simply determined as the one named. This is most evident in that when one addresses God in prayer, one also addresses another person. Insofar as one is speaking *to*, the address carries itself beyond its own limits, addressing another in friendship even as it seems to be addressed solely to one. Address to the other as wholly other (*tout autre*) cannot guard itself from becoming address to *each* other.

The multiplicity of pure address is manifest in a restricted form within apophatic theology. Mystical treatises are written to another—Pseudo-Dionysius writes to Timothy, Augustine's *Confessions* is written to Christian brothers, and—to extend the line of apophatic theology, in light of chapter 3—Aquinas' *Summa* is addressed to novices in the study of theology. These works never simply address one other, or God, and it is via the text of the name that the address "turns aside."[50] These texts are also addressed to brothers; the address to God extends itself to the fraternal order, as love of God unfolds into love of neighbor. As prayers to God and others, the performative address of this speech exceeds its object. At the same time, insofar as the authors try to maintain the necessity of linking prayer with praise, they seem destined to think

---

one carefully attends to his distinction between prayer as such, and prayer as joined to the encomium, which is how it is thought within apophatic discourse.

Caputo's interpretation of this point, it seems to me, is closely linked to his radical separation of Derrida's discourse on *khôra* from theological discourse. *Khôra*, it seems to me, is the secret of theology; one cannot simply distinguish them. This is not a minor point, since it ultimately shapes his view of "religion without religion." See John Caputo, *The Prayers and Tears of Jacques Derrida: Religion Without Religion* (Bloomington: Indiana University Press, 1997), pp. 38-9. By contrast, if prayer can be thought as freed from encomium, even if it always appears in and through structures of predication, prayer is conceivable *within* theological discourse (as well as outside of it).

49 Derrida, "How Not to Speak," p. 111.
50 Ibid., p. 117.

the address as nonetheless limited, particularly insofar as it is signified by fraternity. Thus, the restriction of prayer's address, in seeing it as determined by praise, also limits the turning of this speech toward others—as Derrida suggests, in a fraternal determination that neutralizes sexual difference.

The beyond of prayer occurs *within* naming God; while we can conceive of it as a separate structure, prayer is not separable from praise in fact. Without the inscription of the name, there would be no address.[51] Naming God goes "over there, toward the name, toward the beyond of the name in the name. Toward what, toward he or she who remains—save the name."[52] This "toward the beyond" in the act of naming—what Derrida and Levinas would call *testimony*—occurs through naming. Only through language and naming is the event possible, but the secret of the singular name cannot be known as such in language; it remains "at once in and on language, then, within and at the surface."[53] Testimony remains secret in its sharing, kept *as* a secret through its dissimulation in language and first and foremost in the name.[54] Insofar as names do not adequately name, they point to an appellation or call beyond the naming of the proper—an expropriating address of prayer or testimony undetermined by knowledge in which an alternative thought of responsibility become possible. This expropriative function of language is connected with Derrida's privilege of writing in his early work, as that which remains open beyond closure. As Richard Kearney describes what Derrida sees at the heart of religion, in naming God there is "a violence which Derrida identifies with a form of writing which remains faithful to the other and yet estranged, which respects the alien precisely by alienating us from it, which refuses the facility of immediate possession or the certainty of decidable affirmation and negation."[55]

Part of the "violence" to which Kearney refers lies in the complex relationship between negative theology and another, subversive form of apophasis within Platonism, one that revolves around the figure of *khora*. *Khora*, as discussed by Plato in the *Timaeus*, is that which receives, or gives space to that which comes into being. It, then, "is" beyond being, neither spatial nor temporal, material nor

---

51 Thus, the difference between prayer and praise, while thinkable, can never appear as such. Address only appears as address in its dissimulation through the name. As Derrida says at the end of "How Not to Speak," there could be no prayer without writing; this marks an affirmation of discourse as holding the impossible possibility of address to the other as other that apophatic theology does not seem willing to recognize, even as it admits it in its practice.

52 Derrida, "*Sauf le Nom*," p. 59.

53 Ibid., p. 58.

54 Derrida makes a similar point regarding the name in "*L'aphorisme à contretemps*," a series of aphorisms that revolve around *Romeo and Juliet*. Juliet calls for Romeo to be beyond his name ('deny thy father, and refuse thy name'); she calls for him—Romeo—to be beyond the name by calling his name. Without the name, he (Romeo) would not be beyond the name. See Jacques Derrrida, "*L'aphorisme à contretemps*," in *Psyché: Inventions de l'autre*, pp. 519-33. See especially aphorisms 17-21.

55 Kearney, "Derrida's Ethical Re-turn," p. 46.

spiritual, and the relation to *khora* is neither singular nor nor universal. The relation is "without"—relation to that which is utterly indifferent, relation without address. The problem that arises is that the theological determination of apophasis, and the hyperessentiality of negative theology, determine the thought of *khora*—either as a material receptacle, or as otherwise derivative from God's creation. Treating *khora* as derivative or secondary, much as a certain form of Platonism does,[56] leads negative theology to a determinate form of address. By dissociating the *khora* from the space of negative theology, and thinking prayer apart from praise, Derrida thinks the apophatic naming of God in its particular historical form, thereby opening the possibility of recognizing other, different modes of address:

> It remains to be known (beyond knowing) if the place is opened by appeal (response, the event that calls for the response, revelation, history, etc.), or if it remains impassively foreign, like *Khora*, to everything that takes its place and replaces itself and plays within this place including what is named God. Let's call this the test of *Khora* ...[57]

By thinking the *khora* beyond this determination, Derrida locates a moment of undecidability, between the *khora* as that which gives rise to everything, and as receiving that which is given by God. In this undecideability would be the condition for any determined or particular address to which negative theology would be destined—yet, also the recognition that other forms of apophatic discourse could likewise take shape.

Derrida's view on the relation between naming God and singularity can be summarized as follows: names enable singular relation through the possibility of testimony, but this singular relation, as a mode of address *to* the other as other, never appears as such in a name. While one can relate singularly through names in testimony, no name would capture or comprehend this singularity. Testimony is related to the belonging-without-belonging of "witness"[58] that divides itself from the singular in order to preserve singularity's possibility. The best name refers singularly by not referring, by not capturing the essence of that to which it refers, but rather by letting its referent be itself beyond its name. The best name is thus replaceable by other names, which can be substituted for it. Singularity is possible only where substitution and replaceability are likewise possible: "Each thing, each being, you, me, the other, each X, each name, and each name of God can become the example of other substitutable X's. A process of absolute formalization. Any other is totally other (*tout autre est tout autre*)."[59]

Thus, a naming of God appropriate to the one so named is found solely in prayer—an address undetermined by encomium or predication and therefore irrecuperable by the subject—which opens onto a messianic structure of witness and testimony. Derrida terms this a "messianic" structure because while the naming does not appear directly,

---

56 See Derrida, *On the Name*, pp. 119-21.
57 Ibid., p. 76.
58 Derrida, *Aporias*, p. 79.
59 Derrida, "Sauf le Nom," p. 76.

it nonetheless conditions and shapes actions and consciousness, opening them to the future. While prayer appears through the specific names of God, its difference from a written or spoken name, like what Levinas terms the Name's "evacuation" of its letters, opens a relation beyond cognition. It guards alterity through the possibility of the name being replaced by another name. In recognizing, through the appellation that occurs within naming God, that God is wholly other, one also recognizes that *each other is wholly other.* It is, in short, a thought of God's alterity that reflects back into immanence, as responsibility before others. By contrast, the hyperessentiality of negative theology risks limiting both the address and responsibility.

Through the name, the thought of a relation that is to-come (*à-venir*) and futural can be thought. This "futural" relation, however, as a messianic possibility, is not an eschatological event unavailable to us. To read Derrida as making this claim completely misses the point of the messianic for Derrida. The messianic futurity of testimony is a condition for politics, decision, and responsibility here and now, even as it likewise renders such concepts impossible in terms of their philosophical formulation; deferral and impossibility remain modes of relation, while disturbing the order of presence. To think their possibility opens the thought of a different politics that Derrida frequently articulated as an alternative thought of *friendship*. The messianic is not an eschatological thought, but rather one that conditions and displaces the possibility of politics and responsibility today.[60] In light of these reflections upon singularity in terms of naming God, an exploration of his views on friendship will show how these two issues converge in the idea of testimony.

III. Friendship and Singularity in Derrida

Friendship and Singularity I: Blanchot on Friendship

Derrida's recent work in ethics and politics has examined the concepts of decision, gift, forgiveness, and responsibility as a path toward reconceiving friendship. In showing how these concepts undo and point beyond themselves, Derrida extends Levinas's pressing of phenomenology to its limits.[61] Levinas's influence is especially apparent in the messianic strain of Derrida's recent work, which emphasizes how the infinitude of responsibility structures the temporality of action by carrying it beyond the limits of the world. While Derrida's work on friendship thus bears an affinity to Levinas, his writings on friendship are also clearly influenced by and in conversation with the thought of Maurice Blanchot. Blanchot's work opens

---

60 An excellent argument to this end is Richard Beardsworth's *Derrida and the Poltical* (London: Routledge, 1996). Beardsworth shows those places at which Gillian Rose's critique of Derrida misreads *différance* as an ideal and thereby fails to recognize that *différance* and undecidability are for Derrida inseparable from the situation in which they arise.

61 Beardsworth often minimizes the importance of Levinas's influence on Derrida, particularly in terms of the inconceivability of responsibility and the unconscious nature of the decision. In my opinion, it is difficult to overstate Levinas's importance to Derrida's work.

the thought of a relation that exceeds likeness, reciprocity, and identity, sharply challenging Aristotelian friendship. Often elliptic in style, evoking and revoking images and themes, Blanchot's literature performatively and narratively points toward a different friendship.

Two texts in which Blanchot reflects upon the possibility of friendship are "The Negative Community" and *Friendship*.[62] Both engage the work of Georges Bataille as it centers on the theme of community. As discussed in "The Negative Community," Blanchot finds in Bataille a suspicion of community as a *communion* that implies a fusion of persons into an indistinguishable, indivisible unity. One could say that Bataille's version of community would make him a "Marxist"—like Groucho, he would not join any club that would have him as a member. Such a pure union or fusion of persons ultimately denies the possibility of singular relation to the other.[63] Blanchot suggests that an absolutely immanent community, perhaps like the necessary identity or equality between Aristotelian friends, ultimately denies each individual's singularity. Bataille's life and work, on the other hand, represent a different thought of community, one that comes together precisely in order to part— a community directed towards a "community of absence" and solitude in which each remains irreducibly other.

A community of absence develops from the *insufficiency* of individuals. For Blanchot, insufficiency is the ability to be put into question.[64] Standing helplessly as the other leaves or passes in death, one's agency is put into question and shown to be insufficient. Furthermore, even while death separates one from the other in irreducible singularity, the event of insufficiency becomes something shared, and thus begins to found a new community where selves do not fuse:

> To remain present in the proximity of another who by dying removes himself definitively, to take upon myself another's death as the only death that concerns me, this is what puts me beside myself, this is the only separation that can open me in its very impossibility, to the Openness of a community ... The mute conversation which, holding the hand of "another who dies," "I" keep up with him, I don't keep up simply to help him die, but to share the solitude of the event which seems to be the possibility that is most his own and his unshareable possession in that it dispossesses him absolutely.[65]

This "dispossession" brings us back to the language of friendship, as a sharing of what is unshareably "most his own." In the "impossible sharing" of solitude, what is shared is not an essence or character, but the radical finitude and historicity of one's dispossession. The community of absence fulfills this insufficiency by deepening it, leading its members into solitude rather than toward a unified, collective being-

---

62 Maurice Blanchot, "The Negative Community", in *The Unavowable Community*, trans. P. Joris (Barrytown, NY: Station Hill Press, 1988); *Friendship*, trans. E. Rothenberg (Stanford: Stanford University Press, 1997).

63 Blanchot, "The Negative Community," p. 2.

64 Ibid., pp. 7-8.

65 Ibid., p. 9.

together. In its solitude and putting-into-question of the subject, this friendship radically displaces the equality and symmetry of Aristotelian friendship.

The dispossession in such a community of absence is central to Blanchot's conception of "worklessness" (*desoéuvrement*).[66] In such worklessness one's activity is irrecuperable by either oneself or another; unable to be directed towards an end outside of its own activity, it is best understood as loss. All that one can do is to substitute oneself for the one who is dying, but this in no way replaces the other; in its limits, such substitution rather confirms the singularity of the other.[67] Such a community that undoes itself, a friendship founded on an abyssal absence, leads to Blanchot's formulation of friendship: "*Friendship: friendship for the unknown without friends.*"[68] This subjectivity that is most one's own in expropriation, in the "sharing of solitude," is very important for Derrida's work, in terms of thinking of absolute asymmetry and generosity as transcendental requirements for the gift. Moreover, Blanchot's thought of friendship reverses the relationship between friendship and consciousness. For, if the possibility that comes from the other is "most my own" and makes singularity possible, then the possibility of friendship is *prior* to consciousness and the ego, founding ipseity before any agency is possible. For Blanchot, friendship is a relationship prior to knowledge; from friendship, consciousness comes-to-be, rather than the reverse. Here, knowledge plays a derivative role in friendship, rather than friendship being directed toward the act of contemplation.

A second aspect of Blanchot's work on friendship that is decisive for Derrida's thought is the association of friendship with address. For Blanchot, one speaks *to* a friend rather than *of* a friend. This is clearest in *Friendship* (*L'Amitié*). Written in memory of Bataille, *Friendship* ranges across numerous issues in the modern world, particularly regarding the status of art; Bataille and his work are mentioned only rarely and obliquely. The essays function as a set of writings *inspired* by Bataille and in mourning of his passing—in memory of the solitude and uniqueness of his thought. The book, in short, is written *to* Bataille rather than about him. As Blanchot writes:

> Friendship, this relation without dependence, without episode, yet into which all of the simplicity of life enters, passes by way of the recognition of the common strangeness *that does not allow us to speak of our friends but only to speak to them*, not to make of them a topic of conversations (or essays), but the movement of understanding in which, speaking to us, they reserve, even on the most familiar terms, an infinite distance, the fundamental separation on the basis of which what separates becomes relation.[69]

---

66 "Worklessness" is closely related to the idea of "general economy" as expenditure and loss in Bataille's work. See Joris's introduction to *The Unavowable Community* for a helpful discussion of this aspect of Bataille's and Blanchot's thought.

67 Blanchot, "The Negative Community," pp. 9-11.

68 Ibid., p. 24.

69 Blanchot, *Friendship*, p. 291.

Only in this abyssal solitude, where one relates to the other in "common strangeness," is friendship truly found. To speak of a friend can only reduce distance and destroy friendship, effacing the "fundamental separation" that establishes this relation. Would a eulogy, in memory of friendship, be its ruin as well?

The importance of address to friendship, and the dangers Blanchot sees in speaking *of* a friend, become clearest in a remarkable essay on Kafka at the end of *Friendship*. "Kafka and Brod" describes what Blanchot sees as the nearly irreparable distortion done to Kafka's work by Max Brod's interpretation—to speak for him and to guide others in approaching his work and life. Brod did so, in the belief that other readings of Kafka were missing something essential. However, in so determining Kafka's texts and the readings of them, Brod limited and circumscribed who Kafka was for others. This was already to describe Kafka, to no longer name him singularly, and to not let him be who he was, a perhaps inevitable distortion. In short, Brod's interpretation denied the "principle of insufficiency" to Kafka by seeking to complete him, answering questions regarding his status and the meaning of his work, and thereby not safeguarding the being-in-question that Kafka's work represented.[70] It is to avoid such violence that Blanchot only obliquely writes of Bataille, choosing instead to address him through the themes and works of others, respecting Bataille's singularity in distancing himself from him.

Yet, in examining this practice of friendship, one notices something deeply troubling within Blanchot's thought of friendship: to speak to *an* other, one must speak of *others*. To deflect predication from the one with whom one wishes to be friends, one must predicate of another. This double bind—the impossibility of address *to another* as such—indicates that the very possibility of responsibility and friendship is also the possibility of violence and enmity, as one risks thematizing (and denying the singularity of) another in attending to the solitude of one friend.[71] Both friendship's openness beyond thematization and the problematic nature of such address establish the field for Derrida's reflections on the possibility of friendship.

Friendship and Singularity II: Derrida on Friendship

Blanchot's work correlates with Derrida's understanding of two events central to the practice of friendship: the gift and testimony. In parallel to Blanchot's formulation of the worklessness of a community of absence, Derrida analyzes the logic of the gift as an event that must exceed the agency and calculation of the subject. Second, Derrida approaches the idea of address (speaking *to*) beyond thematization (speaking *of*) through the notion of testimony or confession. Both of these events of friendship are

---

70 Ibid., pp. 240-51.
71 This last point is only a problem for attempts to read Blanchot's work as having a political sensibility, which Derrida does. However, some have criticized Derrida as *reducing* the significance of Blanchot's work in emphasizing these political points. See Georges Leroux, "A L'ami inconnu: Derrida, lecteur politique de Blanchot," *Etudes Françaises* 31 (1995-6), pp. 111-23.

highly intertwined with the possibility of language; as we shall see, they converge with his interpretation of testimony in the naming of God. For the gift and testimony to be events of friendship, they must be events of singular relation, and Derrida's analysis starts from the aporias entailed within this condition.

First, the gift. According to Derrida's analysis, the phenomenon of the gift requires three features: a giver, a given, and a receiver. Moreover, a gift must be a generous giving from which the giver does not profit, a giving without expectation of return or economic exchange. However, these transcendental requirements also undermine the possibility of a gift's actualization. For, if there is a giver who is aware of giving, and who *intends to give*, consciousness of the intention already returns to the subject. As soon as there is a given, the gift has a certain value; moreover, precisely to the extent that there is a giver who is conscious of this value, and knows what she gives, she *receives* the consciousness of having given the gift. Since she thus receives in giving, the giving is not without return, and thus already collapses into an economic exchange. Likewise, the receiver, in knowing that he has received a gift, finds himself indebted to the one who gave it. This is a debt without debt, in the sense that the receiver must give back to the giver, even just in receiving. Like a receiver in football who "gives a target" to the passer, by receiving a gift the recipient gives back to the giver the possibility of giving.

Thus, from all angles, in terms of the phenomenon of the gift, the appearance as such of a gift without return is impossible. This does not mean that there is no gift, but that the gift *is not*: it must be thought according to the modality of the impossible, and one cannot know that a gift has been given, since the conditions that make it possible also make it impossible. Only possible as impossible, the gift escapes any thematizable demands of practical reason or morality:

> The gift would be that which does not obey the principle of reason: It is, it *ought* to be, it owes itself to be *without any reason*, without wherefore, and without foundation. The gift, if there is any, does not even belong to practical reason. It should remain a stranger to morality, to the will, perhaps to freedom, at least to that freedom that is associated with the will of a subject.[72]

Since the gift, in order to be aneconomic, must not return to the giver (it must not be intentional), there must be chance in order for there to be a gift, even while it also must be an intentional giving. This is why the gift remains an inviolable secret at the heart of any economic act of giving, including the act of giving words. The idea of the gift as irreducible to any economic formulation thus opens the thought of a certain worklessness (*desoéuvrement*) of language; insofar as narrative and description cannot present the event as such, they guard its absence in their very presentation; narrative (or literature) becomes an activity that undoes itself and points beyond its own formulation, manifesting the secret that only "is" on the edge of language.[73]

---

72 Jacques Derrida, *Given Time I. Counterfeit Money*, trans. P. Kamuf (Chicago: University of Chicago Press, 1992), p. 156.
73 This "nonfunctional function" of narrative is discussed by Blanchot as a *recit*.

For example, in Derrida's reading of Baudelaire's story "Counterfeit Money," neither the gift nor the *confession* of the narrator's friend can appear as such; the narrator's "gift of nature" is a speculative, economic faculty that forecloses the possibility of the gift and friendship. Based on what he knows, that which he is able to thematize, the narrator condemns the friend. The friend's failure to know is, on the narrator's view, unforgivable. "I could almost have forgiven him the desire for the criminal enjoyment of which a moment before I assumed him capable ... but I will never forgive him the ineptitude of his calculation."[74] The friend's gift of nature, it would seem, grants certainty as to how knowledge, economy, friendship and forgiveness circulate, as he calculates the cost of the friend's deceit in giving a counterfeit coin. But the narrator's condemnation of the friend for the friend's poor calculation simply highlights the problematic: if the friend had told the narrator what he had done, recounted his evil deed, would the friend really have *forgiven* him? Can forgiveness only be given in exchange for remorse, and thus economically, or must forgiveness be prior to remorse in order to be a forgiveness that does not remain calculative?[75] Against the narrator, Derrida suggests that the gift or forgiveness resides at the point where one would give in the absence of knowledge or calculation, even as this breaks with morality or what we often conceive as responsibility.

In its impossibility, the gift's connection with asymmetry and nonreciprocity leads to a new conception of friendship. If a gift is an event of friendship that cannot involve economic exchange, then friendship must break with reciprocity, since the determination of the giver and recipient would render friendship as a singular event impossible. As an event of friendship, the gift inscribes an incalculable asymmetry within the equality and reciprocity of Aristotelian friendship. For, while complete friendship in the Aristotelian sense is not reducible to utility, it still serves the end of contemplation. Derrida, by contrast, dissociates wishing the other well from this cognitive focus:

> A logic of the gift thus withholds friendship from its philosophical interpretation ... This logic calls friendship back to non-reciprocity, to dissymmetry or to disproportion, to the impossibility of a return to offered or received hospitality; in short, it calls friendship back to the irreducible precedence of the other.[76]

While friendship, as equal and reciprocal, can be known in its presence, the thought of an asymmetrical friendship beyond presence and to-come (*à-venir*) displaces the spatiotemporal limits of Aristotelian friendship.[77]

---

74 Charles Baudelaire, "Counterfeit Money," in Derrida, *Given Time*.

75 This question indicates Derrida's own position as stated in a paper titled "To Forgive: The Unforgivable and the Imprescriptable," at the Religion and Postmodernism conference, Villanova University, October 1999. Published in J. Caputo and M. Scanlon (eds), *Questioning God* (Bloomington: Indiana University Press, 2000), pp. 21-51.

76 Derrida, *Politics of Friendship*, p. 62.

77 This is the thesis of the first chapter of *Politics of Friendship*, pp. 1-24.

Much as his analysis of the gift is very close to the idea of worklessness in Blanchot's writings, Derrida's articulation of friendship as an event of testimony also bears a strong affinity to Blanchot on the theme of address. As we have seen in Derrida's discussion of naming God, testimony or confession must be thinkable apart from predication or any intentional act on the part of the subject. Testimony is an address beyond thematization, a *speaking-to* prior to *speaking-of*. In the purity of address, it is indistinguishable from prayer.[78] For Derrida, Augustine's *Confessions* exemplify the irreducibility of testimony or confession to knowledge: "The eidetic purity of confession stands out better when the other is already in a position to know what I confess. That is why Saint Augustine wonders so often why he confesses to God who knows everything."[79] As a response prior to saying anything—in a sense, a response-ability prior to the subject—testimony remains irreducible to knowledge; it cannot appear as such within a text or narrative, even as it only gives itself *within* such inscription. Like the gift, it manifests a relation that exceeds canonical friendship.

However, while prior to any predication, testimony nonetheless only gives itself as a trace through the predication of language. One never encounters "pure" testimony, factically speaking. Much as prayer only gives itself in conjunction with praise even though they are conceptually distinct, testimony reveals itself by concealing itself in language. This address only presents itself, it would seem, as a disruption of the essential or predicative relation, opening toward a "who?" beyond the bounds of "what?" Derrida raises this possibility in a reading of Aristotle's discussion of the essence of friendship:

> It is true that right in the middle of this series of questions [by Aristotle], between the one on the being or the being-such of friendship and the one on the possible plurivocity of a saying of friendship, there is a question which is itself terribly equivocal: *kai tís o philos*. This question asks *what* the friend is, but also asks *who* he is. This hesitation in the language between the what and the who does not seem to make Aristotle tremble ... as if the question "who?" had to bend or bow in advance of the ontological question "what?" or "what is?"
>
> This implicit subjection of the *who* to the *what* will call for question on our part. The question will bring with it a protestation: in the name of the friend or in the name of the name. If this protestation takes on a political aspect, it will perhaps be less properly political than it would appear. It will signify, rather, the principle of a possible resistance to the reduction of the political, even the ethical, to the ontophenomenological.[80]

The reduction of the question "who" to the limits of the question "what" would be the reduction of singularity to that which could appear within the ontological field. Derrida's challenge resonates with both Blanchot's concern for address and Levinas's thought of the "who?" that opens one to ethical Desire. Moreover, Derrida's

---

78 Though Derrida would distinguish testimony from the determinate form of apophatic prayer that is linked with praise.
79 Derrida, *Given Time*, p. 168. See also *Sauf le Nom* for how testimony, in its being-written, opens itself to other humans as well as to God.
80 Derrida, *Politics of Friendship*, p. 6.

emphasis on the address prior to the ontological unsettles the limits established by Aristotle in his determinations of *who* can be a friend on the basis of character, essence, and especially natural origin. As the quote makes plain, this is a question of naming, of identity, and of friendship at the same time. The problem here is that Aristotle writes as though one can know or determine in advance who is capable of being friends on the basis of scientific inquiry. This circumscription of friendship by cognition effaces responsibility because of its determination of friendship in terms of knowledge, suppressing the decision for friendship.

As a friendship that is "already" as prior to the subject, a belonging-without-belonging in speaking to one another, but also a friendship that is not-yet since it remains futural, calling *for* friendship in calling to the other who may not be present,[81] Derrida thus sees testimony as connected with the structure of mourning. A testimonial friendship presupposes an address to another who is not present, to whom one nonetheless speaks in *hope* of friendship. As testamentary, one's address to the other holds both the possibility of putting to death (effacing/forgetting the other) *and* the possibility that the other will live on (*sur-vivre*) through one's address. Giving without reserve opens both the possibility of good and evil; both possibilities coexist together within the same event, as one gives the other the chance to appear and to speak, but in this openness to the event one also risks the possibility of violence. This does not mean that evil is necessary, on Derrida's view, but rather that its *possibility* is coeval with the possibility of goodness, responsibility, and ethics. Through reflection on the gift and testimony, Derrida thus rethinks friendship as an event in its singularity, rather than as a stable, enduring entity, thereby opening a space for rethinking Aristotelian friendship and its accompanying politics.

C. Friendship and Messianic Politics

Derrida's reflections on the gift and testimony provide the basis for his displacement of philosophical friendship. Derrida focuses upon several structural oppositions that determine this form of friendship. In particular, he analyzes and questions how friendship is defined as fraternity, in opposition to the feminine, and as opposed to enmity, thus establishing the internal and external limits of friendship. In analyzing how friendship is defined through these oppositions, and thus questioning such determination, Derrida articulates his conception of friendship. By displacing the natural, fraternal, and political boundaries of philosophical friendship, Derrida moves beyond the canonical view of friendships of virtue, "turning the virtue of virtue against itself" in a neo-Nietzschean gesture.[82]

Derrida examines the turning of friendship into enmity through a reading of Carl Schmitt's *The Concept of the Political*.[83] For Schmitt, the distinction of friend from

---

81 Ibid., pp. 235-6.
82 Ibid., p. 33.
83 In addition to the importance of Carl Schmitt's work to this thesis, Derrida's *Politics of Friendship* reflects at length on Nietzsche's inversion of a phrase that has permeated the

enemy is the essence of politics. This distinction is actualized in the act of war, in which one is willing to kill the enemy. Even if one does not actually kill the enemy, war as the horizon of politics always already informs all properly political decisions, such that politics is war by other means.[84] Since the political distinction between friend and enemy is properly actualized in war's killing of the enemy, the proper locus of politics is the state. In emphasizing the role of the state, Schmitt's concern is the disappearance of the "proper" concept of the political through its dissemination into all spheres of life. Writing in Weimar Germany, Schmitt watched the fracture of the state as the unit of modern politics, as disputes within the state (along religious, class, or party lines) were becoming political in nature. Such an absolute politics allows for *no* politics on Schmitt's view, since the treatment of internal disputes as political usurps the power of the state and blurs the line between friend and enemy. Only when one knows who one's friends and enemies are can politics in the pure, proper sense be practiced.

Schmitt's argument hinges on the distinction between disputes within the state (civil war) and war between states. By maintaining this distinction in a rigorous manner Schmitt can uphold the sovereignty of the state in political matters. The border of the state becomes the boundary; those within the state are to be treated as friends and those outside of the state as enemies. This does not mean that there cannot be disputes within the state, but Schmitt would label such disputes as between "private" enemies (*inimicus*) and thereby distinguish them from the public, properly political enmity (*hostis*). One may have private disputes and enmities with those of one's state, who are also one's political friends, but these must not become political decisions; conversely, one cannot have friendship with political enemies. Friend and enemy would then no longer intersect, and love of one's political enemies becomes inconceivable. As Schmitt puts it in a famous quote:

> The often quoted "Love your enemies" (Matt. 5:44; Luke 6:27) reads *diligite inimicos vestros, agapâte tous ekhthrous umôn* and not *diligite hostis vestros*. No mention is made of the political enemy. Never in the thousand-year struggle between Christians and Moslems did it occur to a Christian to surrender rather than defend Europe out of love toward the Saracens or Turks. The enemy in the political sense need not be hated personally, and in the private sphere only does it make sense to love one's enemy, that is, one's adversary.[85]

---

philosophical canon on friendship. Where Aristotle is often cited as having stated, "O my friends, there is no friend!" Nietzsche inverts the phrase to "Foes, there are no foes!" (Derrida, *Politics of Friendship*, p. 50; Nietzsche, *Human, All too Human*, 2, para. 376).

84 As Schmitt interprets Clausewits, "To be precise, war, for Clausewits, is not merely one of many instruments, but the *ultima ratio* of the friend-and-enemy grouping. War has its own grammar, but politics remains its brain." Carl Schmitt, *The Concept of the Political*, trans. G. Schwab (New Brunswick: Rutgers University Press, 1976), p. 34.

85 Derrida, *Politics of Friendship*, p. 88. Quoting from Schmitt, *The Concept of the Political*. Derrida attends to Schmitt's reading of this scriptural passage in *The Gift of Death*, arguing that in the context of discussions of the neighbor, one cannot maintain the public/private distinction of enemies in the way Schmitt intends. Jesus' saying seems, if anything, to be saying, love your political enemies. Thus, Schmitt's politics (as manifest in this point of

Thus, for Schmitt, difference must be conceived as oppositional in order to make a political distinction. Political friendship must be distinguished from love, which would be private, whereas friendship becomes an impersonal relation. Where the friend is not strictly opposed to the enemy, politics—the essence of humanity for Schmitt—disappears.

By raising two questions regarding Schmitt's discourse on politics, Derrida points toward a messianic idea of friendship and a politics of deconstruction. First, Derrida shows that on Schmitt's terms, friendship is defined through its opposition to enmity. Schmitt never says what friendship is in and of itself; in a classic Hegelian gesture, he defines its identity through its difference from hostility. The thought of friendship is thus inseparable from the thought of war. From a Schmittian point of view, the violence of war necessarily precedes the possibility of friendship and love; he presupposes that humanity is essentially evil and, that this recognition founds politics in the proper sense. Furthermore, for Schmitt to read the statement "love your enemies" (*diligite inimicos vestros*) as a *purely* private love of enemies is only possible once one has made the political distinction between "private" and "public" enemies. Schmitt's reading does not confirm the private nature of Christian love, but rather presupposes it. By so restricting love, Schmitt's friendship thus bears within it hostility toward political enemies, toward those who would question this determination of the political, and even, as Derrida points out, toward women— never mentioned once in connection with the political sphere, and thus excluded from friendship in the political sense as well.

As part of his analysis, Derrida questions Schmitt's reading of the Gospel passage, as only regarding one's personal enemies. Since "love your enemies" is treated as love that goes beyond a circumscribed love of neighbor, it intends *precisely* the love of political enemies that Schmitt would exclude:

> If one's neighbor is here one's *congener*, someone from *my* community, from the same people or nation ('*amith*), then the person who can be opposed to him or her [the one to be loved] is the non-neighbor *not as private enemy but as foreigner*, as member of another nation, community, or people ... the frontier between *inimicus* and *hostis* would be more permeable than he [Schmitt] wants to believe.[86]

By dislocating the opposition between friend and enemy, this "Christian politics" (over against that of Schmitt) would make conceivable a love without return, and also an asymmetrical friendship that goes beyond the friend/enemy opposition. As such a friendship goes beyond the calculative, cognitive determination on which Schmitt founds politics, this gospel command opens the thought of a friendship and politics that would dislocate the limits of the canonical conception of friendship.

However, it is important to note the modality in which such a possibility exists, for one could never be certain that this politics would actually break with the

---

interpretation) are called into question from within. See Jacques Derrida, *The Gift of Death*, trans. D. Wills (Chicago: University of Chicago Press, 1994), pp. 103-5.

86 Derrida, *The Gift of Death*, p. 105. See also *Politics of Friendship*, pp. 88-9.

economic, determinate friendship figured by fraternity. This possibility, for Derrida, would exist in the mode of the "perhaps," as even within the scriptural passage itself, the love without return of loving an enemy still reverts to an economic formulation. As Derrida describes in *The Gift of Death*, insofar as God "sees in secret," knows what one does and compensates one's giving (so that there is a return here), the asymmetrical relation to the other is also inscribed within an exchange, even if the economy is heterogeneous to finite calculation.[87] Such a reinscription of economy is not simply negative: however, Derrida's point is that the Christian thought of love of enemies *testifies* to the possibility of a noncanonical, nonphilosophical friendship, but cannot render it present as such. Thus, while Schmitt's work reinscribes the limits of Christian friendship ever more forcefully, by deconstructing this reinscription Derrida points toward both the possibility of a friendship and politics that goes beyond this limit from within Christian thought.

Derrida's second point regarding Schmittian politics turns on the maintenance of the opposition between friend and enemy through the figure of *fraternity*. Like many authors throughout the history of philosophy, Schmitt evokes the figure of brotherhood to represent a determinate, present friendship—in this case, the friendship arising from the cognitive distinction between friend and enemy.[88] However, Schmitt's work also points to another possibility: when he seeks to know who his enemy is, here too he invokes the figure of the brother.[89] Derrida makes several points with regard to the figure of the brother who marks the limit of the state: in Schmitt's work, fraternity marks the opposition between friendship and enmity; it allows one to separate friend and enemy in a rigorous fashion; it lets one wage war on behalf of the brother/friend against the enemy, and to do so marks a political judgment. However, it also allows one to determine, or know the enemy, as a brother, in a metaphorical sense. The figure that divides friend and enemy, politically, undoes their opposition.[90] Fraternity would seem to rest undecidably between friendship and enmity, and it problematizes and contaminates the very political distinction Schmitt wishes to make. "Fraternity," as a name for friendship, marks both a particular relation with a concrete friend, and the possibility of a universal relation, in which the concrete enemy would be included, both founding and ruining Schmitt's concept of the political.

Given that fraternization is at once natural and symbolic, Derrida argues for a radical inversion: where kinship would seem to be the basis for friendship, enmity, and politics, the delimitation of these boundaries indicates that its symbolic form precedes and produces its natural appearance. The "given" of kinship must be

---

87 "This concept (that God pays back infinitely more) founds and destroys the Christian concepts of responsibility and justice and their 'object.'" Derrida, *The Gift of Death*, p. 112.

88 Derrida, *Politics of Friendship*, p. 149. *Politics of Friendship* is full of references to other authors and texts on the subject of friendship that give Derrida's work a richness and subtlety that cannot be reproduced here. As already noted with the example of Nietzsche, I cannot do justice to all of the strands of thought in this dense and rich book.

89 Ibid., p. 163.

90 Ibid, p. 115. This thought of the border is developed at more length in Derrida, *Aporias*, esp. pp. 6-21.

"reproduced" rhetorically in order to appear originary. Through its repetition and differing from itself, fraternity as a symbolic process manifests itself in the form of a natural fraternity that would conceal and forget its symbolic underpinnings. As Derrida writes:

> What we are calling here "fraternization", is what produces symbolically, conventionally, through authorized engagement, a *determined politics*, which, be it left- or right-wing, alleges a real fraternity or regulates spiritual fraternity, fraternity in the figurative sense, *on the symbolic projection of a real or natural fraternity*. Has anyone ever met a brother? ... In nature?[91]

In short, legal equality establishes natural equality as a necessary fiction that legitimates the political opposition of friend and enemy, and gives an appearance of necessity to the political order.

The real danger of such "naturalization" of fraternity is that its self-naturalizing presentation limits the field of political action and friendship. This determination shares its logic with nationalism, sexism, and other forms of exclusion. While one's nature need not determine relations in the strong sense, so that there is no choice or will involved, nature does limit the range of options available to one as human. Thus, to conceive of brotherhood as natural, and friendship as fraternal, not only allows for "effective" politics based on the "real possibility" of war and the friend/enemy distinction, it forecloses other political options, as well as other sorts of friendship. Insofar as friendship proceeds only on the basis of "natural" fraternity, it remains within the bounds of knowledge and fails to be open to the other. Such determinate friendship is without risk, contingency, or decision—and thus without responsibility. Such a "natural friendship" is enmity, since it does not welcome the other as other; a friendship within nature, proceeding on the basis of cognition, would be no friendship at all:

> What would a future be if the decision were able to be programmed, and if the risk [*l'aléa*], the uncertainty, the unstable certainty, the inassurance of the "perhaps", were not suspended on it at the opening of what comes, flush with the vent, within it and with an open heart? ... This suspension, the imminence of an interruption, can be called the other, the revolution, or chaos; it is, in any case, the risk of an instability.[92]

Nature, on this view, in stabilizing friendship, would be the first *technique*—that which mechanizes friendship and turns it into a repeatable, nonsingular relation.

The naturalization of fraternity is thus a *neutralization* of difference, limiting it to that which is conceived oppositionally, here along the lines of the friend/enemy opposition. The thought of fraternity, as the limit of friendship and politics, limits friendship to that which can be known as "present," thereby inscribing friendship within an ontology or what has come to be known as a "metaphysics of presence." Derrida often broaches this in terms of the neutralization of sexual difference in

---

91 Derrida, *Politics of Friendship*, p. 93, my emphasis.
92 Ibid., p. 29.

ontology and philosophy. Thus, one of the primary questions of *Politics of Friendship*: can a man and woman, or women, or even two brothers, across their differences, *as* nonidentical, be friends, if friendship is fraternal? For, as long as friendship is thought on fraternal terms, a certain hierarchy is inevitably built into the relationship, and has been determinative for both philosophical and theological conceptions of friendship. Unmasking the symbolic, unnatural character of fraternity lets friendship be beyond that limit. To think friendship differently "would therefore be a matter of thinking an alterity without hierarchical difference at the root of democracy" which "would free a certain interpretation of equality by removing it from the phallogocentric schema of fraternity."[93] For Derrida the privilege of presence is interconnected with a political order, a determinate order that limits friendship and politics. The deconstruction of fraternity opens friendship beyond both presence and fraternity, to a messianic friendship that addresses the other as singular other in a nonoppositional thought of difference.[94]

IV. Incalculable Friendship

Derrida's work, as explored above, poses several challenges to the canonical version of friendship. The naturalization/fraternization of friendship always already involves a *neutralization* of difference and is thus never original. Within the canonical understanding of friendship, singularity and equality are thought within the limits of fraternity. Fraternity, in some sense, makes friendship knowable and thereby determinate, and this limitation of friendship therefore leads to a determinate politics. *Politics of Friendship* exhibits the philosophical determination of friendship as fraternal in a fascinating and deeply troubling manner; conceiving of a friendship without fraternity seems nearly impossible. This is as true of the thought of friendship in Nietzsche, Bataille, Blanchot, and Nancy, even as they seek to disrupt Aristotelian friendship from within, as of those friendships conceived in explicitly Aristotelian terms.[95] It is true, to be sure, that the brotherhood of a "community of separation" is far different from that of a friendship of virtue, yet the underlying dependence upon the figure of fraternity to produce a likeness or sharing remains. In thus neutralizing difference and limiting thought, the figure of fraternity also neutralizes or effaces the thought of singularity as relation to the other as other.

However, as Derrida explores toward the end of *Politics of Friendship*, the symbolic production of fraternity also contains the possibility of its own deconstruction. For

---

93 Ibid., p. 232.

94 The literature on deconstruction and feminism is ever-growing. Derrida's most explicit formulation of sexual difference as indicating a nonoppositional difference, even if it is not itself equatable with this difference, is in "*Geschlecht*: Difference sexuelle, difference ontologique."

95 Derrida, *Politics of Friendship*, pp. 46-8. For Blanchot, see "The Negative Community," p. 44; for Nancy, see Jean-Luc Nancy, "Partage de liberté. Égalité, fraternité, justice," in *L'Experience de la Liberté* (Paris: Galilée, 1988), pp. 91-107.

while friendship in the present appears to be irreducibly fraternal, this fraternity must be heterogeneous to itself at its origin. Friendship, to be friendship, must be with *more than one*. To love the other as wholly other is also to open oneself to *any* other as wholly other.[96] Singular relation is singular by dissimulating itself in its repetition. The relation to the third (what Levinas terms justice) is already at the heart of the ethical relation, making possible singular responsibility before *this other* and for this other in the repetition and differing of alterity from itself.[97] In the more than one ($n+1$) of friendship, we see a structure of address that exceeds thematization. This address must exceed its determined form in order to be an address to a singular other. In this openness of friendship—much like the openness of testimony or prayer— an address beyond the limits of fraternity may be possible. The canonical form of friendship testifies to singular relation, and deconstruction brings this testimony to light.

At the same time, the $n+1$ formulation of friendship is not simply addressed to *all*, in a universal, homogeneous sense. Rather, the openness of address, which can only be thought through its determinate form, demonstrates the messianic logic of friendship in Derrida's recent work, which seeks to address the universal singularity of each one, or the universality of the exception.[98] This address, open to more than one, exceeds the one named as addressee or friend. This possibility of a friendship that exceeds a determinate, fixed addressee, is at the heart of Derrida's conception of both naming God and friendship. In the asymmetric, nonreciprocal love that provides a condition for friendship without ever appearing as such, a different thought of friendship emerges, even if one can never know that it exists, in certainty. Likewise,

---

96 For Derrida, the necessity of this thought of friendship as with "more than one" is engaged through the puzzling mantra-like repetition of Aristotle's reputed statement "O my friends, there is no friend!" In *Politics of Friendship*, Derrida puzzles over the nonappearance of this phrase in Aristotle's opus; however, if one changes the Greek accent, there is a phrase from the NE that fits: "He who has too many friends has no friend."

Derrida's analysis of this second phrase (in the chapter "Recoils") focuses on the opposed forms of speech in these two translations: the first (canonical) moves from performative to constative, while the second would seem to be simply constative, but thereby depends upon an even more open form of address. In this open address, the possibility of a friendship across difference may be thinkable. Perhaps; Derrida is wary of presenting this as an objective possibility. The primary point he seeks to make from this reading is that both phrases intersect in the thought that there is no single friend. Derrida, *Politics of Friendship*, pp. 194-226.

97 See Derrida, *Adieu*, pp. 49-85.

98 For Derrida's repudiation of "universal friendship" or "universal humanity" as itself a concept that effaces the aleatory and conditional status of politics and friendship, and thereby the messianic possibility of nonfraternal friendship, see Jacques Derrida, "Faith and Knowledge," in *Acts of Religion*, pp. 50-53. Of particular concern to Derrida on this count is the use of such a concept by European powers, in the name of a "universal humanity" that is in fact Christian (and thus not universal), and thus under the name of democracy and the liberal state effaces or neutralizes those differences which exceed its own form, often in the process promoting the spread of global capitalism.

deconstruction, as the witness to that which the name *seeks* to name, opens friendship beyond the limits of necessary identity.

As this chapter has shown, the possibility of a messianic structure of address arises both within the naming of God, and as an alternative politics, such that testimony shapes Derrida's understanding of both naming God and friendship. As Derrida puts it, his understanding of the naming of God and the politics of such a friendship are "with and against" the Judeo-Christian-Islamic traditions. Take, for example, the Christian love of the neighbor that is apparently determined as fraternal love, as in Augustine's *Confessions*. Even while Augustine thematizes charity as fraternity, a friendship and brotherhood in light of the love for God, the event of testimony and confession will have contested this determined address and opened itself beyond this predicative determination to the other as singular other.[99] Precisely by exceeding the order of representable friendship synonymous with fraternity, Derrida's work opens the thought of a relation that goes beyond cognition to a singular responsibility, a relation that both remains internal to and exceeds the thought of friendship within Christian theology.

For Derrida, then, the openness of testimony is connected with the responsibility that rests at the heart of both naming God and friendship. Yet as we have seen in both the discussion of naming and of friendship, testimony as a radically open address cannot appear *as such*, since it cannot be thematized and yet remain radically open at the same time. Its appearance must be irreducibly dissimulative. Testimony— speaking *to* an other in friendship or in prayer—cannot be certain; this possibility that unsettles ontotheology and fraternity exists in the mode of the "perhaps." Derrida draws this thought of the perhaps from Nietzsche:

> This is the moment when the disjunction between thinking and knowing becomes crucial ... This does not amount to conceding a hypothetical or conditional dimension but to marking a difference between "there is" and "is" or "exists"—that is to say, the words of presence.[100]

Nietzsche thinks the "perhaps"—the possibility that philosophy and Christianity, in seeking to be founded on truth, are nothing but a *fiction* that efface their own literary status—so as to unsettle the order of knowing and open the possibility of a genealogy. If "there is friendship" (*il y a l'amitié*) that can only be thought and not known, then the literary, fictive modality of thought is precisely what allows for a relation beyond cognition. "For to love friendship, it is not enough to know how to bear the other in mourning; one must love the future. And there is no more just category for the future than that of the 'perhaps.'"[101] The same "perhaps," it seems, could be said of the naming of God in prayer.

For Nietzsche, the "perhaps" opens a possibility of a friendship beyond charity or Christian love of one's neighbor. To carry out his genealogical project, however,

---

99 Derrida, *"Sauf le Nom,"* pp. 50-55.
100 Derrida, *Politics of Friendship*, p. 39.
101 Ibid., p. 29.

Nietzsche must think that he knows what the "perhaps" is, so that he can rigorously distinguish Christianity from that which would come thereafter. Yet nothing is less certain than the necessity of this genealogy; this literary modality of the "perhaps" may be against the Enlightenment, democracy, and humanity—or, contra Nietzsche, it may in fact be *for* it. Derrida disputes Nietzsche's reduction of Christianity; while he agrees with Nietzsche that theology remains economic, he sees it nonetheless as testifying to a noneconomic relation. This relation, as a messianic possibility beyond Christianity and beyond fraternity, may only be thought *through* fraternity, and in the possibility of its deconstruction. It may thus be *internal* to Christianity as well.[102] This would be, then, a theology that does *not* view the command to "Love your enemies" as a strictly private command, but rather one that opens up the very limits of political thought. At the same time, a faithful reading of Derrida's logic requires that one recognize that both the aneconomic possibility *and* the economic reduction of responsibility arise together, so that one can never be certain that a truly singular relation has occurred. This dual possibility, while recognizing the hope that resides within a theological conception of friendship, demands that such hope remain vigilant and responsible, against the constant possibility of losing the relation to singularity.

Furthermore, for Derrida, in spite of this appearance in Nietzsche's texts, the radically open form of the "perhaps" need not oppose itself to democracy or Enlightenment ideals, or to theology. Rather, the "perhaps" opens the thought of democracy to its most proper form—beyond the state, fraternity, and parties. The thought of every other as wholly other is the thought of radical democracy, even if as a messianic possibility it can only be testified to and never rendered present.[103] Such a deconstructive friendship renders contingent the concrete deployment of politics, bears in mind the aleatory nature of activity, and effaces its own presentation so as to keep itself open to others. This is why Derrida consistently raises questions of sexual difference. His project is wary of the risks of concrete political determination;[104] still, by opening the limits of established communities and interpretations, his work seeks to make them hospitable to singular relation to the other.[105]

---

102 Derrida's clearest distancing of himself from Nietzsche on this point is at the end of *The Gift of Death*, where (pp. 113-15) he wonders how Nietzsche can presume to know what faith is.

103 "Shall we say that this responsibility which inspires (in Nietzsche) a discourse of hostility towards 'democratic taste' and 'modern ideas' is exercised against democracy in general, modernity in general; or that, on the contrary, it responds in the name of a hyperbole of democracy ... to come?" Derrida, *Politics of Friendship*, p. 38.

104 A very good discussion of this facet of Derrida's work, particularly with regard to questions of sexual difference, is Drucilla Cornell's "Where Love Begins: Sexual Difference and the Limit of the Masculine Symbolic," in E. Feder, M. Rawlinson, and E. Zakin (eds), *Derrida and Feminism* (New York: Routledge, 1997), pp. 161-206.

105 Derrida's work, then, may remain unsatisfactory from a feminist standpoint. I find it valuable in opening canonical philosophical and religious understandings of names and friendship to new possibilities that may be more open to sexual difference and singularity.

The analysis to this point has argued for the convergence of Derrida's analysis of naming God and friendship in the idea of testimony. As in the earlier chapters, naming God and friendship exhibit logics similar to one another, but here we move beyond an Aristotelian or Thomistic approach. Naming God and friendship converge again—in this case, in the *impossibility* of appearing as such, and their connection with testimony—thereby pointing to an alternative conception of singularity and love that goes beyond cognition. By seeking to think relation *beyond* cognition rather than within its limits, this counter-convergence poses an important challenge to the essentialist understanding of names and friendship in Aristotle. In light of this analysis, it is now possible to rethink the significance of friendship with God in Aquinas. This involves both comparing their work directly, and reading Derrida in relation to two of his critics in Christian theology—John Milbank and Jean-Luc Marion. It thereby gives us an alternative standpoint from which to examine the Thomistic convergence between naming God and friendship, and this comparative analysis will constitute this work's conclusion.

That may remain the limits of its efficacy in terms of practical politics, but it strikes me as an important role nonetheless. I am grateful to Ellen Armour for raising questions that have helped me to think about the parameters of deconstruction's efficacy.

Chapter 6

Conclusion: In the Name of Friendship

I. Testifying to Friendship with God

The preceding chapters have demonstrated that for Thomas Aquinas and Jacques Derrida, friendship constitutes the pragmatic or political correlate of naming God. In light of how one names God, either in eminent discourse or in prayer and testimony, one conceives the possibility of singular relation, and thereby opens the field of possibility for friendship with human others. In charity as friendship with God, or in singular responsibility before the other, Thomas' and Derrida's understandings of the communal *telos* of human life grow from their views on language and signification, whether in terms of beatitude or the self-deconstructing pursuit of justice for singular others.

In light of this research, we may now draw several preliminary conclusions. First, this exploration of their work confirms the correlation between naming and friendship, as semantic and pragmatic modes of singularity. Thus, the examination of these concepts within the work of Derrida and Thomas has elucidated their respective understandings of singularity, and these concepts provide a way to relate the linguistic and pragmatic dimensions of singularity for other authors as well. Examining the relationship between naming God and friendship can illuminate singularity more fully, and each concept may serve as an interpretive key for understanding a particular author's work on the other concept as well.

Second, the correlation between naming God and friendship opens new avenues of thought for considering the political or pragmatic significance of particular approaches to religious thought. For both Thomas and Derrida, their views on naming God converge with specific understandings of friendship and charity, thereby leading their conceptions of friendship away from the Aristotelian conception of friendship with which this work began. In light of these transformations, one must consider what each approach to naming God offers for imagining and constructing responsible, just communities.

In the *Summa Theologiae*, naming God eminently plays a decisive role in the possibility of becoming friends with God. While we cannot know or name God properly by natural reason—as seen in the vagueness of the five ways' reference—sacred doctrine's eminent mode of signification names God properly (if still with deficient understanding). Through the *via negativa*, and its incorporation of both concrete and abstract signification, one directs one's language and thought toward the eminent discourse Dionysius described in *The Divine Names*. This discursive transformation in sacred doctrine's eminent discourse allows the human soul to take on the habit of charity, and to begin loving God for God's sake, in a voluntary action that moves us from servitude to friendship, participating in the science of God.

For Thomas, then, the supernatural possibility of naming God ruptures the closed world of Aristotelian friendship, as God's name signifies God's being with and for humanity. In this solidarity that traverses the distance between human and divine, the impossible friendship between God and humans becomes possible. Through adoption, a friendship between those of infinitely different natures becomes conceivable, calling into question the Aristotelian determination of friendship as an essential, natural and necessary identity. In thus dislocating friendship, this also reshapes the relation between friendship and justice, as charity acts to inform and transform the virtues of the soul.

The political implications of charity's transformation of friendship become clearest in the precept to love one's enemies, which extends the concern for distributive justice beyond the family or the *polis*. This command, one could say, serves as an apophatic moment that negates and displaces familial, natural love, reforming these bonds in the light of charity and God's love for creation. Like the eminent signification of divine names, charity incorporates and transcends both the particular responsibilities and universal precepts of scripture, forming an eminent love that seeks to love particular others without excluding all others. Particular friendships and familial relations, often interpreted as preferential and exclusive relations, become the secondary causality of God's providence and predestination, enacting a rich, agapic conception of distributive justice through the relations that constitute us as political animals. Thus, much as our naming of God affirms and denies concrete and abstract modes of signification to represent God's simplicity within our composite language, the eminent love of charity incorporates the varied aspects of our social, embodied life into the habit of Trinitarian love. Furthermore, strictly speaking, since our naming and understanding is deficient, it is through the activity of charity that we discover most fully who God is. By attending to the particular distribution of God's justice and mercy, in developing charity and friendship in the world, we participate in God's love and perfect our knowledge of God: "By the works which we perform with the body we can come to the perfect knowledge (*fruitionem*) of God" (ST II-II.25.8). Here, we see the pragmatic dimension of naming God at its fullest expression, as Thomas' speculative, Dionysian theology comes to its completion in charity.

Derrida's work points toward a different convergence, as naming God and friendship are both conceived as impossible, unable to appear as such. The impossibility of such singular relation thereby extenuates the quest for justice and opens the possibility of testimony. The unmotivated movement of the trace, which appears only in its effacement or erasure, allows one to name, but it also lets the other be other since the name and its referent are only arbitrarily related. What we call a "proper name" is always already classificatory, descriptive, and thus not really *proper* to that which it names. However, the failure of reference is for the good, as the dissociation between names and their referents allows prayer—as supplicating, undetermined, address to the other—to emerge, even if the language of praise *both* enables *and* effaces this relation, such that it only is as a trace.

The trace, then, is the thought of a radical alterity and friendship that goes beyond language even while remaining within it. When one thinks of language in light of the trace and difference, it becomes the site of the event, the gift, the friendship that relates to the other *qua* other. Without appearing as such, there *will have been* this event. This possibility of friendship is perhaps exemplified in the singular relation to God in prayer, which refers to the wholly other in a language that is both proper and inadequate, and thus remains unknowable in the strict sense. Such naming testifies to singular relation, holding out its possibility without ever determinately presenting it as such.

The inadequate propriety of naming not only makes singular relation possible, it also opens a concern for justice. Naming the wholly other, in its very respect for the other, cannot guarantee its reference; it may refer to any other, or *each* other as wholly other. For Derrida, this possibility of iteration and destinerrancy is at the heart of any singular relation—the condition for its possibility even while being its ruin. Since other others are therefore always already implicated within the singular relation of naming, the hyperbolic tautology of *tout autre est tout autre* reflects the singularity of friendship and naming into a concern for justice. Like naming, the singular relation of friendship finds its possibility in the impossibility of its appearing as such.

Derrida argues that this friendship that breaks with calculation is also suggested by the command to love one's enemies, when this command is interpreted in a *political* (i.e., non-private) sense. This command of an impossible love founds responsibility and justice, because it opens one to the possibility of loving any other, allowing love or friendship for another to be truly singular. Furthermore, in deconstructing the boundary between friend and enemy, friendship is rendered undecidable, which opens the space for decision and relation.

Bearing in mind both their reworkings of Dionysius and their interpretations of friendship in light of the command to love one's enemies, several intriguing comparisons between Thomas and Derrida emerge. First, and most basically, there is no friendship without justice for either thinker. Friendship is, in a sense, both a private and public relation; charity is between one and God as a spiritual communication, but it also seeks friendship with others, and pursues justice as the form of the virtues. Likewise, for Derrida, there is never a single friend; the third, as Levinas would say, will have been at the inception of friendship between two. Furthermore, it is important to note that Thomas, like Derrida, interprets the command to love one's enemies as a political command, and at its perfection charity would love enemies singularly, in spite of any natural or political borders of separation. The concerns of both thinkers with the political dimension, moreover, are not meant to deny the significance of individual, singular relations. Rather, for both Thomas and Derrida, without attending to this political dimension, a truly responsible attention to singularity would be impossible; in Thomas' terms, it is only through the political dimension that one fully embodies an *imitatio Christi*, and reaches the perfection of charity. Friendship is both relation within community, and that which unsettles communal bonds, self-deconstructively opening beyond itself.

The similarities discussed above are significant, as they show that both the Thomistic and deconstructive approaches require openness to the other, as concern for justice, in order for friendship to be responsible, and truly to pursue what is good. However, within these similarities, a specific difference emerges that demands more consideration. This difference is in terms of how one loves one's enemy, even a political one. For Thomas, there are three ways to love one's enemy—as an enemy, according to her nature, or as an individual—and the first possibility is excluded from charity as "perverse" and "contrary to charity." Thomas deems it impossible to love one who does one harm, or has enmity toward oneself, insofar as he or she is an enemy. One cannot love someone for the evil they would do, and so this is both irrational and impossible. In light of chapter 5, one could say that a certain fraternization is at work here; one conceives one's enemy as a brother, a fellow child of God, and thus as lovable, but thereby one also neutralizes the opposition and hostility between oneself and the enemy.

By contrast with Thomas, Derrida argues that one must love one's enemy as an enemy, in order for love, friendship, or forgiveness to be possible. This is a difficult and complex point, but it is clear that his thought of love of enemy goes beyond that of Thomas. For Derrida, to love an enemy *as* an enemy is to do the impossible, and it is, as for Thomas, a moment of madness. However, this moment of madness opens up the possibility of the impossible, which for Derrida is the only possibility that truly engages responsibility.[1] Only in such love could one truly forgive the singular other, or establish friendship with the other, even as such a hyperbolic love seems to go against all morality and ethics. Furthermore, such a love of the enemy is particularly important in opening the possibility of decision and responsibility within friendship; it immediately opens the question of whether or not one is to love one's friends, thereby allowing one to appropriate and decide for a love that would otherwise seem to be natural, programmed, or already decided. To love an enemy makes friendship with others responsible by opening the possibility of a decision that goes beyond what one knows or can rationalize. Thomas' disagreement on this point may be a recognition of our embodied finitude, yet the need to recognize this possibility, as founding responsibility, remains central.

The parallels between Thomas and Derrida can thus be summarized as follows. Both thinkers *extenuate* the conceptions of naming and friendship operative within their philosophical and theological settings, such that the significance of naming God is political—in the sense of both establishing and unsettling the limits of community. Thomas opens the closed world of Aristotelian friendship, transforming it into the eminent love of charity through a Pseudo-Dionysian discourse. Derrida's work likewise questions the limit of Thomas' work on charity, which remains predicative and restricts charity to fraternity. Testimony, in short, unsettles the stability, and knowability, of charity's eminent love.

---

1   For more on how love of enemy as an enemy is both demanded and impossible, see Jacquces Derrida, "On Forgiveness" in S. Critchley and R. Kearney (eds), *On Cosmopolitanism and Forgiveness* (New York: Routledge, 2001), esp. pp. 34-5.

Derrida's position could simply be read as adopting a quasi-Nietzschean critique of Christian love. However, in light of Thomas' commentary on John, and given that love of enemies is the perfection of charity, another possibility arises. For, if charity is friendship with God, it is friendship with the one who loves us even in our enmity toward God. To love one's enemy as an enemy, in the face of one's own death, is what God does for us, in divine ecstasy; thus, perhaps deconstruction points more starkly to the incarnational ethic that charity commands, calling Thomistic charity to be faithful to its vocation unto its limits.

The convergence of naming God and friendship in each author's work thus points toward an important difference in their respective positions. In light of this, we can now turn to the work of two of Derrida's most prominent theological critics, Jean-Luc Marion and John Milbank, both of whom engage Thomas and the Dionysian tradition in response to deconstruction. The conceptual association between naming God and friendship allows us to consider both the linguistic and political aspects of their criticisms of Derrida. In light of the above comparison, the inadequacies of both of their readings can be demonstrated, as will be shown below.

II. Giving Distance: Jean-Luc Marion and the Saturated Phenomenon

In his work, Jean-Luc Marion has consistently and thoroughly engaged Derrida in an ongoing conversation regarding the position of theology vis-à-vis philosophy, and its relation to phenomenology in particular. Marion's work is particularly relevant for several reasons: first, his commitment to a Dionysian theology places his views on divine names in direct conversation with Derrida. Second, his alternative reading of Husserlian phenomenology and Cartesian philosophy opens the possibility of a philosophy which might free theology from ontological, cognitive determination. Third, and very intriguingly, at least in his early work Marion criticized Thomas for reasons analogous to his criticisms of Derrida. He takes issue with Thomas for reducing goodness to the level of Being, and with Derrida for treating all difference as an "effect" of *différance*, in both cases foreclosing the possibility of a non-ontological metaphysics of the given. The subsequent change in his views regarding Thomas' thought can thus clarify the relationship between Marion and Derrida. Through these criticisms, his approach thus leads to an alternative understanding of naming God and friendship. To briefly summarize Marion's position, he argues for a conception of the good that transcends Being, breaks with the ontological difference while exceeding *différance*, and names God iconically, which leads to the envisaging of charity.

Marion generally maintains a distinction between his philosophical and theological investigations; nevertheless, he clearly philosophizes with a view toward theological reflection. It therefore makes sense to approach his criticism of Derrida first from a philosophical standpoint, and then elaborate the constructive theology that ensues. Marion directs his criticism of Derrida at the generalization of Derrida's conclusions regarding the working of *différance* as the quasi-cause of particular differences. In this generalization, he sees Derrida as falling into one of the frequent pretensions of philosophical atheism. For Marion, atheism is always and only a conceptual atheism: it denies a concept of God, as being truly infinite or being truly God. Rigorous atheism, as a denial of such concepts, can never accede to a denial of God's own self. As Marion writes, "Otherwise said, conceptual atheism remains rigorous only in never passing beyond the limits of its operative concept; in brief, its rigor regionalizes its power. In consequence, since all conceptual atheism must remain regional, it opens the possibility of other concepts of God in eliminating a concept of God (that which it denies)."[2] In thus recognizing the possibility of a God beyond or other than the concept that it denies, atheism would carefully recognize its own limits. This would allow one to *see through* atheism, iconically, to a new thought of God beyond an anthropomorphic concept.[3] Atheism would thus become a discourse of the *via negativa*, with its denial of concepts opening the possibility of an eminent theological discourse: "The succession of conceptual atheisms would thereby imitate, on the terrain of philosophy, the critical remotion of divine names in speculative theology."[4]

By contrast, an atheism which fails to recognize its limits becomes dogmatic, or even idolatrous. In failing to recognize that it has only destroyed or deconstructed a concept, atheism pretends to become absolute, forgetting the possibility of a God who passes the limits of human thought. As Marion writes in *God Without Being*:

> When a philosophical thought expresses a concept of what it then names "God," this concept functions exactly as an idol. It gives itself to be seen, but thus all the better conceals itself as the mirror where thought invisibly has its forward point fixed, so that the invisible finds itself, with an aim suspended by the fixed concept, disqualified and abandoned; thought freezes, and the idolatrous concept of "God" appears, where, more than God, thought judges itself.[5]

To act as if the negated concept is itself God is to be frozen by one's own reflection. These criticisms both indicate the limited, regional legitimacy that Marion accords to phenomenological criticism of theology, and suggest that the possibility of an eminent naming of God always exceeds the criticism that one could level against it. Broadly speaking, Marion applies this general criticism to Derrida's claim that God is "an effect of the trace" (in "Différance"), but his criticisms can also be more specifically located in two distinct moments.

---

2   Jean-Luc Marion, "De la «mort de dieu» aux noms divins: l'itinéraire théologique de la métaphysique," *Laval théologique et philosophique* 41 (1985), p. 27. My translation.

3   For an example along these lines, see Marion's reading of Anselm's *Proslogion*, which frees the argument from the strictures of Kant's refutation of the ontological argument. Jean-Luc Marion, "Is the Argument Ontological? The Anselmian Proof and the Two Demonstrations of the Existence of God in the Meditations," in *Cartesian Questions: Method and Metaphysics* (Chicago: University of Chicago Press, 1999), pp. 139-60.

4   Marion, "De la «mort de dieu»," p. 28.

5   Jean-Luc Marion, *God Without Being (Hors-Texte)*, trans. T. Carlson (Chicago; University of Chicago Press, 1991), p. 16.

First, in *The Idol and the Distance*, a work explicating the Dionysian alternative to contemporary continental conceptuality, Marion levels a sharp criticism against Derrida's conception of *différance* on several levels. First, Marion argues that *différance*, as the nonsimple origin of both ontic differences and ontological difference, is ultimately indifferent to any particular differences whatsoever. The generality of its movement ultimately reduces all differences to the same level. Second, in this indifference, as well as its conceptual similarity to the ontological difference, *différance* ultimately remains within the fold of ontological difference. Because it does not positively exceed ontological difference or its showing-forth of ontic differences, but only "is" in making them possible, *différance* is reducible to the ontological difference itself. Third, in his rejection of nostalgia, and his determination of theology as an effect of the trace, Derrida appears to think of theology as only conceiving God in ontotheological terms. Marion takes this to mean that Derrida does not consider the possibility of an eminent theology that would think of the differential relation between God and creation as a distance that exceeds the ontological difference and frees God from the idolatrous conceptuality of Being. This early criticism largely remains intact through *God Without Being*, the title of which (*Dieu Sans L'Être: Hors-Texte*) can be translated as "God Without the Letter," implying thinking God beyond writing, or outside the text.[6] This criticism is also reworked and intensified in more recent writings.[7]

Second, Marion's later work develops the idea of the gift and givenness as a phenomenological trait that elides conceptual circumscription. Turning his attention to Derrida's reading of Husserl in *Speech and Phenomena*, Marion argues that Derrida's criticism of Husserl fails to register the extent to which signification exceeds intuition in the *Logical Investigations*. In *Speech and Phenomena*, Derrida criticizes Husserl for limiting signification by intuition, as represented by Husserl's claim that the intended meaning of an occasional signification ("this," "now," etc.) can only be fulfilled (and grasped) in the presence of an accompanying intuition. Husserl, on Derrida's view, still thinks of the occasion in terms of a fullness of presence, rather than constituted by the trace through a play of differences, and it is on this point that Derrida argues that he remains within the metaphysical tradition even as he ends it.

For Marion, Derrida errs by making this regional demand for intuition within occasional signification into a general rule for Husserlian phenomenology.[8] Husserl argues that for other, nonoccasional forms of speech, signification need not be accompanied by an intuition, and that in some cases it must exceed intuition.

---

6 Or, again, as "God Without Being (It)," meaning "God Without Being God"; for more on the title, see Jacques Derrida, "How Not to Speak: Denials," in Coward and Foshay, *Derrida and Negative Theology*, p. 133 n. 3.

7 Marion, *God Without Being*, p. 85 (with footnotes citing *L'Idole et la Distance* (Paris: B. Grasset, 1977)).

8 Jean-Luc Marion, *Reduction and Givenness: Investigations of Husserl, Heidegger, and Phenomenology*, trans. T. Carlson (Evanston: Northwestern University Press, 1998), pp. 27-8.

Marion therefore claims that while Derrida is correct that Husserl thinks through a "metaphysics of presence," his phenomenology points to a notion of "presencing" that exceeds intuition; on Marion's view, the independence of signification from intuition indicates that a metaphysics of givenness precedes and exceeds the restricted, ontological presence targeted by Derrida's criticism.[9] Thus, while accepting Derrida's criticism of Husserl's account of occasional signification, the generalization from this regional argument is unwarranted, and occludes the possibility of a givenness and a "presencing."

Marion argues that Heidegger likewise follows this alternative thought of givenness in at least a limited fashion, as the "*es gibt*" ("There is/it gives") as a givenness of the Being of beings opens the thought of the ontological difference. He then moves beyond Heidegger's thought of givenness by inverting the relation between the moods of anxiety and boredom. Rather than think of boredom as that which opens us to being as a whole, such that anxiety can open us to the Nothing and thereby to the call of Being, he argues that a more radical boredom leads to the indeterminate call of anxiety *beyond* Being. "Could not boredom also—or even first—intervene in order to free us from the call through which Being claims us?"[10] This call, bored with everything and nothing, leads beyond being, such that I am called (*interloqué*) to respond before even *being* myself—a call very close, as Marion notes, to Levinas' envisaging of responsibility. Boredom functions as an apophatic mood that calls one beyond conceptuality and ontology to sheer givenness, in which both caller and called are anonymous. As Carlson suggests in reading the debate between Marion and Derrida, Marion accepts that for the subject to be properly surprised in the event of interlocution, the caller must remain unnamed. The "call as such" is precognitive and prior to any denomination.[11] "The imprecision, the indecision, and indeed the confusion of the claiming instance attests much rather that in the beginning is found the pure form of the call, as such."[12] This is, however, a break with both ontology and deconstruction. Givenness simultaneously liberates thought from intuition—as exemplified by the thought that goes beyond Being—*and* from the play of signification, the trace, and writing, as the pure call would be beyond any name or sign.

More recently, building on *Reduction and Givenness*, Marion has developed an approach that he considers a third reduction, alongside and beyond those of Husserl

---

9 Ibid., p. 37: "The broadening [of signification] must be understood not only as an extension of intuition and of signification through givenness, but especially as 'the demand for a liberation of the ground.' Givenness broadens presence in that it frees it from any limits of the faculties, as far as to let beings play freely—eventually beings in their Being. And only such a liberating broadening will be able to claim to surpass the 'metaphysics of presence,' which, in fact, does not cease to *restrain* the present and to *hold back* its givenness."

10 Ibid., p. 189.

11 Carlson, *Indiscretions*, p. 231.

12 Ibid., p. 202.

and Heidegger, and thus escaping the parameters of deconstruction. This reduction emphasizes the givenness of phenomena, as an aspect of phenomenality that exceeds objectivity, and thus precedes and encompasses both Husserlian and Heideggerian thought. Givenness is present both in everyday phenomena (such as a painting[13]) and revealed phenomena, such as Jesus teaching the disciples in the resurrection.[14] Marion labels such phenomena "saturated phenomena," as they overflow the categories of objectivity, while giving themselves to our senses. One of the central features of saturated phenomena is their overturning of consciousness. Whereas, within the field of objectivity, consciousness intends knowledge of objects, a saturated phenomenon inverts the gaze, and makes consciousness realize that it is subject to another—it finds itself called (*interloqué*), in a relation that exceeds cognition. Since such phenomena cannot be thought within the terms of objectivity, Marion argues we must expand our understanding of phenomena.

Marion thereby challenges Derrida's understanding of naming God and of friendship by interpreting them as exemplary saturated phenomena. The crux of his argument is that the practice of eminently naming God, in the Dionysian sense, goes beyond being, and does not seek to hyperessentialize God. In *Being Given*, Marion further identifies this indeterminacy with the name of God from Exodus 3:

> Moreover the name of God par excellence, such as God revealed it to Moses, attests precisely the impertinence of all names of essence or description in referring itself to an empty tautology—I am who I am—which opens the field to the litany of all names without end ... all phenomena of revelation (according to its possibility) and above all a Revelation (according to its effectivity) would imply the radical anonymity of the one who calls.[15]

As eminent signification, the naming of God is neither affirmative nor negative, and the effect of its "anonymity" is to pull the one who names God out of the realm of intentionality. This occurs most fully in the language of praise, which will still have the form of predication, as such attribution is necessary for prayer to occur (on Marion's view, this distinguishes his position from Derrida's). However, eminent signification is a "de-nomination," what Marion terms a "pragmatic theology of absence," opening a distance that places God beyond cognition and yet brings the subject into relation with the unnameable one:

> The Name does not name God as an essence; it designates what passes beyond every name ... This pragmatic theology is deployed, in fact, under the figure of the liturgy, where it is never a matter of speaking of God, but always of *speaking to God in the words of the Word*

---

13 Jean-Luc Marion, *Being Given: Toward a Phenomenology of Givenness*, trans. J. Kosky (Stanford: Stanford University Press, 2002), pp. 39-53. See also *The Crossing of the Visible*, trans. J. Kosky (Stanford: Stanford University Press, 2004).

14 Jean-Luc Marion, "'They Recognized Him; and He Became Invisible to Them," trans. S. Lewis, *Modern Theology* 18 (2002), pp. 145-52.

15 Marion, *Being Given*, p. 296. See also Marion, *L'Idole et la Distance*, pp. 186-7.

... Concerning God, this shift from the theoretical use of language to its pragmatic use is achieved in the finally liturgical function of all *theo*-logical discourse.[16]

Clearly, Marion here makes use of his earlier writing on atheism, as a form of negative theology that undoes the conceptual naming of God. Yet, in the pragmatics that he describes, eminent theology transcends negative theology, and thus remains free from Derrida's charge of hyperessentialization. Eminent theology, in transcending cognition, shifts the emphasis of naming to relation to the other, opening onto love and friendship.

Moreover, Marion has recently argued that friendship presents itself as an exemplary saturated phenomena. In "The Event or the Happening Phenomenon," Marion analyzes the friendship of Montaigne and Étienne la Boétie. In friendship, which "makes it my duty to cast a gaze on him,"[17] the one partner does not simply view the other; rather, the one makes himself subject to the other's gaze. In friendship, one becomes *interloqué*. The crossing of their gazes, in their meeting, and their mutual recognition, is only attributable to the event itself; it is an event "such that it gives itself without contest or reserve." What is intriguing, here, is that Marion's emphasis on friendship as an *event* highlights that it opens a distance for the subject, emphasizing that it asymmetrically opens one to the other, more than its reciprocity or equality.

Marion strikes a similar note in his interpretation of John 15, where he describes Jesus' friendship with the disciples. Jesus calls the disciples friends, insofar as they keep his commandments. What this signifies is that Jesus creates a space for the disciples, in which they can repeat, or perform, his acts and commands in their own way. Yet Jesus' act is also, simultaneously, a return to the Father, such that their repetition of his life is a participation in the life of the Trinity. It is in his return to the Father that he sends the Spirit to them—creating distance, opening alterity, and crossing the distance as well.[18] Jesus calls them to friendship—and they become friends, *by creating distance in their relations to one another*, participating in the divine creation of other subjects:

> Only charity (or however one would like to call it if one is afraid to acknowledge its name) opens the space where the gaze of the other can shine forth ... It is up to me to set the stage for the other, not as an object that I hold under contract and whose play I thus direct, but as the uncontrollable, the unforeseeable, and the foreign stranger who will affect me, provoke me, and—possibly—love me. Love of the other repeats creation through the same withdrawal wherein God opens, to what is not, the right to be, and even the right to refuse Him.[19]

---

16 Jean-Luc Marion, "In the Name: How to Avoid Speaking of It," in *In Excess: Studies in Saturated Phenomena*, trans. R. Horner and V. Berraud (New York: Fordham University Press, 2002), p. 157.

17 Jean-Luc Marion, "The Event or the Happening Phenomenon," in *In Excess*, pp. 37-8.

18 Jean-Luc Marion, "The Gift of a Presence," in *Prolegomena to Charity*, trans. S. Lewis (New York: Fordham University Press, 2002), pp. 141-5.

19 Jean-Luc Marion, "What Love Knows," in *Prolegomena to Charity*, pp. 166-7.

In this passage, we see Marion emphasize the asymmetry of relations, and that charity as friendship is a *repetition of God's unilateral gift*. Friendship, too, is anonymous, in that it is not simply an act of love toward God, but also an act that opens toward any stranger. Its unilateral character is highlighted, moreover, by the right to refusal granted to the other; it does not demand or require reciprocity. In short, for Marion, charity, as the height of love, requires the openness to love of the other as an enemy, and it is in this openness that love truly participates in the divine charity of the Trinity. Marion's construal of distance as constitutive of the triune relations will be discussed further below, in relation to Milbank's Trinitarian theology.

Marion articulates the theological implications of this anonymous givenness in terms of the gift that arises through non-ontological presencing. Liturgically the call that sends the gift occurs in the Eucharist. The Eucharist is not an event to be interpreted by a hermeneutics: it *is* a hermeneutics, the event in which the Son speaks to us of who the Father is. Theology, beginning from the Eucharist, is a discourse *of* God in both senses, as both "speaking and spoken," in which we address God, and thereby a saying that elides the predicative and thematic violence of human discourse. "The Word is not said in any tongue, since he transgresses language itself, seeing that, Word in flesh and bone, he is given as indissolubly speaker, sign and referent. The referent, which here becomes locutor, even if he speaks our words, is not said in them according to our manner of speaking."[20] The Eucharist, in which God signifies (and is signified) eminently, exceeds the effects of human language, even while appearing within them. It is God's interpretation of our language and subjectivity, interpreting and calling *us*.

Since the Eucharist is a communal event, it must occur in some form of presence. But which presence? This eucharistic hermeneutic plays itself out in the notion of the gift—a "present" without the ordinary notion of presence. Marion appropriates Heidegger's critique of the "ordinary conception of time" in which presence is conceived as *hic et nunc*—here and now, or in Heideggerian terms present-at-hand (*Vorhandenheit, maintenant*). A present that is a gift, however, is not simply here and now, but rather a present extenuated between a past pledge, and an (eschatological) future.[21] This gift, this act of love, can only be "justified" or demonstrated by further acts of love—by charity. And, indeed, this is not a justification or assurance in the ordinary sense, since it only comes to its fruition in the testimony of martyrdom. Here, Marion's reflections on eminent language unfold into practice, as one confesses Jesus' lordship, and authenticates such confession in one's martyrdom or self-abandon as an act of charitable love.[22] Such martyrdom, beyond a metaphysical notion of presence, likewise exceeds the limits of a deconstructive criticism.

---

20 Marion, *God Without Being*, p. 141.
21 Ibid., pp. 170-73.
22 Ibid., pp. 196-7.

While the preceding discussion summarizes the main points of Marion's project and his response to Derrida, his reading of Thomas also plays a central role in the development of his reflection. This criticism is most explicit in *God Without Being*, though also suggested in earlier works as well.[23] As Marion writes:

> If the imagination can produce the idol that takes the place of the absent, and if the *ens* falls largely in the conception of imagination, can one not hazard that, according to what Saint Thomas himself freely insinuates, the *ens*, related to "God" as his first name, indeed could determine him as the ultimate—idol?[24]

By privileging "Being" as the most proper name of God, whose essence is to exist, Thomas supposedly thinks divine goodness within the parameters of Being, and thus in the terms of onto-thelogy. On Marion's view, this is a decisive moment in the history of theology: "The divine certainly did not await Saint Thomas to enter into metaphysics; but it is only with Saint Thomas that the God (crossed out) revealed in Jesus Christ under the name of charity finds himself summoned to enter the role of the divine of metaphysics, in assuming *esse/ens* as his proper name."[25] To treat God as Being, in this sense, is to enter decisively into onto-theology, privileging speculative access over the knowledge of God that, in the name of the good, apprehends God primarily as love.

For Marion, Thomas thus departs from the Dionysian tradition of conceiving God as the good beyond being. This criticism is quite close to that of Michel Corbin discussed in chapter 3. By contrast with the ontological approach that forecloses distance, as we have seen the Dionysian naming opens beyond ontotheology:

> To begin with, he [Denys] does not pretend that goodness constitutes the proper name of the Requisite (*aitia*), but that in the apprehension of goodness the dimension is cleared where the very possibility of a categorical statement concerning God ceases to be valid, and where the reversal of denomination into praise becomes inevitable. *To praise* the Requisite *as* such, hence *as* goodness, amounts to opening distance ... The first praise, the name of goodness, therefore does not offer any "most proper name" and decidedly abolishes every conceptual idol of "God" in favor of the luminous darkness where God manifests himself, in short, where he gives himself to be envisaged by us.[26]

Goodness, then, moves one beyond naming, opening the unnameable thought of God in a self-effacing "luminous darkness."

In response to criticism, Marion has revised his approach to Thomas' thought. Briefly put, he has recognized that Thomas' privilege of Being as the name most proper for our understanding does not *absolutely* privilege Being over goodness. Indeed, given the indeterminacy of this name, it may be the way that God remains unknowable for us, preserving the transcendence and eminence of God that Marion

---

23 See Marion, *L'Idole et la Distance*, pp. 270-71.
24 Marion, *God Without Being*, p. 82.
25 Ibid., p. 82.
26 Ibid., p. 76.

sees as signified more properly by goodness. In more recent work, he has suggested that Aquinas distinguishes between divine being and the Being that one finds in Heidegger, thus reinterpreting Being itself as an eminent discourse.[27] Marion's complex attitude toward Thomas illustrates the difficulty in interpreting Thomas' appropriation of Aristotelian grammar and metaphysics. On the one hand, as Marion has argued, one can read Thomas as reducing or misinterpreting the Dionysian, eminent approach to theology, bringing it within the parameters of ontotheology. On the other hand, one could argue, as in chapter 3, that Thomas actually directs Aristotelian philosophy beyond its limits, emptying it of its worldly content in a theological remotion, remaining more faithful to Dionysius than he would initially appear.

In thinking this second possibility, one must reflect upon the *necessity* of appropriating Aristotelian philosophy, through which Thomas differs from the earlier Dionysian heritage. Namely, when Thomas takes this approach, he distances himself, and humanity, from divine presencing, as our access to the eminent world of charity only comes through the dissimulation of being. Charity only appears to us as a trace within our language. Thus, while affirming the Dionysian idea of God as the self-diffusing good in whom all creatures move and have their being, and participate in goodness to that extent, Thomas also makes any immediate, cognitive understanding of God impossible, such that it is only through faith and the practical working of charity that a knowledge of God becomes possible. In short, by opening a path to charity through the metaphysics, causality, and ethics of Aristotelian philosophy, Thomas affirms the imminent, worldly life of the wayfarer, while recognizing the transcendence and nonappearance of the beatific vision that completes the life of charity. It may be in the language of being that God's goodness becomes manifest to us.[28]

Still, the category of the saturated phenomenon, and the emphasis on givenness, open new possibilities for conceiving of theological language and ethics. As Marion strongly argues, this suggests that phenomena of revelation—including Christian scriptures, but those of other traditions as well—should be accorded a legitimate place in phenomenological discussion. However, in his attempts to argue that givenness is not subject to deconstruction, he pristinates the saturated phenomenon in a way that is not warranted. For instance, in *God Without Being*, Marion describes the justification or assurance that marks a truly Christian speech, as epitomized in the phrase "Jesus is Lord." In this phrase, he argues that the speaker is distanced from its referent, and ultimately the assurance for the phrase can only come through

---

27 Jean-Luc Marion, "Saint Thomas d'Aquin et l'Onto-théo-logie," *Revue Thomiste* 95 (1995), pp. 31-66.

28 See, for instance, Richard Kearney, "The God Who May Be," in J. Caputo and M. Scanlon (eds), *Questioning God* (Indianapolis: Indiana University Press, 2001), p. 169: "It (naming God as being) shows that God's self-nomination cannot dispense with the detour through being, lest it become so unknown as to pass us by unseen, unheard ... to pass beyond being you have to pass through it."

the Son himself. Thus, whereas other discourse, whether constative or performative, relies to a certain degree upon the assurance and promise of the speaker, in this language of faith the speaker denies his own legitimacy as a speaker, and refers the statement to God:

> The Christian is not attested as such by calling himself Christian, but by saying: "Jesus is Lord," and expecting of Jesus alone that he confirm both the utterance and the one who speaks [*énonciateur*] … He thus endures, as much as the suffering of an often persecuted minority, the pain of not knowing the one he names, and especially of knowing himself disqualified from every qualification to know him, and even to confess him.[29]

Clearly, the believer's relation to Christ, and his statement, in its authenticity, would be a statement that goes beyond cognition. Insofar as this is the case, the statement "states" martyrdom or testimony.

However, one must recognize, as well, that this same statement can become dogmatic, speculative, or otherwise predicative, and this possibility is internal to the possibility of testimony or martyrdom. The anonymity of the name can be lost in its enunciation. As Jesus states in the Sermon on the Mount:

> Not everyone who says to me, "Lord, Lord," will enter the kingdom of heaven, but only the one who does the will of my Father in heaven. On that day, many will say to me, "Lord, Lord, did we not prophesy in your name, and cast out demons in your name, and do many deeds of power in your name?" Then I will declare to them, "I never knew you; go away from me, you evildoers."[30]

In this statement, and the contrast between building upon rock and sand that follows, Jesus dissociates *doing* God's will from the words that are spoken. At the least, the words themselves provide no assurance of their reference. Relation to God, distance, and friendship reside in responsibility and openness to the other, and this statement of faith itself remains open to contamination, violence, and evil. In this statement— and the ethic of the Sermon on the Mount that accompanies it—the certainty or assurance of faith differs from itself, in a pragmatic openness to the other.

In this quote, then, we see a scriptural warrant for accepting Derrida's approach to prayer and praise, as radical openness to the other must, in some sense, remain beyond the language of praise. This would, likewise, counter Derrida's hypothesis that the distinction is "inadmissible" for a Christian theologian. It points, I think, to a deeper issue in Marion's thought of givenness as falling outside the purview of deconstruction. By arguing that givenness is constitutive of the appearance of all phenomena, Marion thereby highlights the way that when something gives itself, it may be mis-taken, and the givenness may not be recognized. It may be objectified, or perceived without charity. This is a condition of the saturated phenomenon itself.

---

29 Marion, *God Without Being*, p. 195.
30 Matthew 7:21-3.

Indeed, this becomes even clearer when Marion discusses how the idol is a saturated phenomenon[31]—and yet, in no way opens onto the gaze of another.

Marion's dismissal of Derrida's arguments regarding negative theology encounters similar problems. The eminent naming of God may go beyond predication to pragmatics, but it still takes the form of predication. It thus gives rise to the possibility of speaking *of* God, and this possibility arises with the emergence of eminent naming itself. This is, in fact, the heart of Derrida's critique of negative theology: not that prayer must be utterly dissociated from attribution, but rather that it must be dissociated from attribution *and* rely on attribution at the same time. Its impossibility is also the condition for naming God.

From this, one can conclude that if one follows Marion to the end, his theo-phenomenology does "hyperessentialize" God. Not by treating God as being, nor in imagining that we can speak of God's goodness beyond being. Rather, insofar as Marion treats the saturated phenomenon as an isolatable, pure event, free from the effects of the trace and onto-theology, he does not admit that it may lose its identity, lapse, or fall into objectification. Likewise, as friendship must give the other the possibility of refusal, in order to be itself friendship must risk its failure. Betrayal and theft are possibilities internal to givenness; in other words, if givenness never appears as such, then it may operate within the parameters of deconstruction, and continued deconstruction may be necessary for the proper thought of givenness to emerge. Thus, insofar as Derrida does not recognize that saturated phenomena *may* exceed the play of the trace, though this cannot be known, his reading of Marion must be qualified. Nonetheless, insofar as Marion refuses to recognize that Derrida's critique still applies to his work, his response remains deficient.

This is not an idle distance between Marion and Derrida; it has profound effects on the role that language plays in ethics. If a "pure call" is possible as such, then the relation to God is, ultimately, knowable: even if one only knows it in knowing oneself to be called, one still *knows* that one has been called. For Derrida, however, it is precisely when relation exceeds cognition that responsibility—and thus friendship—can be found. Derrida's emphasis on the impossibility of address, testimony, and friendship opens a space for responsibility beyond thematization, and his concern with Marion's work seems to be its risk of reinscribing responsibility within a thematic or conceptual framework, despite Marion's protests to the contrary.

III. Derrida and Radical Orthodoxy

In the wake of Heideggerian philosophy and its challenge to theology, the radical orthodoxy movement founded by John Milbank, Catherine Pickstock, and Graham Ward[32] has appropriated Aquinas' work as the basis for a challenge to postmodernity.

---

31 Jean-Luc Marion, "The Idol or the Radiance of the Painting," in *In Excess*, pp. 54-81.

32 In what follows, the discussion will focus primarily upon Milbank's own work, though occasional reference will be made to the work of others in the radical orthodoxy movement. For the purpose of simplicity, I will refer here to *Truth in Aquinas* (Oxford: Blackwell, 2000)

In turning to patristic theology (up to and including Thomas), while locating the roots of modern and postmodern thought in late medieval nominalism, radical orthodoxy has argued for an alternative, theological ontology and a conception of difference that questions the parameters of deconstructive and postmodern thought. Milbank's argument often proceeds from a shared starting ground, but then diverges from postmodernity with respect to the conclusions. As he writes in *Theology and Social Theory*:

> The strategy which the theologian should adopt is that of showing that the critique of presence, substance, the idea, the subject, causality, thought-before expression, and realist representation do not necessarily entail the critique of transcendence, participation, analogy, hierarchy, teleology and the Platonic Good, reinterpreted by Christianity as identical with Being. This strategy ... points out an unexpected fissure traversing its blank face of refusal ... By exposing the critical non-necessity of the reading of reality as conflictual, and the hopelessly metaphysical nature of even this ontology, an alternative possibility of reading reality as of itself peaceful is gradually opened to view, and the notions of transcendence, participation, analogy, hierarchy, teleology and the Platonic Good will be shown to belong inextricably to this reading.[33]

While accepting the poststructural refusal of modernity, radical orthodoxy thus argues that a Christianized Platonism offers an alternative logic that can respond to the crisis of nihilism.[34] Specifically, a Trinitarian "theoontology" can, on Milbank's view, imagine an alternative way of thought and thus of human community. As he writes, "God as Trinity is therefore himself community and even a community in process, infinitely realized beyond any conceivable opposition between 'perfect act' and 'perfect potential.' A trinitarian ontology can therefore be a differential ontology surpassing the Aristotelian 'actus purus.'"[35]

Milbank's challenge to deconstruction is part of a larger challenge to the preeminence of the transcendental project in modern theology. By refusing to treat phenomenology as the limit of thought and metaphysics, Milbank's work moves beyond the scope of possibility and impossibility as framed by Derrida, Marion, and other recent continental thinkers. His account develops an alternative metaphysics whose originality exceeds the bounds of onto-theology, and thereby frees Thomas' conceptions of analogy, participation, and reciprocal gift-exchange from the bounds of Heideggerian thought. While his work is important constructively, I will argue below that his critique of Derrida fails, particularly as regards the contrast between Thomas and Derrida. Namely, Derrida's critical work retains its importance even

---

as a part of Milbank's opus, though that is in no way meant to minimize Catherine Pickstock's original contributions to this work.

33 John Milbank, *Theology and Social Theory: Beyond Secular Reason* (Oxford: Blackwell, 1990), p. 296.

34 See John Milbank, "The Programme of Radical Orthodoxy," in Hemming, *Radical Orthodoxy? A Catholic Enquiry*, pp. 33-45.

35 John Milbank, "Postmodern Critical Augustinianisms: A Short Summa in Reply to Forty-Two Unasked Questions," *Modern Theology* 7 (1991), p. 234.

in light of Milbank's writings, precisely in terms of explicating the asymmetry of the relationship between God and creation, and the deficiency of our acts and significations in response to divine charity and speech.

Taking up the language of gift-giving, and as a challenge to Derrida's conception of the gift as impossible, Milbank lays out an alternative to the deconstructive project. Beginning from the notion that "gift" is a proper name for the Holy Spirit—as discussed by Thomas in I.37 of the *Summa*—Milbank argues that gift is properly conceived in *reciprocal* rather than unilateral terminology, as the Spirit is the exchange between the Father and Son. Whereas gift is often taken to mean a unilateral act of expenditure without return that disrupts the exchange of economics, if "gift" is the proper name for the communion of the Father and Son, then it should be thought as a noneconomic reciprocity. Two features constitute such noneconomic reciprocity: indefinite delay and nonidentical repetition, and their import is twofold. First, it indicates that the initial gift is a gift, in part, by creating a space and time for the agency of the other; it gives subjectivity to the recipient in hoping that its gift will lead to activity by the other. Whereas a contractual or legal exchange precludes the responsibility of the other, foreclosing it in its programmatic detail, a gift permits the other agency from its first reception. Second, delay and the nonidentical repetition of a gift take on further importance for Milbank's argument in that they require judgment, *phronesis*, and virtue, so that one gives at the right time and in the right way.[36] Delay and nonidentical repetition "might be construed as a requisite *attention* to the other, her character, situation, and mood, such that we know how to surprise and not to annoy."[37] Gift-exchange, then, would only be fulfilled by a careful attention to particulars.

As opposed to unilateral gift-giving, gift-exchange exhibits two central characteristics of Milbank's theological project. First, he undertakes a critical retrieval of the scholastic and patristic tradition, finding the primary analogate of all gift-exchange in the Trinity. Human gift-exchange, then, is a human participation in the reciprocal relations of love between the Father, Son, and the Spirit. The resources for such primary gift-giving are found in both Jewish culture and the Jewish and Christian scriptures:

> Even in its origin, the Church begins as an exchange and not as a simple reception of a unilateral gift ... An aspect of Christ's kenosis is his entering into irreducible dependence and sociality, yet by virtue of his trinitarian existence there is no shedding of aseity involved here ... One receives gift *as* the gift of an always preceding gift-exchange. Only such a perspective makes sense of why *agape* arrives as an interpersonal event and not simply as a new command ... To be a Christian is *not*, as piety supposes, spontaneously and freely to love, of one's own originality and without necessarily seeking any communion. On the contrary, it is to *repeat differently*, in order to repeat, *exactly*, the content of Christ's

---

36 John Milbank, "Can a Gift Be Given? Prolegomena to a Future Trinitarian Metaphysic," *Modern Theology* 11 (1995), p. 151.

37 Ibid., p. 132.

life, and to wait, by a necessary delay, the answering repetition of the other that will fold temporal linearity back into the eternal circle of the triune life.[38]

The significance of delay and nonidentical repetition are clearly evident in this passage. In thinking of gift-exchange as an interpersonal event that repeats divine relationality, Milbank shifts away from contractual obligation and technique toward personal and social relations. As represented in the primary analogate of the triune life, one could say the following: *what* is given, in its concreteness and ontological specificity, is always already shaped by the donnee: ontology is a manifestation of personal relation, rather than a substance into which personal relation may then intervene. For Milbank, this is represented in created being in that we only *are* insofar as we receive from God and return praise to God. Being, as participation, is itself the nonidentical repetition of triune exchange.

Second, Milbank seeks a further, critical retrieval of Greek metaphysics and its accompanying conception of virtue. While Milbank is admittedly more Platonist than Aristotelian, his conception of gift-exchange as nonidentical reciprocity based on virtue and *phronesis* resonates strongly with the reciprocal activity of Aristotelian friendship.[39] Like Aristotle, he reads a concern for justice as a *prerequisite* for friendship; contractual obligation, on his view, is undertaken precisely so that the generosity of gift-exchange can extend itself—or at minimum can avoid the egoism that would restrict giving to a preferential friendship that neglected others. [40] Such generous *agape* finds its fulfillment not as a purely disinterested ethical relation, but rather as a relation that seeks to extend generosity in and through its attention to particularity. The generosity of giving, for Milbank, only finds its fulfillment when what is given is appropriately correlated to its recipients, so that giving courses in and through being—personalizing being in this event.

Milbank has further emphasized the import of particularity and embodiment in his recent writings, contrasting an ensouled selfhood (which is both spirit and embodiment) with the dualistic subjectivity of Descartes and modernity. Here, he further develops the connection with friendship noted above, and argues that this reciprocity need not be exclusive or enclosed. In contrast with the disinterested love of Kantian and post-Kantian ethics, he writes that for Aquinas, "one will find ... not a word which construes charity as the neutral altruistic love for the remote, but much about a hierarchical, preferential exercise of charity according to specific relations and affinities—of course including that toward the arriving stranger."[41]

---

38 Ibid., p. 150.

39 In *Theology and Social Theory*, Milbank does argue against the agonistic, exclusive components of Aristotelian virtue (and, thus, of Aristotelian friendship); see pp. 355-60. This criticism has received less emphasis in more recent writings, but it must be acknowledged.

40 Ibid., pp. 151-2.

41 John Milbank, "The Soul of Reciprocity (Part One): Reciprocity Refused," *Modern Theology* 17 (2001), p. 343. While I disagree with his assessment of Levinas, Milbank's proposal bears striking and promising affinities with the conception of embodiment set forth in Luce Irigaray's recent work, *To Be Two* (New York: Routledge, 2001).

Drawing on Aquinas' order of charity, Milbank rightly notes that we exercise charity as "finite animals," and thereby argues that the "asymmetrical reciprocity"[42] of the soul to others and the world provides a richer and more accurate conception of both subjectivity and moral action than any Cartesian or post-Cartesian approach.

Milbank's proposal is notable both for its emphasis on the importance of justice to a proper gift, *and* in its emphasis on concrete particularity as represented by the "suitability" of a gift, as well as the embodied nature of reciprocity. As part of his relational ontology, he also reconceives the act of naming God. As he writes: "The name 'Jesus' does not indicate an identifiable 'character', but is rather the obscure and mysterious hinge which permits shifts from one kind of discourse to another."[43] The name "Jesus" finds its meaning not only in the events and acts of Jesus' life, but also in the metanarrative interpretations of this life that are already internal to the gospel. This indicates a complexity to how we "identify" Jesus that is often overlooked: the meaning of Jesus, on Milbank's view, can only be understood in light of the continued, non-identical *repetition* of the name—the name's meaning is its use.

Much as a gift is only fully received in its use and delayed return, we only understand who Jesus is, and what it means to say that God is incarnate in Jesus, through embodied reception of Jesus—textually in scripture, but in the Church as well. This network of interpretations and repetitions gives the name "Jesus" its radical uniqueness. The relational properties of the name constitute its ontological reference: "It [personal identity] resides purely on the 'surface' of a series of events which exhibit a certain pattern and coherence. It is, paradoxically, the unique singularity and incommunicability of this pattern which makes it 'repeatable' and further definable beyond the confines of its possession by a single 'individual'."[44] Only in the passage from one to the other does a name truly achieve its uniqueness. Again, the participatory ontology is evident, as our speech participates in God's own speaking of the Son. Such participation, moreover, is clearly formative of community: "Jesus is the name of the new law, because now the word of God is found to be located ... in true, strong, peaceful relationships, beginning with the practice of Jesus."[45] Ontology and pragmatics go hand in hand.

In Milbank's work, Thomas' importance lies largely in his development of a theological metaphysics. Natural reason has a limited knowledge of God; the participation of natural reason in sacred doctrine (in faith) is thus a growth into the

---

42 By asymmetrical reciprocity, Milbank means "not a fixed circle, but an unending spiral, in which each response only completes the circle by breaking out of it to reestablish it." John Milbank, "The Soul of Reciprocity (Part Two): Reciprocity Granted," *Modern Theology* 17 (2001), p. 486. The contrast, here, is with a "fixed circularity" that would be ontotheological, and that Milbank associates with Aristotle; such a "fixed" circularity would be close to the essentialism discussed in chapter 2.

43 John Milbank, "The Name of Jesus," in *The Word Made Strange: Theology, Language, Culture* (London: Blackwell, 1997), p. 149.

44 Ibid., p. 157.

45 Ibid.

divine life, an *intensification* of our participation in the divine life. Milbank thus argues that for Thomas, we do have a vision of the divine essence in this life—indirectly, perhaps, but nonetheless still a knowledge of who God is. The central argument, here, is that theology understands creation as participating in the divine life, rather than as something that can be known independently.[46] Furthermore, our knowledge (or faith, in and through sacred doctrine) is in some sense a repetition of God's knowledge of God's self, and the truth of what we "know" lies in the correspondence between human and divine cognition, as the human mind grows in conformity to the divine way of knowing through the Son.[47]

While Milbank's approach takes Thomas as a prototype for the development of a theo-ontology, questions have been raised regarding the limits of this appropriation. For example, as Frederick Bauerschmidt has argued, Milbank's Christology appears to identify the Church and Christ, at least insofar as the Church's practice becomes determinative of the reference of the name "Jesus."[48] Bauerschmidt's argument points toward an important tension within Milbank's work; for, while he rightly recognizes that Aquinas' doctrine of analogical participation qualitatively differentiates God from creation, in practice it often would appear that this differentiation is lost. For example, in a paper responding to Derrida's reflections on forgiveness, Milbank writes, "Forgiveness, therefore, perfects gift-exchange as fusion," and glosses this as shared character, "one shared identity." This is, at once, the union of the Incarnation, and the union toward which creation is directed as well.[49] Such language of fusion evokes Augustinian friendship, in which friends are "one soul in two bodies,"[50] but it also raises questions as to whether the singularity of the participants is suitably recognized.

While it would be overstating the case to say that Milbank emphasizes participation to the point of obscuring the difference between divine simplicity and creaturely existence, the emphasis on reciprocity (even on asymmetrical reciprocity) indicates that Bauerschmidt has located symptoms of what could be a deeper problem in Milbank's work. Namely, to emphasize the reciprocity of divine-human friendship with God, and the participation of the Church in the life of the Trinity, obscures the unilateral, universal activity of grace in this process of sanctification. For, while on the one hand the acts by which we reciprocate are ours, on the other hand the ability to reciprocate, and the very possibility of reciprocating, are initiated by God (see the section in chapter 4 on the universal and particular causality of grace and

---

46 See John Milbank, "Intensities," *Modern Theology* 15 (1999), pp. 445-97. This essay is reprinted as the second chapter of Milbank, *Truth in Aquinas*.

47 Here, see Catherine Pickstock's opening essay on Thomas' "correspondence theory" of truth in *Truth in Aquinas*, pp. 1-18.

48 Frederick Bauerschmidt, "The Word Made Speculative: John Milbank's Christological Poetics," *Modern Theology* 15 (1999), pp. 417-32.

49 John Milbank, "Forgiveness and Incarnation," in Caputo and Scanlon, *Questioning God*, pp. 117-18.

50 St. Augustine of Hippo, *The Confessions*, trans. E. Hampl (New York: Vintage, 1999), p. 61.

free will for further elaboration). This is clear for Thomas, from Jesus "calling" the disciples to friendship, or teaching them the first principles of charity, to the Spirit's creating the habit of charity in the soul. Even, it seems to me, within the life of the Trinity, Thomas' emphasis upon the innascibility of the Father indicates that a unilateral logic works in tandem with reciprocity, precisely so as to open it beyond any restrictive or essential limits.

Two related problems arise from this first issue. First, our participation is given an overwhelmingly speculative character—as, for instance, in glossing faith as an increase in knowledge. The sense that we may participate in the divine life in charity, or through the practice of friendship itself, largely recedes from view. As we have seen, for Thomas, the eminent language of mystical unknowing opens onto friendship, as the way that we come to the fullest cognition of God available in this life. In spite of radical orthodoxy's explicit political commitments, the overriding emphasis on ontology and metaphysics may shift the focus to a more speculative theology than Thomas himself would hold.

Second, the emphasis on ecclesial participation risks underplaying the relationship of the Church to the world. The emphasis on reciprocity and liturgy may leave one with the impression that the Church, in its own identity, is a vibrant and full participation in the divine life, in isolation from the surrounding world. While Milbank does, as in the above quote, recognize that gift-giving must be "open to the stranger" to reflect divine charity, the emphasis on friendship as shared commitment to the good, liturgical naming of God as participation, and the exclusivist aspects of Platonist and Aristotelian friendship leave the relationships with those outside Christian community largely undeveloped. This can raise the suspicion that such relationships are not an integral aspect of Christian life for radically orthodox theology.[51] For example, while *Truth in Aquinas* emphasizes embodiment as the way that we come to know God as Trinity,[52] centrally through the Incarnation, such knowledge is glossed as primarily liturgical. By contrast, if one centralizes the importance of friendship as the form of embodied contemplation Christians are called to undertake, the significance of ethics, relations beyond the community, and liturgy can all be given appropriate play in considering the embodied, lived form of contemplation that grows from Thomas' account of naming God in Christ. While Milbank's work expresses a commitment to such openness, his growing antipathy toward Derridean and Levinasian thought raises the question of just how central such openness is to his reflection. At the least, there is a tension here.

Milbank's retrieval of more traditional modes of theological discourse, the imagining of analogy as non-identical repetition, and the argument for a distinctively Christian relational metaphysics are all significant and helpful achievements. However, whereas Milbank argues that these constructive developments likewise

---

51 For an argument along these lines, see Mark Dooley, "The Catastrophe of Forgiveness: Derrida, Milbank, and the (Im)possibility of Forgiveness," in Caputo and Scanlon, *Questioning God*, p. 135.

52 Milbank, *Truth in Aquinas*, pp. 60-87.

imply the refutation of deconstruction and an overcoming of nihilism, it is precisely in recognizing the importance and innovation of Milbank's work that Derrida's thoughts regarding the gift, friendship, and naming God regain their significance. This can be demonstrated through consideration of several features of his arguments.

First, as mentioned above, one wonders if Milbank's emphasis on ecclesiological participation in the divine life obscures or marginalizes the specific differences by which we share in such activity. While Aquinas does emphasize analogical participation, and our ability to become friends with God, he also strongly differentiates the causality of God and humanity within charity, and the mode of our participation is clearly deficient (as is the mode of signification in naming God, even eminently).

The distinction by Derrida between prayer and praise may be helpful here, in terms of recognizing the limited manner of our participation in charity. For, as Derrida argues that it is in the opening of oneself to the other in prayer, which accompanies the praise of faith but is in principle dissociable from it, for Thomas it is in the acts of charity, the works of the body, that we most fully relate to God and participate in charity. To be sure, these acts come about through faith, and in the context of liturgical and scriptural language. Yet one may wonder if the priority Thomas accords to charity—which, of the theological virtues, is the only one to remain *in patria*—might be well served by the prayer/praise distinction by which Derrida interrogates negative theology. For, while faith relates to God as God is in our intellect—and thus, within ontology and the realm of the same—Thomas does say that charity relates to God as God is, beyond what we may thematize or know. It may only be through faith that charity becomes possible, yet Thomas does still distinguish the respective places of these theological virtues, a point that could be further clarified in Milbank's work. Charity, like prayer, goes beyond the language of predication in relation to the other.

Second, and perhaps most importantly, while Milbank conceives of the unilateral gift as inherently violent, and reductive of the contingency and embodiment of giving, one must ask if the asymmetrical reciprocity of gift-exchange necessarily excludes or overcomes violence. This is, in large part, to consider the ethical implications of the difference between God and creation. To be sure, when discussing the Trinity, the gift-exchange of love between the persons (in which the persons are the gifts, so complete is the love and exchange) is perfect. To imagine such love, to believe it in the faith and the practice of the Church, is to believe in the possibility of a perfectly peaceful love and exchange. However, at the same time, Milbank himself recognizes that the human repetition of such gift-giving is imperfect, and frequently marked by violence and failure. Milbank notes, for example, that the need for contracts and law can be interpreted as a regulation upon the injustice of human giving, and its failure to repeat properly the divine generosity that it seeks to imitate anew (see p. 196 above). Furthermore, at the end of *Theology and Social Theory*, he argues that the Church's failure to live up to the practice that it imagined unleashed a worse violence, as law and politics became dissociated from the church communities, with secularity emerging from this dissociation of Church and state.⁵³

These ruinations of peaceful gift-giving do not, of themselves, preclude the possibility of a peaceful ontology. One could argue, therefore, that such a radically orthodox approach advocates, and seeks to practice, an ontology of peace, over against a poststructural or deconstructive theology that takes violence as foundational and necessary, or that there can be a peacefully predicative form of discourse and naming. Yet the contrast between radical orthodoxy and deconstruction is not so simple. As we have seen with respect to both naming God and friendship for Derrida, it is not the case that reference simply fails, or that friendship and giving are immediately violent. Rather, the point is that reference and friendship are constituted by the *possibility* of their failure and violence. The possibility of their failure and their success are one. This possibility thus structurally determines them, and thereby is inevitable; in the human desire to love is the possibility of evil, betrayal or treachery. Because this possibility haunts the very possibility of a peaceful act, one cannot know if naming or friendship has occurred, and yet it is possible that there will have been friendship.

In this light, if ontological violence emerges from within the desire for pure peacefulness, then it is necessary to consider more carefully the potential violence Milbank notes above. For, it would seem that in imagining the peaceful exchange of the *ecclesia*, as an imitation of the Trinity, there is also the possibility of the betrayal of this peace, and that this possibility structures the *poiesis* of radical orthodoxy. If this is the case, then so that one does not say there is peace when there is no peace, and so that one does not wrongly declare a contractual agreement to be a free and forgiving reconciliation, and to prevent the "fusion" of charity from becoming hegemonic, the need for deconstructive "ethical purism" may remain within radical orthodoxy itself, precisely so as to allow it to move toward its desired goal.⁵⁴ At this point, Derrida's emphasis on the centrality of love of enemies to a friendship worthy of the name may need to take priority, so as to bring such peaceful relations to fruition.

To recognize the potential for violence within one's participation in charity is, first of all, to recognize the difference between God and creation, a difference that remains even in redemption and even in one's participation in *scientia Dei* through sacred doctrine. Indeed, Thomas himself makes space for such a deconstructive awareness in his constant recognition of the deficiency of our modes of signification and action. While the names we can give to God do refer, this is because of who God is, while the meanings that we intend necessarily stray from their signification. To

---

53 See Milbank, *Theology and Social Theory*, pp. 432-4.

54 In fairness, this may be implicitly recognized by Milbank himself. In "Can a Gift Be Given?" he argues that the idea of peaceful gift exchange, as Christian agape, can be defended "only by purging it of all archaic agonistic components" (p. 131). It remains unclear to me how such purging could be accomplished without attending to the unilateral acts that constitute the exchange, and thus to some degree without a deconstructive turn.

call God good, or even to call God Father, Son, and Spirit, still is to use terms in a creaturely way on the part of how we signify. Indeed, the best way for us to signify, in Dionysian fashion, is to recognize that while our words signify qualities which exist pre-eminently in God, and only in creatures by participation, our language works in the inverse order, signifying the creatures we know and only indirectly signifying God. Drift or errancy is internal to any speech, even the possibility of analogical language.

Likewise, our acts of friendship with God remain limited and deficient in their signification of God's simple, unchanging love. One cannot have a "special movement of love" toward all neighbors, nor can one seek to reconcile with all enemies as Jesus did in calling them to become friends. These limitations are not of themselves evil, as it is in our particularity (community, embodiment, language) that God's charity becomes friendship *for us*. Nevertheless, they illustrate that it remains possible for human charity to become exclusive, to seek its own, and to become determined by essentialist identity, undercutting the asymmetry through which charity opens itself beyond the determinate boundaries of a community. Again, to retain the critical tension that Thomas recognizes within human activity opens a space for deconstructive reflection *within* systematic thought.

To this end, integrating Milbank's emphasis on ecclesial life, with its focus on particularity and embodiment, must serve as a central moment in contemporary appropriations of Thomism. Nonetheless, it should be countered by both the work of Marion and Derrida, as Marion's focus on distance helps us to recognize both the infinite distance that divine generosity opens for us, and that the giving of distance to others may be the real gift of friendship. Derrida's reminder of the necessity of love of enemies, which destabilizes the friend/enemy opposition, serves as an extension of Marion's point that can test and open the boundaries of radically orthodox communities. Noting the places where deconstruction retains its value actually allows for increased, deeper emphasis on particularity and embodiment, and would allow radical orthodoxy to more fully commit itself to a reappropriation of Thomas. It may be that the full constructive potential of radical orthodoxy will emerge not from its polemic against deconstruction, but rather from their solidarity.

IV. In the Name of Friendship

In the introduction, the connection between naming God and friendship emerged from reflection on a statement by Franz Rosenzweig regarding the name of God: "God does not have a name so that he may be called by it ... It is for our sake that He permits Himself to be named and called by that name, since it is only by jointly calling upon Him that we become a 'We.'"[55] For Rosenzweig, it does not affect God's life if we name God properly or improperly; however, the names that we give to God do affect us, binding communities together and establishing relationships. In some

---

55 Rosenzweig, *Understanding the Sick and the Healthy*, p. 91.

ways, this is not far from Thomas' position, as our naming of God, in its deficient signification, does not effect a change in God. However, the names we give to God can bring a change in us, orienting us toward charity, and reshaping community.

However, Rosenzweig's critical reflection goes further, in his awareness that the "We" that emerges from naming God carries within it a pretense of false universality. For as the "We" is spoken, it implies a "you" (or a "y'all") that stands outside it.[56] Even when unfolding into the act of love, the community is not-yet whole. In its pragmatic dimension, then, our naming of God always remains incomplete. As Rosenzweig writes of Psalm 115, which both invokes and revokes proximity to God, "In one breath they thus move the we into the fulfillment constituted by immediate proximity to the divine name, and from this conclusion withdraw it back into the not-yet of the present—'not to us but.'"[57] Thus, it is in the recognition that our names for God do not refer, and that they open onto God's infinite mystery and love which transcend our conceptions, that the communities established in light of the name are opened beyond their borders as well.

In a world where acting "in the name of God" is most frequently associated with fanaticism, irrationality, and violence, the connections between naming God and friendship explored in this work provide a more hopeful interpretation of pragmatics of Christian discourse. There are two levels to this hope: first, the retrieval of Thomas' account of naming God shows that for the most profound thinkers of Christianity, the name of God commences a journey into mystery, an ecstasy of human knowledge and intensification of love. It also demands the pursuit of justice, and the opening onto new forms of friendship and peacefulness within the world. To thus explore how the name of God can be peaceful, rational, and establish friendships in the world shows the resources for repair and correction with Christian theology, and the ability of Christian communities to draw from their tradition to make such corrections.

At the same time, such repair is not simply an internal matter for Christianity, but is a question of the relations between Christian and other communities. Here, the language of friendship is risky; friendship may unite hearts and increase devotion between parties, but it may also lend itself to exclusivism and sectarianism. Furthermore, even if the friendship of charity does actualize peace, to practice it solely within the terms of the Christian community still limits the possibilities of understanding, both within Christian communities and between various religious groups (and with secular groups as well). Thus, as a gesture of friendship, the adoption of alternative philosophical language, which today would be that of postmodernism, may be necessary. It is at this level that Derrida's discourse can be seen as particularly helpful; not so much in the development or articulation of doctrine, but rather in attending to the practice of friendship with critical vigilance.

The question that remains, it seems, is how best to relate a Trinitarian naming of God to friendship, in a way that integrates both a commitment to particularity and an

---

56 Rosenzweig, *The Star of Redemption*, pp. 236-8, 250-3. See also Gibbs, *Why Ethics? Signs of Responsibilities*, pp. 184-7. I owe the translation of "y'all" to Robert Gibbs.

57 Rosenzweig, *The Star of Redemption*, p. 251.

openness to the other, as signified for both Thomas and Derrida by the command to love one's enemies. Drawing on Marion, Derrida, and Milbank, I would suggest the following dynamic as a way to conceive friendship with God in terms that suggest its participation within the triune life.

The exchange of love between Father and Son constitutes the person of the Holy Spirit; this is a gift, but it is also a person. Friendship with God is a relation that gives being to the other, creating the other as subject, and hospitably extending relations of peace and friendship. If the Spirit is a divine person, then the extension of friendship must open itself to the subjectivity of others, even those not, initially, part of the friendship. *There must always be more than one friend.* Such creation of subjectivity must mean, however, that the giving relation must also be one of listening, of engagement, of anticipation of an unexpected response. This includes, of course the possible response that criticizes one's actions and judgments. Without this, how can one know that one's gift is truly suitable, and attentive to the embodied particularity of the other?

Second, in the Trinity the persons give without reserve: their giving of themselves also gives the possibility of creating new friendships. The Spirit is, itself, the embodiment of the openness of the love of the Father and Son to the inclusion of others. As Thomas writes, Father and Son love the Spirit, in itself, but also as it is in us (ST I.37.2). Exchange opens, of itself, to extension to others. As in Thomas' commentary on John, moreover, the creation of friendship requires the openness to love one's enemies, as it is precisely with those hostile to God, namely ourselves, that God seeks friendship.

Third, friendship with God is a mutual relation, but the mutuality is less one of reciprocity than of *shared giving*. Here, one could follow the thought of Richard of St. Victor, who emphasizes that in the life of the Trinity, the Father and Son do not only exchange gifts, but give together to the Spirit.[58] Our "shared love" (*condilectus*) is a sharing in this giving-together of the Trinity, which, as shared giving, *need* not depend on a return. This creates a way to understand friendship as shared commitment, but one that still attends to the finite, deficient, secondary ways in which we participate in this commitment. Thus, rather than emphasize reciprocity, friendship with God may be best conceived in terms of a shared commitment of giving. This shared commitment may be unilateral, particularly when we consider Marion's argument that unilateral giving, in which the giver becomes anonymous, is the only possible modality for the gift to exist. In sharing such giving, we may be adopted by the one who gives freely to us.

By analogy to such Trinitarian exchange, and drawing on a Dionysian conception of the good, one can counter radical orthodoxy's envisaging of charity as a process of fusion with the idea of charity as a *diffusive unity*, in which the one who names God strives to emulate the diffusive, kenotic, unilateral goodness of God. The friendship then becomes an active participation, which establishes relations only through their

---

58 Richard of St. Victor, *Book Three of the Trinity* (New York: Paulist Press, 1979), pp. 390-392.

deconstruction and extension to others. Here, a deconstructive approach to naming God and friendship would be less a determination of ontological conclusions than a habit of life and thought that would contribute to the shaping of Christian discourse, interpretation, and ethics, by critically recognizing the ongoing possibility of intensification and extension of charity, as well as the ways our cognition and friendship can become irresponsible.

It would be easy, in light of the above description, to say that this conception of friendship with God abstracts from practices and relations, becoming purely interior. Yet, this need not be the case, on two levels. First, clearly, listening and the creation of friendship can be practiced, over time, in particular, concrete settings, in relation both to one's own community and with others. Second, such "shared giving" need not be simply an inner commitment, but rather could be a scripturally informed conforming of oneself to God. And, perhaps it is in the interplay of these two commitments—both worship and study within the Church, and engagement in listening to others outside it—that shared giving most fully conforms to the triune life. Indeed, in the activity of scriptural reasoning, where readers from different traditions join together, such shared commitment, listening to the outsider, *and* scriptural study merge. From the pragmatic dynamics of these two relations, charity in the Augustinian sense, that enjoys God and loves one's neighbors, may most fully emerge.

Perhaps, as with Gregory of Nyssa, it is in recognizing the imperfection of our naming God and our friendship, the limits of our reason and our love, that we can also find the true perfection of humanity in the *epektasis* of virtue, such that "we regard falling from God's friendship as the only thing dreadful and we consider becoming God's friend the only thing worth of honor and desire."[59] In striving for a friendship that is virtuous beyond classical virtue, turns enmity to friendship, extends to the stranger (*philoxenia*), loves beyond fraternity and across sexual difference, and seeks to live in the light of the transcendent Name, then with and beyond Aelred of Rievaulx, one may "from being a friend of his [or her] fellow-man become the friend of God."[60]

---

59 Gregory of Nyssa, *The Life of Moses*, p. 137.
60 Aelred of Rievaulx, *Spiritual Friendship*, p. 73.

Bibliography

Adams, Don, "Loving God and One's Neighbor: Thomistic Charity," *Faith and Philosophy* 11 (1997): 207-10.

Aelred of Rievaulx, *Spiritual Friendship*, trans. M. Laker, SSND (Kalamazoo: Cistercian Publications, 1977).

Andrews, Isolde, *Deconstructing Barth: A Study of the Complementary Methods in Karl Barth and Jacques Derrida* (New York: Peter Lang, 1996).

Annas, Julia, "Self-Love in Aristotle," *The Southern Journal of Philosophy* 27 (1988): 1-18.

St. Anselm of Canterbury, *Proslogion*, in E. Fairweather (ed.), *A Scholastic Miscellany: Anselm to Ockham* (Philadelphia: Westminster Press, 1956).

St. Thomas Aquinas, *Aristotle: Peri Hermeneias*, trans. J.T. Oesterle (Milwaukee: Marquette University Press, 1962).

———*Commentary on Aristotle's Nicomachean Ethics*, trans. C. Litzinger (Notre Dame, IN: Dumb Ox Books, 1993).

———*Commentary on Aristotle's De Anima*, trans. K. Foster and S. Humphries (Notre Dame, IN: Dumb Ox Books, 1994).

———*De Caritate*, trans. L.T. Kendzierski (Milwaukee: Marquette University Press, 1960).

———*Faith, Reason, and Theology: Questions I-IV of His Commentary on Boethius' De Trinitate*, trans. A. Maurer (Toronto: Pontifical Institute of Medieval Studies, 1987).

———*In Librum Beati Dionysii De Divnis Nominibus* (Rome: Marietti, 1950).

———*The Literal Exposition of Job: A Commentary on Providence*, trans. A. Damico (Atlanta: Scholars' Press, 1988).

———*On Being and Essence*, trans. A. Maurer (Toronto: The Pontifical Institute of Mediaeval Studies, 1968).

———*Summa Contra Gentiles*, trans. C.J. O'Neil (Notre Dame, IN: University of Notre Dame Press, 1975).

———*Summa Theologiae* (Madrid: Biblioteca de Autores Cristianos, 1951).

———*Summa Thelogiae*, trans. Fathers of the English Dominican Province (London, 1920).

———*Super Evangelium S. Iohannis* (Rome: Marietti, 1951).

Aristotle, *Nicomachean Ethics*, trans. D. Ross (Oxford: Oxford University Press, 1980).

Aubenque, Pierre, "The twofold natural foundation of justice according to Aristotle," trans. R. Heinaman, in R. Heinaman (ed.), *Aristotle and Moral Realism* (London: UCL Press, 1995), pp. 35-47.

St. Augustine of Hippo, *The Confessions*, trans. E. Hampl (New York: Vintage, 1999), p. 61.

Barth, Karl, *Anselm: Fides Quaerens Intellectum*, trans. J. Robertson (Richmond: John Knox Press, 1960).

Bauerschmidt, Frederick, "The Word Made Speculative: John Milbank's Christological Poetics," *Modern Theology* 15 (1999): 417-32.

Beardsworth, Richard, *Derrida and the Political* (London: Routledge, 1996).

Bell, David, "Reference and Sense: An Epitome," *Philosophical Quarterly* 34 (1984): 369-372.

Bennington, Geoff, "Derridabase," in *Jacques Derrida*, trans. G. Bennington (Chicago: University of Chicago Press, 1993).

Bernasconi, Robert, "The Trace of Levinas in Derrida," in D. Wood and R. Bernasconi (eds), *Derrida and Différance* (Evanston: Northwestern University Press, 1988).

Blanchot, Maurice, *Friendship*, trans. E. Rothenberg (Stanford: Stanford University Press, 1997).

——*The Unavowable Community*, trans. P. Joris (Barrytown, NY: Station Hill Press, 1988).

Bobik, Joseph, "Aquinas on Friendship with God," *New Scholasticism* 61 (1986): 257-71.

Bowlin, John R., *Contingency and Fortune in Aquinas' Ethics* (Cambridge: Cambridge University Press, 1999).

Bradley, Denis J., *Aquinas on the Twofold Human Good: Reason and Human Happiness in Aquinas' Moral Science* (Washington, DC: The Catholic University of America Press, 1997).

Burrell, David, *Aquinas: God and Action* (Notre Dame, IN: University of Notre Dame Press, 1979).

——*Knowing the Unknowable God: Ibn-Sina, Maimonides, and Aquinas* (Notre Dame, IN: University of Notre Dame Press, 1986).

Caputo, John, *The Prayers and Tears of Jacques Derrida: Religion Without Religion* (Bloomington: Indiana University Press, 1997).

Caputo, J. and Scanlon, M. (eds), *Questioning God* (Indianapolis: Indiana University Press, 2001).

Carl, Wolfgang, *Frege's Theory of Sense and Reference* (Cambridge: University of Cambridge Press, 1994).

Carlson, Thomas, *Indiscretions: Finitude and the Naming of God* (Chicago: University of Chicago Press, 1998).

Cates, Diana Fritz, *Choosing to Feel: Friendship and Compassion in Aristotle and Thomas Aquinas* (South Bend: University of Notre Dame Press, 1997).

Chenu, M.D., *La théologie comme science au XIIIème siécle* 3rd edn (Paris: J. Vrin, 1957).

Cole, Darrell, "Thomas Aquinas on Virtuous Warfare," *Journal of Religious Ethics* 27 (1999): 57-80.

Cooper, John, "Aristotle on Friendship," in A. Rorty (ed.), *Essays on Aristotle's Ethics* (Berkeley: University of California Press, 1980), pp. 301-340.

Corbin, Michel, *Le Chemin de la Théologie chez Thomas d'Aquin* (Paris: Beauchesne, 1974).

———"Le Pain de la Vie: La lecture de Jean VI par S. Thomas d'Aquin," *Recherches des Sciences Religieuses* 65 (1977): 107-38.

———"Négation et transcendance chez Denys," *Recherches des Sciences philosophiques et theologiques* 69 (1985): 41-76.

Cornell, Drucilla, "Where Love Begins: Sexual Difference and the Limit of the Masculine Symbolic," in E. Feder, M. Rawlinson, and E. Zakin (eds), *Derrida and Feminism* (New York: Routledge, 1997), pp. 161-206.

Della Rocca, Michael, "Essentialists and Essentialism," *Journal of Philosophy* 93 (1996): 186-202.

Derrida, Jacques, *Acts of Religion*, ed. G. Anijar (New York: Routledge, 2002).

——— *Adieu: à Emmanuel Levinas* (Paris: Galilée, 1997).

———*Aporias*, trans. T. Dutoit (Stanford: Stanford University Press, 1994).

———"At this Moment in This Work Here I Am," trans. R. Berezdivin, in R. Bernasconi and S. Critchley (eds), *Re-reading Levinas* (Bloomington: Indiana University Press, 1991).

———*The Gift of Death*, trans. D. Wills (Chicago: University of Chicago Press, 1994).

———*Given Time I. Counterfeit Money*, trans. P. Kamuf (Chicago: University of Chicago Press, 1992).

———"How Not to Speak: Denials," trans. K. Frieden, in H. Coward and T. Foshay (eds), *Derrida and Negative Theology* (Albany: State University of New York Press, 1992).

———*Margins of Philosophy*, trans. A. Bass (Chicago: University of Chicago Press, 1982).

———*Of Grammatology*, trans. G. Spivak (Baltimore: Johns Hopkins University Press, 1976).

———*On Cosmopolitanism and Forgiveness*, ed. S. Critchley and R. Kearney (New York: Routledge, 2001).

———*On the Name*, trans. T. Leavey (Stanford: Stanford University Press, 1997).

———*Politics of Friendship*, trans. G. Collins (New York: Verso, 1994).

———*Psyché: Inventions de l'autre* (Paris: Galilée, 1987).

———*Speech and Phenomena and Other Essays on Husserl's Theory of Signs*, trans. D. Allison (Evanston: Northwestern University Press, 1973).

———*Writing and Difference*, trans. A. Bass (Chicago: University of Chicago Press, 1978).

Dewan, Lawrence, "The Number and Order of St. Thomas's Five Ways," *The Downside Review* 92 (January 1974): 1-18.

Diamond, Cora, *The Realistic Spirit* (Cambridge, MA: MIT Press, 1991).

Fodor, James, *Christian Hermeneutics: Paul Ricoeur and the Refiguring of Theology* (Oxford: Oxford University Press, 1995).

Forgie, J. William, "The Cosmological and Ontological Arguments: How St. Thomas Solved the Kantian Problem," *Religious Studies* 31 (1995): 89-101.

Frege, Gottlob, "On *Sinn* and *Bedeutung*," trans. M. Black, in M. Beaney (ed.), *The Frege Reader* (Oxford: Blackwell, 1997).
Geach, P.T., *Reference and Generality: An Examination of Some Medieval and Modern Theories* (Ithaca: Cornell University Press, 1980).
Gibbs, Robert, *Why Ethics? Signs of Responsibilities* (Princeton: Princeton University Press, 2000).
——*Correlations in Rosenzweig and Levinas* (Princeton: Princeton University Press, 1992).
Gilson, Etienne, *The Christian Philosophy of St. Thomas Aquinas*, trans. L. Shook (New York: Random House, 1956).
Goetschel, Roland, "Exode 3,14 dans la Pensée Juive Allemande de la Première Partie du xxème Siècle," in *Celui Qui Est: interpretations juives et chrétiennes d'Exode 3:14* (Paris: Les Editions du Cerf, 1986), pp. 265-76.
Gregory of Nyssa, *The Life of Moses*, trans. A. Malherbe (New York: Paulist Press, 1978).
Hankey, Wayne, *God in Himself: Aquinas' Doctrine of God as Expounded in the Summa Theologiae* (Oxford: Oxford University Press, 1987).
Harak, G. Simon, *Virtuous Passions: The Formation of Christian Character* (New York: Paulist Press, 1993).
Hart, Kevin, *The Trespass of the Sign: Deconstruction, Theology, and Philosophy* (Cambridge: Cambridge University Press, 1989).
Heidegger, Martin, *Pathmarks*, ed. W. McNeill (Cambridge: Cambridge University Press, 1998).
Hemming, Lawrence, "*Quod Impossibile Est*! Aquinas and Radical Orthodoxy" in L. Hemming (ed.), *Radical Orthodoxy? A Catholic Enquiry* (Burlington: Ashgate, 2000).
Hunsinger, George, *Karl Barth and Radical Politics* (Philadelphia: Westminster Press, 1976).
Jenkins, John, *Knowledge and Faith in Thomas Aquinas* (Cambridge: Cambridge University Press, 1997).
Johnson, James Turner, "Aquinas and Luther on War and Peace: Sovereign Authority and the Use of Armed Force," *Journal of Religious Ethics* 31 (2003): 3-20.
Jones, L. Gregory, "The Theological Transformation of Aristotelian Friendship in the Thought of Saint Thomas Aquinas," *New Scholasticism* 61 (1987): 373-99.
Jordan, Mark, "The Names of God and the Being of Names," in A. Freddoso (ed.), *The Existence and Nature of God* (Notre Dame, IN: University of Notre Dame Press, 1983).
Kearney, Richard, "Derrida's Ethical Re-turn," in G. Madison (ed.), *Working Through Derrida* (Evanston: Northwestern University Press, 1993).
Keaty, Anthony W., "Thomas' Authority for Identifying Charity as Friendship: Aristotle or John 15?" *The Thomist* 62 (1998): 581-601.
Kenny, Anthony, *Aristotle on the Perfect Life* (Oxford: Clarendon Press, 1992).
——*The Five Ways: St. Thomas Aquinas' Proofs of God's Existence* (New York: Schocken Books, 1969).

Kerr, Fergus, "Charity as Friendship," in *Language, Meaning, and God* (London: Chapman, 1987).
Kierkegaard, Søren, *Works of Love*, trans. H.V. Hong and E.H. Hong (Princeton: Princeton University Press, 1995).
Kripke, Saul A., *Naming and Necessity* (Cambridge, MA: Harvard University Press, 1980).
———"Identity and Necessity," in S. Schwartz (ed.), *Naming, Necessity, and Natural Kinds* (Ithaca: Cornell University Press, 1977).
Lear, Jonathan, *Aristotle and Logical Theory* (New York: Cambridge University Press, 1980)
———*Love and Its Place in Nature: A Philosophical Interpretation of Freudian Psychoanalysis* (New York: Noonday Press, 1990).
———*Aristotle: The Desire to Understand* (Cambridge: Cambridge University Press, 1988).
Leroux, Georges, "A L'ami inconnu: Derrida, lecteur politique de Blanchot," *Etudes Françaises* 31 (1995-6): 111-23.
Levering, Matthew, *Scripture and Metaphysics: Aquinas and the Renewal of Trinitarian Theology* (Oxford: Blackwell, 2004).
Levinas, Emmanuel, *Beyond the Verse: Talmudic Readings and Lectures*, trans. G. Mole (Bloomington: Indiana University Press, 1994).
———*Basic Philosophical Writings*, ed. A. Peperzak and R. Bernasconi (Bloomington: Indiana University Press, 1996).
———*Dieu, la mort, et le temps* (Paris: Grasset, 1993).
———*Totality and Infinity*, trans. A. Lingis (Pittsburgh: Duquesne University Press, 1968).
Linsky, Leonard, *Names and Descriptions* (Chicago: University of Chicago Press, 1977).
Lowe, Walter, *Theology and Difference: The Wound of Reason* (Bloomington: Indiana University Press, 1993).
Mackey, Louis, *Peregrinations of the Word: Essays in Medieval Philosophy* (Ann Arbor, MI: University of Michigan Press, 1997).
MacIntyre, Alasdair, *Three Rival Versions of Moral Inquiry: Encyclopedia, Genealogy, and Tradition* ((Notre Dame, IN: University of Notre Dame Press, 1990).
Maimonides, Moses ben, *The Guide for the Perplexed*, trans. M. Friedlander (New York: Dover, 1956).
Malet, A., *Personne et amour dans la theologie trinitaire de Saint Thomas d'Aquin* (Paris: Librairie Philosophique J. Vrin, 1956).
Marion, Jean-Luc, *Being Given: Toward a Phenomenology of Givenness*, trans. J. Kosky (Stanford: Stanford University Press, 2002).
———"De la «mort de dieu» aux noms divins: l'itinéraire théologique de la métaphysique," *Laval théologique et philosophique* 41 (1985): 25-41.
———*God Without Being (Hors-Texte)*, trans. T. Carlson (Chicago: University of Chicago Press, 1991).

———*In Excess: Studies in Saturated Phenomena*, trans. R. Horner and V. Berraud (New York: Fordham University Press, 2002).
———"Is the Argument Ontological? The Anselmian Proof and the Two Demonstrations of the Existence of God in the Meditations," in *Cartesian Questions: Method and Metaphysics* (Chicago: University of Chicago Press, 1999), pp. 139-60.
———*Prolegomena to Charity*, trans. S. Lewis (New York: Fordham University Press, 2002).
———*Reduction and Givenness: Investigations of Husserl, Heidegger, and Phenomenology*, trans. T. Carlson (Evanston: Northwestern University Press, 1998).
———"Saint Thomas d'Aquin et l'Onto-théo-logie," *Revue Thomiste* 95 (1995): 31-66.
———"They Recognized Him, and He Became Invisible to Them," trans. S. Lewis, *Modern Theology* 18 (2002): 145-52.
Marshall, Bruce, *Christology in Conflict* (Oxford: Blackwell, 1988).
———"Absorbing the World," in *Theology and Dialogue: Essays in Conversation with George Lindbeck* (Notre Dame, IN: University of Notre Dame Press, 1990).
Maurer, Armand, "St. Thomas on the Sacred Name 'Tetragammaton'," *Mediaeval Studies* 34 (1972): 275-77.
McCormack, Bruce, *Karl Barth's Critically Realistic Dialectical Theology: Its Genesis and Development 1910-36* (New York: Oxford University Press, 1995).
McDowell, John, *Meaning, Knowledge, and Reality* (Cambridge, M. A.: Harvard University Press, 1998).
———*Mind, Value and Reality* (Cambridge, MA: Harvard University Press, 1998).
McGinn, Bernard, *The Foundations of Mysticism*, vol. 1 of *The Presence of God* (New York: Crossroad, 1991).
McInerny, Ralph, *Aquinas and Analogy* (Washington, DC: The Catholic University of America Press, 1996).
———"Ethics," in N. Kretzmann and E. Stump (eds), *The Cambridge Companion to Aquinas* (Cambridge: Cambridge University Press, 1993).
Milbank, John, *Being Reconciled: Ontology and Pardon* (London: Routledge, 2003).
———"Can a Gift Be Given? Prolegomena to a Future Trinitarian Metaphysic," *Modern Theology* 11 (1995): 119-61.
———"Intensities," *Modern Theology* 15 (1999): 445-97.
———"Postmodern Critical Augustinianisms: A Short Summa in Reply to Forty-Two Unasked Questions," *Modern Theology* 7 (1991): 225-37.
———"The Programme of Radical Orthodoxy," in L. Hemming (ed.), *Radical Orthodoxy? A Catholic Enquiry* (Burlington: Ashgate, 2000), pp. 33-45.
———"The Soul of Reciprocity (Part One): Reciprocity Refused," *Modern Theology* 17 (2001): 335-91.
———"The Soul of Reciprocity (Part Two): Reciprocity Granted," *Modern Theology* 17 (2001): 485-507.

―――Theology and Social Theory: Beyond Secular Reason (Oxford: Blackwell's, 1990).
―――Truth in Aquinas (with Catherine Pickstock) (Oxford: Blackwell, 2001).
―――The Word Made Strange: Theology, Language, Culture (Oxford: Blackwell, 1997).
Miskotte, Kornelis, When the Gods Are Silent, trans. J. Doberstein (New York: Harper and Row, 1967).
Mosès, Stephane, Système et Révélation: La philosophie de Franz Rosenzweig (Paris: Éditions du Seuil, 1982).
Moss, David, "St. Anselm, Theoria, and the Convolution of Sense," in J. Milbank, C. Pickstock, and G. Ward (eds), *Radical Orthodoxy: A New Theology* (Oxford: Routledge, 1999), pp. 00–00.
Nancy, Jean-Luc, L'Experience de la Liberté (Paris: Galilée, 1988).
Nelson, Daniel Mark, *The Priority of Prudence: Virtue and Natural Law in Thomas Aquinas and the Implications for Modern Ethics* (University Park, PA: Pennsylvania State University Press, 1991).
Norris, Christopher, *The Deconstructive Turn: Essays in the Rhetoric of Philosophy* (New York: Meuthen, 1983).
Nussbaum, Martha, *The Fragility of Goodness: Luck and Ethics in Greek Tragedy and Philosophy* (Cambridge: Cambridge University Press, 1986).
―――Love's Knowledge: Essays on Philosophy and Literature (Oxford: Oxford University Press, 1992).
Ochs, Peter, "Scriptural Logic," in G. Jones and S. Fowl (eds), *Rethinking Metaphysics* (Oxford: Blackwell, 1995).
―――"Three Postcritical Encounters with the Burning Bush (in memory of Emmanuel Levinas)," in S. Fowl (ed.), *The Theological Interpretation of Scripture* (Oxford: Blackwell, 1997).
O'Rourke, Fran, *Pseudo-Dionysius and the Metaphysics of Aquinas* (Leiden: E.J. Brill, 1992).
Owen, G.E.L., "Tithenai ta Phenomena," in S. Mansion (ed.), *Aristote et les Problèmes de Methode* (Louvain: Publications Universitaires, 1961), pp. 83-103.
Porter, Jean, "De Ordine Caritatis: Charity, Friendship, and Justice in Thomas Aquinas' *Summa Theologiae*," *The Thomist* 53 (1989): 197-213.
―――"Salvific Love and Charity: A Comparison of the Thought of Karl Rahner and Thomas Aquinas," in E.N. Santurri and W. Werpehowski (eds), *The Love Commandments* (Washington, DC: Georgetown University Press, 1992), pp. 250-9.
Preller, Victor, *Divine Science and the Science of God: A Reformulation of Thomas Aquinas* (Princeton: Princeton University Press, 1967).
Pseudo-Dionysius, *The Complete Works*, ed. C. Luibheid (New York: Paulist Press, 1988).
Putnam, Hilary, "Thoughts to an Analytical Thomist," *The Monist* 80 (1997): 487-99.
Ricoeur, Paul, *Figuring the Sacred*, ed. M. Wallace (Minneapolis: Fortress Press, 1995).

―――― *Interpretation Theory: Discourse and the Surplus of Meaning* (Fort Worth: Texas Christian University Press, 1976).

Richard of St. Victor, *Book Three of the Trinity* (New York: Paulist Press, 1979).

Roche, Timothy D., "The Perfect Happiness," *The Southern Journal of Philosophy* 27 (1988): 103-26.

Rogers, Jr., Eugene F., "How the Virtues of an Interpreter Presuppose and Perfect Hermeneutics: The Case of Thomas Aquinas," *Journal of Religion* 76 (1996): 64-83.

―――― *Sexuality and the Christian Body: Their Way into the Triune God* (Oxford: Blackwell, 1999).

―――― *Thomas Aquinas and Karl Barth: Sacred Doctrine and the Natural Knowledge of God* (Notre Dame, IN: University of Notre Dame Press, 1995).

Rosenzweig, Franz, *Scripture and Translation*, trans. L. Rosenwald and E. Fox (Bloomington: Indiana University Press, 1994).

―――― *The Star of Redemption*, trans. W. Hallo (South Bend: University of Notre Dame Press, 1970).

―――― *Understanding the Sick and the Healthy: A View of World, Man, and God*, trans. T. Luckman, ed. N. N. Glatzer (Cambridge, MA: Harvard University Press, 1999).

Schmitt, Carl, *The Concept of the Political*, trans. G. Schwab (New Brunswick: Rutgers University Press, 1976).

Schollmeier, Paul, *Other Selves: Aristotle on Personal and Political Friendship* (Albany: State University of New York Press, 1994).

Schoot, Henk, *Christ the "Name' of God": Thomas Aquinas on Naming Christ* (Leuven: Peeters, 1993).

Searle, John, *Philosophy and Ordinary Language*, ed. C. Caton (Urbana: University of Illinois Press, 1963).

Seneca, "On the Tranquility of the Mind," trans. G. Hadas, in *The Stoic Philosophy of Seneca* (New York: W.W. Norton, 1958).

Sherman, Nancy, *The Fabric of Character: Aristotle's Theory of Virtue* (Oxford: Clarendon Press, 1989).

Soskice, Janet Martin, "The Gift of the Name," *Gregorianum* 79 (1998) : 231-46.

―――― "Philo and Negative Theology," in M. Olivetti (ed.), *Théologie Négative*,(Padova: Biblioteca dell'Archivo di Filosofia, 29: CEDAM, 2002).

―――― *Metaphor and Religious Language* (Oxford: Oxford University Press, 1985).

Soulen, Kendall, *The God of Israel and Christian Theology* (Minneapolis: Augsburg Fortress, 1996).

―――― "YHWH the Triune God," *Modern Theology* 15 (1999): 25-54.

Spikes, Michael, "Self-Present Meaning and the One-Many Paradox: A Kripkean Critique of Derrida," *Christianity and Literature* 37 (1988): 13-28.

―――― "Present Absence versus Absent Presence: Kripke Contra Derrida," *Soundings* 75 (1992): 333-55.

Stern-Gillet, Suzanne, *Aristotle's Philosophy of Friendship* (Albany: State University of New York Press, 1995).

Stump, Eleonore, "Providence and the Problem of Evil," in *Christian Philosophy*, ed. T.P. Flint (Notre Dame, IN: University of Notre Dame Press, 1990), pp. 53-61.

Tanner, Kathryn, *God and Creation in Christian Theology: Tyranny or Empowerment?* (London: Blackwell, 1989).

Timmerman, Jens, "Why We Cannot Wish Our Friends to Be Gods," *Phronesis* 40: 2 (1995): 209-15.

Vattimo, Gianni, "The Trace of the Trace," in G. Vattimo and J. Derrida (eds) *Religion*, (Stanford: Stanford University Press, 1998), pp. 79-94.

Von Balthasar, Hans Urs, *The Theology of Karl Barth*, trans. E. Oakes (San Francisco: Ignatius Press, 1992).

von Leyden, W., *Aristotle on Equality and Justice: His Political Argument* (New York: St. Martin's Press, 1985).

Wadell, Paul, *Friendship and the Moral Life* (Notre Dame, IN: University of Notre Dame Press, 1989).

——— *The Primacy of Love: An Introduction to the Ethics of Thomas Aquinas* (New York: Paulist Press, 1992)

Ward, Graham, *Barth, Derrida, and the Language of Theology* (Cambridge: Cambridge University Press, 1995).

Wawrykow, Joseph, *God's Grace and Human Action: "Merit" in the Theology of Thomas Aquinas* (Notre Dame, IN: University of Notre Dame Press, 1995).

Wedin, Michael V., "Singular Statements and Essentialism in Aristotle," in F.J. Pelletier and J. King-Farlow (eds), *New Essays on Aristotle* (Guelph, Ontario: Canadian Association for Publishing in Philosophy, 1984), pp. 67-98.

Weisheipl, James A., F.P., *Friar Thomas D'Aquino: His Life, Thought, and Work* (New York: Doubleday, 1974).

Westberg, Daniel, *Right Practical Reason: Aristotle, Action, and Prudence in Aquinas* (Oxford: Clarendon Press, 1994).

Wilcox, John R., "The Five Ways and the Oneness of God," *The Thomist* 62 (1998): 245-68.

Williams, A. N., *The Ground of Union: Deification in Aquinas and Palamas* (New York: Oxford University Press, 1999).

——— "Mystical Theology Redux: The Pattern of Aquinas' *Summa Theologiae*" in L.G. Jones and J.J. Buckley (eds), *Spirituality and Social Embodiment* (Oxford: Blackwell, 1997): 53-72.

Wittgenstein, Ludwig, *Philosophical Investigations*, trans. E. Anscombe (Oxford: Blackwell, 1953).

Yearley, Lee, "St. Thomas Aquinas on Providence and Predestination," *Anglican Theological Review* 49 (1967): 409-23.

Young, William W. III, "Ritual as First Phenomenology: A Response to Robert Gibbs," *Modern Theology* 16 (2000): 335-9.

Index

Ackrill, J.L. 49 n. 111
Aelred of Rievaulx 5, 110, 205
Annas, Julia 39 n. 65, 41
Anselm of Canterbury, Saint 9, 12-13, 63-4, 77, 184 n. 3
Apophasis 8, 63, 67, 74, 76, 77, 83, 95, 96, 148, 156, 158-60, 167, 180, 186
Aquinas, *see* Thomas Aquinas, Saint
Aristotle 19-23, 32-53, 65, 102, 115-17, 124-5, 137, 141-3, 167-8, 196-7
    Metaphysics 46 n. 99, 65 n. 46, 90-91, 116
    Nicomachean Ethics 20-21, 32-52, 104, 111
    Peri Hermeneias 61 n. 16, 81, 87
Aubenque, Pierre 37 n. 57
Augustine of Hippo, Saint 58, 84-5, 87, 125, 167, 175, 198

Barth, Karl 6-8, 12-13, 15
Bauerschmidt, Frederick 198
Beardsworth, Richard 161 n. 60
beatitude, *see* happiness
Bennington, Geoff 146
Blanchot, Maurice 161-5, 167-73
Bowlin, John 104 n. 10, 114 n. 48
Buber, Martin 3-4
Burrell, David 56, 70-71, 80 n. 66, 84 n. 74

Caputo, John 157-8
Carl, Wolfgang 25 n. 13
Carlson, Thomas 11, 186
Cates, Diana Fritz 130 n. 86, 134
charity 58, 97, 99-105, 107-8, 110-13, 119-37, 175, 180-83, 188-92, 195-6; *see also* friendship, with God; Thomas Aquinas, on charity as friendship
Chenu, M.D. 61 n. 17
Cole, Darrell 127-8
contemplation (*theoria*) 42, 44-50
Cooper, John 33 n. 39, 38 n. 60, 45

Corbin, Michel 59-62, 75-7, 94 n. 90, 96, 129, 190

deconstruction 7, 9, 11, 18, 139-41, 143, 148, 155, 170, 173-7, 183, 186-7, 191-5, 200-202, 205
Della Rocca, Michael, 31 n. 25
Derrida, Jacques 6-11, 18-19, 139-43, 184, 200-202
    on friendship 161, 164-77, 180-83, 192-3
    on naming God 148, 154-61, 180-83, 192-3
    on proper names 143-8
descriptions 23-30, 55, 65, 67-8, 79, 94
Dewan, Lawrence 95 n. 93
différance 143-5, 148, 155, 161, 183-5
Dionysius 2, 6, 57-8, 74-9, 82, 95-6, 99, 137, 140, 155, 158, 179, 181, 191

efficient cause 46, 65-8, 81, 87, 89-90, 93, 117-18, 131
election 16-18, 102, 107-9, 121, 152
embodiment 100-101, 116, 118, 130, 135, 196, 199-200, 202
eminent sense 3, 7, 64, 74, 76-9, 83, 94-6, 139, 179-82, 184-9, 193, 199
    charity as eminent sense 135-7
epistemology 29; *see also* knowledge of God
equality: between friends 36-9, 42, 44-6, 51-2, 101, 173
    between names 25-6, 31
    in charity 102, 104, 107, 109, 126, 135-6
    in justice 35-6
essentialism 20, 30, 51, 85, 136, 138, 197 n. 42
Eucharist 129 n. 85, 198; *see also* sacraments
Exodus 3:14-15 1-3, 5, 69-70, 83, 91, 150, 187

face, the 17, 149-52
Father, God the 5, 84-93, 95, 102, 109-10, 125, 133, 188-9, 192, 195, 199, 202, 204; *see also* God; the Trinity
fear 112, 130-35
final cause 99, 106
five notions 57, 88-96,
five ways 57, 59, 63-70, 83, 89-96, 179
Fodor, James 17 n. 46
Frege, Gottlob 21-6
fraternity and friendship 154, 159, 168, 171-6, 182, 205
friendship, in Aquinas, *see* Thomas Aquinas, charity as friendship
    in Aristotle 32-53
    in Blanchot 161-5
    in Derrida, *see* Derrida, on friendship
    with God 99-113, 135-8, 181-2, 200, 204-5

Gibbs, Robert 1 n. 1, 4 n. 12, 13 n. 32, 155 n. 39, 203 n. 56
gift 8-10, 58, 74, 84, 92, 163-9, 189, 194-202, 204
God 1-20, 37, 46-8, 55-98, 99-113, 116-38, 148-61, 175-7, 183-5, 187-205
Gregory of Nyssa 3-4, 205

habits 100-101, 116-17, 122, 127, 135
happiness
    in Aquinas (beatitude) 64, 101, 113-16, 119
    in Aristotle (*eudaimonia*) 44-51
Hart, Kevin 140
Heidegger, Martin 148-50, 153-4, 186-7, 189
Hemming, Lawrence 9 n. 20
Holy Spirit 58, 84-7, 92-5, 107, 116-18, 195, 204-5; *see also* God; the Trinity

id quod/ id a quo distinction 73, 85

Jenkins, John 61 n. 17, 68 n. 33
Jeremiah 10:7 131 n. 89
Jesus Christ 57, 76, 83, 90, 96, 102, 109-11, 116, 125, 169 n. 85, 187-92, 197-9, 202
John (gospel of) 87, 125, 135, 102, 108-13, 119, 121, 125-6, 129, 131, 132, 188

Jones, L. Gregory 105 n. 12
Jordan, Mark 78 n. 63, 79 n. 65
justice 33-7, 100, 103-5, 128-30, 133-5, 150, 174, 180-82, 196-7

Kearney, Richard 143 n. 6, 155 n. 39, 149, 182 n. 1, 191 n. 28
Keaty, Anthony 102
Kenny, Anthony 44, 67
Kerr, Fergus x, 119
Kierkegaard, Søren 121-2
knowledge of God 1, 5, 7, 56, 59, 74, 80, 101, 126, 190-91; *see also scientia*, *scientia Dei*
    by natural reason 64-5, 67-8, 87, 118, 197-8,
Kripke, Saul 22-31, 32, 37, 42, 51-2, 55, 67, 143, 145-7

Lear, Jonathan 33 n. 40, 41 n. 74, 43, 46, 48-51
Levering, Matthew 8, 58, 63 n. 22, 85 n. 75, 113
Levinas, Emmanuel 4, 6, 17-18, 140, 148-54, 161, 174
    and the face 17, 148-52
    and Talmudic commentary 4, 17, 19, 148, 150-51
Linsky, Leonard 25 n. 12
love of enemies 5, 8, 10, 100, 122-9, 146, 140, 169-71, 176, 180-81, 183, 201-2, 204-5
love of God, *see* friendship, with God
Luke (gospel of) 6: 32-5 10, 169; 14:26 133-4; 18:19 78 n. 64

McDowell, John 27 n. 17, 37 n. 58, 44 n. 90, 147
McInerny, Ralph 72, 80-81, 115 n. 52
MacIntyre, Alasdair, 127
Mackey, Louis 66 n. 29, 28 n. 32
Maimonides, Moses ben 2, 80, 82 n. 72
Malachi 1:6 131 n. 89
Malet, A. 73 n. 46, 85
Marion, Jean-Luc 7, 9, 18, 183-93, 202-4
    on idolatry 184-5, 187, 190, 193
Marshall, Bruce 8 n. 18, 20 n. 49
material cause 46, 90, 99, 106, 131,
Matthew (gospel of) 5 126; 7:21-3 192

Maurer, Armand 58 n. 7, 68, 82
metaphysics 2, 3, 7, 17, 29-30, 63, 65, 70,
    137-8, 139, 145, 183, 186, 190-91,
    194, 196-7, 199
Milbank, John 9-11, 18-19, 193-202
Miskotte, Kornelis 3, 4, 15-16
mode of signification (*modus significandi*)
    57, 68-74, 77-83, 86-9, 92, 94-7,
    136-7, 179-80, 187, 195, 200-203
Moses 1-4, 82, 91, 150, 187
Moss, David 9 n. 22

names of God 1-8, 10-21, 55-8, 63-85,
    89-91, 93, 95, 97, 148-61, 175,
    179-80, 187-8, 192, 195, 197-8,
    202-5
negative theology *see* Apophasis
Nelson, Daniel Mark 114 n. 50, 116 n. 55
Neoplatonism 74-5, 77
Norris, Christopher 145 n. 13
Nussbaum, Martha 32-3, 39 n. 64, 40 n. 69,
    41-4, 49-50

Ochs, Peter ix, 3 n. 8-9, 93 n. 88
ontology 8, 10, 30, 56, 73, 149, 153-4,
    172-3, 186, 194, 196-201
ontotheology 148, 153-4, 175, 190-91
O'Rourke, Fran 75, 77 n. 59, 78, 82 n. 71,
    96 n. 97
Owen, G.E.L. 39

persons, divine 72, 83-9, 92-3, 95-6
Porter, Jean 111 n. 38, 113, 120, 123 n. 68,
    127 n. 81
practical wisdom 32-5, 38, 42, 44, 46, 50,
    52, 100, 110, 115
pragmatic reference 5-8, 13-16, 18-20, 101,
    135, 137-8, 179-80, 187-8, 192, 203
praise 7-8, 12, 18, 75, 82, 142, 156-60, 167,
    187, 190, 192, 196, 200
prayer 6, 12, 18, 139-40, 156-61, 167,
    174-5, 179-81, 187, 192-3, 200
predestination 101-9, 117-18, 120-21, 135
principle of insufficiency 162-4
proper names 21-32, 55, 87, 139-40, 143-8
propter quid demonstrations 67-8
providence 101-6, 120-21, 128
Preller, Victor 56, 67, 68 n. 33, 69, 90-94, 97
Pseudo-Dionysius, *see* Dionysius

quia demonstrations 67-8

radical orthodoxy 8-9, 19, 193-204
reciprocity 9-10, 35, 101-2, 111, 188-9, 195,
    197-200, 204
remotion *see* Apophasis
res significata (thing signified) 57, 69, 79,
    81, 90
Richard of St. Victor 204
Ricoeur, Paul 2, 14-18
rigid designators 22-4, 26-30, 38, 51, 143
Roche, Timothy 49
Rogers, Eugene ix, 20, 59 n. 11, 60 n. 14,
    61 n. 16, 62 n. 18, 94, 95, 97 n. 99,
    116 n. 55
Rosenzweig, Franz 3, 6, 12-15, 157 n. 48,
    202-3

sacraments 57, 97, 112, 128-9
sacred doctrine 7, 11, 19, 56-63, 69-70, 74,
    83, 88-90, 93-4, 97, 99-100, 110-12,
    116, 124-6, 129, 179, 197-8, 201
sanctification 4, 101, 198
saturated phenomenon 187-8, 191-3
Saussure, Ferdinand de 144-5
Schmitt, Carl 168-71
Schoot, Henk 72, 79 n. 15, 83 n. 73
scientia (Aristotelian science)
    in Aquinas 20, 59-63, 100-102, 110
    in friendship 23, 39, 43-6
    scientia Dei 56, 59, 61-2, 64, 69, 70, 80,
        101, 110, 118, 125, 201
Searle, John 26 n. 16
self-love
    in Aristotle 39-42, 141-3
    in Aquinas 113-16, 132
semantic reference 1-2, 4-8, 11, 15, 18, 99,
    137, 139
Seneca, Lucius 110 n. 30
Sherman, Nancy 33-4, 43, 52
simplicity of God 56, 71, 73-4, 77, 83, 86,
    92-3, 202
singularity 6-7, 11-12, 18, 57, 69, 87, 92,
    125, 137, 139, 142-3, 147-52, 154-5,
    160-64, 167-8, 174, 176-7, 179, 181,
    197-8
Son, God the 58, 83-93, 95, 107, 109-10,
    122, 189, 192, 195, 198, 202, 204;
    see also God; the Trinity

Soskice, Janet Martin 2-4, 56
soul 100-101, 110-11, 113-20, 123-7, 129-32, 137, 179-80, 196-9
Spikes, Michael 145 n. 13
state and politics 169, 174, 201
Stern-Gillet, Suzanne, 48 n. 106
suppositum 51, 72-3, 83, 86, 92

Tanner, Kathryn 105 n. 13
testimony 11, 140, 159-61, 164-5, 167-8, 174-7, 179-80, 182, 189, 192, 193
Tetragrammaton, the 2, 76, 80-83, 88, 97, 148; *see also* Exodus 3
theoria 43-6; *see also* contemplation; *scientia*
Thomas Aquinas, St. 6-11, 19, 158, 179-83, 190-91, 195, 201-2
  on analogy 57, 81
  on charity as friendship 99-113, 135-8, 181-2, 200
  on the five ways, *see* five ways
  on knowledge of God 59-63, 197-8
  on naming God 55-9, 63, 70-83, 93-8, 99
  on scriptural interpretation 108-13, 122-9
  on the Trinity 83-93, 94-8
  on virtues and passions 116-18
Trinity, the 9, 57-8, 63, 83-98, 109, 129, 157, 188-9, 194-202; *see also* God

vague individual 65, 86-7
Vattimo, Gianni 151 n. 29
virtue 33-4, 37-42, 46-8, 52, 97, 99-101, 114-18, 123-4, 128-35, 168, 180-81, 195-6, 205

Wadell, Paul 101-2, 108 n. 19, 130 n. 87, 131 n. 88
war 127-9, 169-72
Wawrykow, Joseph 106-8
Weisheipl, James, 108, 126 n. 79
Westberg, Daniel 103, 115, 134
Williams, Anna 59 n. 9, 101, 112 n. 46
Wittgenstein, Ludwig 26 n. 16

Yearley, Lee 103, 105 n. 14
Young, William 4 n. 12

For Product Safety Concerns and Information please contact our EU
representative GPSR@taylorandfrancis.com
Taylor & Francis Verlag GmbH, Kaufingerstraße 24, 80331 München, Germany

www.ingramcontent.com/pod-product-compliance
Lightning Source LLC
Chambersburg PA
CBHW071354290426
44108CB00014B/1537